COMICS GONE APE!

The Missing Link To Primates In Comics

by
MICHAEL EURY

ARTHUR ADAMS 9-29-99

TwoMorrows Publishing

Raleigh,
North Carolina

COMICS GONE APE!
The Missing Link to Primates in Comics
by Michael Eury

Book design by Pamela Morrow • Logo designed by John Morrow • Edited by Michael Eury
"Q & Ape" telephone interviews transcribed by Rose Rummel-Eury • Proofread by Christopher Irving

Published by TwoMorrows Publishing
10407 Bedfordtown Drive • Raleigh, NC 27614
919-449-0344 • www.twomorrows.com

ISBN 978-1-893905-62-7
First printing, April 2007 • Printed in Canada

The front cover's recreation of the cover to *The Avengers* #4 was a surprise gift by artist Arthur Adams to art collector David Mandel after David's purchase of several of Arthur's "JLApe" original covers; cover colors by Tom Ziuko. The Avengers TM & © 2007 Marvel Characters, Inc.

Artist Jay Stephens' back cover homage to the cover of *Wonder Woman* #170 was won by Michael Eury at the charity event Wonder Woman Day, organized by Andy Mangels and taking place on October 29, 2006 at Portland, Oregon's Excalibur Books and Comics. Wonder Woman TM & © 2007 DC Comics.

No primates were harmed during the writing of this book (except for the author's sleep deprivation).

DEDICATION

This book is dedicated to H. A. Rey's Curious George, the mischievous monkey that made most of us go ape long before we read our first comic book.

Illustration from *Curious George* by H. A. Rey. © 1941, and renewed 1969 by H. A. Rey. Copyright assigned to Houghton Mifflin Company in 1993. Curious George is a registered trademark of Houghton Mifflin Company. Used by permission of Houghton Mifflin Company. All rights reserved.

ACKNOWLEDGMENTS

The author extends a Kong-sized THANK YOU!! to the one-and-only Arthur Adams for the eye-popping cover art, and to David Mandel for its use.

Also, very special thanks to Art Adams and the other Q & Ape interview participants: Nick Cardy, Frank Cho, Tim Eldred, Carmine Infantino, Joe Kubert, Tony Millionaire, Doug Moench, Bob Oksner, Jeff Parker, and Anne Timmons. You fine folks helped make *Comics Gone Ape!* special.

In researching this book, I found the following online sources invaluable and recommend them to any comics fan, scholar, or monkey boy: Grand Comic-Book Database (*comics.org*), Scott Shaw!'s Oddball Comics (*oddballcomics.com*), Comic Book Gorillarama (*members.shaw.ca/comicbookgorillarama/cbgindex.htm*), the Pulse (*comicon.com*), Dial B for Blog (*dialbforblog.com*), DarkMark's Comics Indexing Domain (*darkmark6.tripod.com/indexintro.html*), Don Markstein's Toonopedia (*toonopedia.com*), the Appendix to the Handbook of the Marvel Universe (*marvunapp.com*), Wikipedia, the Free Encyclopedia (*en.wikipedia.org*), the Gorilla Age of Comics (*lethargiclad.com/gorilla*), Monster Blog! (*monsterblog.oneroom.org*), Lambiek (*lambiek.net*), the Internet Movie Database (*imdb.com*), Hoknes' *Planet of the Apes* Chronology (*hoknes.com/apechronology.htm*), "Archer St. John and the Little Company That Could" by Ken Quattro from Comicartville (*comicartville.com/lib.htm*), and Welcome to the Clubhouse (*geocities.com/Area51/Labyrinth/7393/index.html*). Also helpful were the publications *Planet of the Apes Revisited* by Joe Russo and Larry Landsman with Edward Gross (2001, Thomas Dunne Books) and the "Lords of the Jungle" essay by Camille E. Cazedessus, Jr., in *The Comic-Book Book* by Don Thompson and Dick Lupoff (1973, Krause Publications).

Finally, the following individuals generously donated their time, artwork, approvals, comic books, support, and/or information, for which the author is sincerely grateful: Phil Amara, Jim Amash, Michael Ambrose, Sergio Aragonés, Mark Arnold, Terry Austin, Alan Bahr, Michael Bair, Dave Ballard, John Bamber, Spencer Beck, Christian Beranek, Edgar Rice Burroughs estate, Gary Chaloner, John Coates, *Comic Book Artist*, Jennifer M. Contino, Colleen Coover, Ray Cuthbert, Dark Horse Comics, DC Comics, Brent E. Erwin, John S. Eury, Mark Evanier, Rich J. Fowlks, Sandra Galfas, Marty Golia, David Hamilton, Jason Harris, Fred Hembeck, Heritage Auctions, Amy Huey, Houghton Mifflin Company, Adam Hughes, Christopher Irving, *The Jack Kirby Collector*, Ryan Jorgensen, Chris Khalaf, Wilf King, Robin Kirby, Ken Knudtsen, Erik Larsen, Mark Levy, Steve Lipsky, Marvel Comics, Alan Maxwell, Todd McFarlane, Gina Misiroglu, *Modern Masters*, NASA, Debbie Olshan, Orangutan Foundation International, Jerry Ordway, Jim Ottaviani, Valerie Parish, Ken Quattro, Dan Ripoll, John Roche, Budd Root, Werner Rosenauer, Rose M. Rummel-Eury, Lew Sayre Schwartz, Scott Shaw!, *Simian Scrolls*, Philip Simon, Dan Slott, Matthew Smith, Anthony Snyder, Chris Staros, Jay Stephens, Ty Templeton, Roy Thomas, Mike Tiefenbacher, Paul Tobin, Scott Trego, Twentieth Century Fox, Universal Studios, Brett Warnock, John Wells, and Tom Ziuko. If I've overlooked any contributor, please accept my sincere apologies for the oversight.

BARREL OF CONTENTS

This original cover painting by an unknown artist pits sword-and-sorcery star Dagar against a large gorilla on the cover of *Dagar #12 (July 1975).* © 1975 Gold Key Comics. Courtesy of Heritage Auctions.

Most of the artists said that they enjoy drawing apes because of their humanlike expressions— **"They're like us,"** I was told.

INTRODUCTION

The other day I was asked by Rachelle, a fellow member of my neighborhood athletic club who knows that I write for a living, about the subject of my next book.

I told her it's about apes in comic books, tossing out trivia about *Planet of the Apes* and Beppo the Super-Monkey. She smiled and nodded, "That sounds fun," but had a slightly vacant stare that suggested she was thinking, "Please, God, let my cell ring…" I've encountered this type of reaction a lot when telling "normal" people about *Comics Gone Ape!*

If you've bought this book, you're not like them—you "get it." You understand that there is something beguiling about a jungle princess scrapping with a mandrill… or a chimpanzee sleuth in a deerstalker's cap… or a super-intelligent talking gorilla mind-blasting a fleet-footed super-hero.

The idea for *Comics Gone Ape!* came to me in December 2005, when I was bored out of my gourd during the earliest scenes in Peter Jackson's *King Kong*—good heavens, man, I paid to see a giant ape, not a poorly cast Jack Black! At least I multi-tasked and brainstormed this project while waiting for the big guy to step in.

Once my research began, I didn't quite know what I was getting into. Sure, I knew a lot about Grodd, Titano, and Congorilla. I remembered Gorr, the Mod Gorilla Boss, and You-All Gibbon. I was even familiar with Monkeyman and O'Brien, Cy-Gor, and BrainiApe. But almost every day as I dug through my collection, scoured back-issue bins, and surfed comics websites, I would be reminded of a character I had forgotten, or discover a new one, or stumble across an obscurity.

Did you know that there are well over 1,000 comic-book covers featuring apes? Additionally, there are thousands of interior pages devoted to them. That's a lot of monkeys! And there is no consistent ape archetype—from the snarling savages of the wild to the future world where apes rule supreme, it's a jungle out there! Consider me your tour guide as we take a safari through those adventures.

You'll note that I've written *Comics Gone Ape!* in a lighthearted voice. I considered a more scholarly approach, but let's face it—it's hard to take Sgt. Gorilla and his ilk *too* seriously!

You'll also notice that throughout this book I use "ape," "monkey," and "primate" inter-changeably. Yes, I know that a gorilla isn't a monkey and that a human is also a primate, but I'm merely parroting the jargon established by dozens of comic-book writers and editors who came before me. This same broad mindset allows us to consider powerless characters like Batman, Green Hornet, and Tarzan to be super-heroes.

Accompanying my fast-paced, fun- and fact-filled history of apes in comic books are interviews—"Q & Apes"—with 11 artists and writers responsible for some of the adventures you'll read about. Most of the artists said that they enjoy drawing apes because of their humanlike expressions—"They're like us," I was told.

That's true, beyond our common evolutionary heritage. Just flip through some of the comics covers in these pages and you'll find apes laughing and growling, playing and fighting, and helping and hurting others—just like us.

"It would speak well of us as a species if we could stop saddling [apes] with our own faults," says Tim Eldred, creator of the wonderful graphic novel *Grease Monkey*. Perhaps we do owe ape-dom an apology for the bank-robbing and world-conquering roles in which we've placed them. However, we also owe them our gratitude for allowing us to explore our own foibles through their actions. Consider *Comics Gone Ape!* that long overdue thank-you to the chimp crusaders and evil gorillas that have entertained, enlightened, and enthralled us for decades!

Author Michael Eury, after reading hundreds of ape comics. *Photo by Rose Rummel-Eury.*

**Michael Eury
Lake Oswego, Oregon
Ape-ril, 2007**

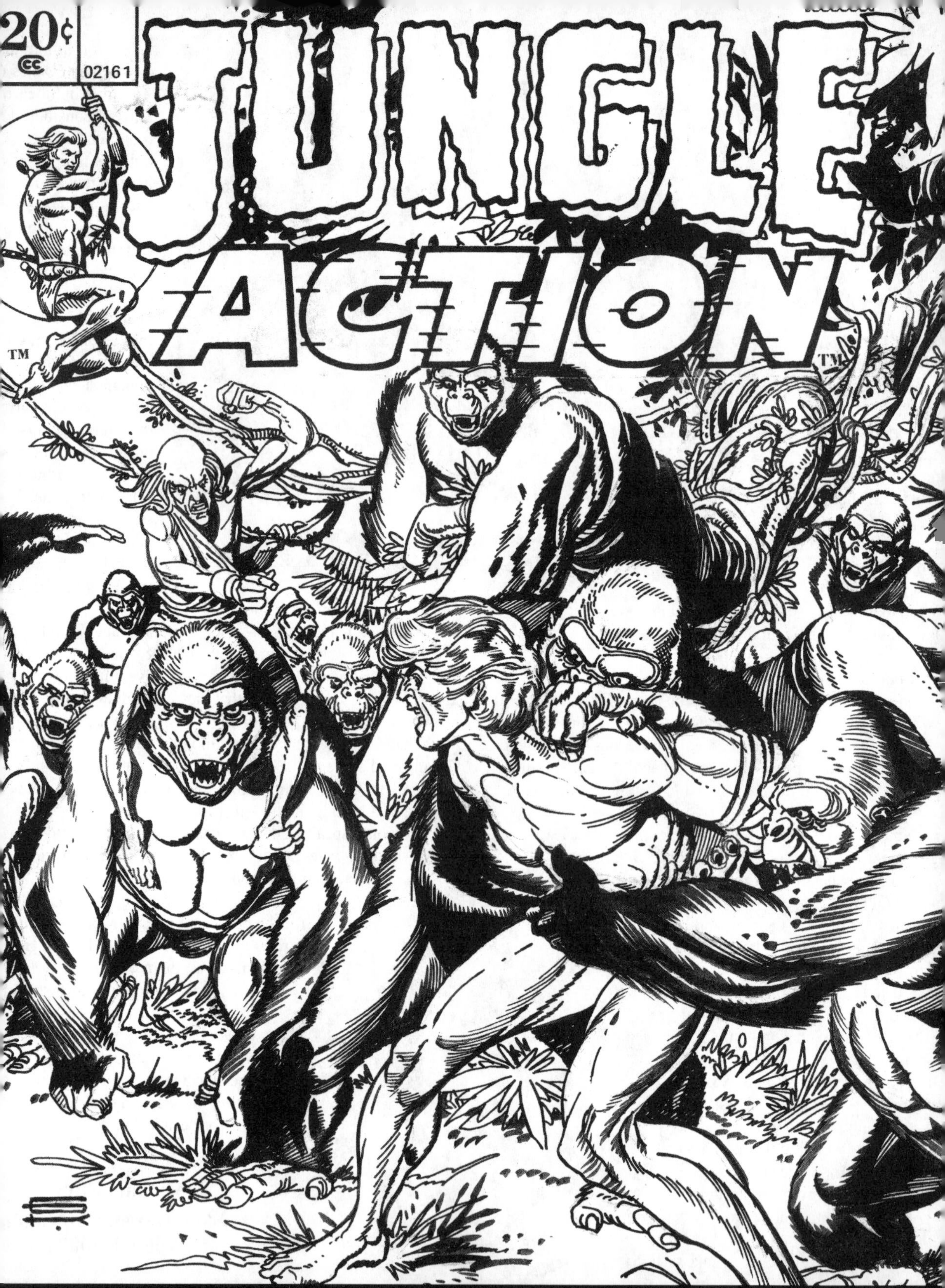
20¢
02161
JUNGLE ACTION
TM
TM

Unpublished 1973 cover art by Gil Kane featuring Marvel's 1950s-era Tarzan-twice-removed, Lo-Zar (alternately Lozar and Lo-Zarr). This "Lord of the Jungle" was renamed Tharn when his stories were reprinted in the 1970s.

Safari-goers and beastmasters never know when they'll meet a monkey with a mad-on!
Watch your step as you bungle into the jungle, where the apes are...

BORN TO BE WILD!

Have you ever seen a jungle movie that *didn't* depict the gorilla as really, really angry? That's fang-snarling, chest-pounding angry.

No, *Gorillas in the Mist* doesn't count.

From the 1930s and through the early '50s, movie houses played lots of cheaply produced jungle serials and pictures. You know the type: They open with a bunch of snooty Europeans in pith helmets on holiday in the jungle, or a gang of ne'er-do-wells out to purloin some weathered artifact. These interlopers inevitably stumble across an enraged bull ape that's jackhammering his pecs and frothing like a busted washing machine, grunting something that, in his language, can only mean "Git off my property!" Or "I'm taking the blonde, sissy-britches, just you try and stop me!" Hollywood knew that a grumpy gorilla was always good for a scare… or a laugh, if you looked close enough to see the zipper in the gorilla suit.

Why the rage, Congo king? Look at it this way: How would *you* feel if a chattering tour group tromped through your back yard? Territorial squabbles have led countless countries to war, so really, these apes are entitled to a little bluster.

Many of the moviegoers watching those jungle serials and pictures were young men (and occasionally, women—you go, Tarpe Mills!) who made serialized pictures of their own in the flourishing field of comic books. And those impressionable writers and artists, marching in step to the

A gorilla beat out neo-star Superman for the spotlight on Leo O'Mealia's cover to *Action Comics* #6 (Nov. 1938).
© 2007 DC Comics.

snorted commands of their middle-aged editors hot to ape Hollywood's lucrative jungle craze, tapped the gorilla on the shoulder (from a safe distance, of course) and knighted him the poster child for cantankerous critters. Sure, you'd find the occasional savage-lord-vs.-lion cover, and the suggestive jungle-queen-vs.-anaconda cover, but the ones that most grabbed readers' attentions featured grumpy gorillas (or other ornery apes). This wasn't the exclusive terrain jungle or "adventure" series—once in a while, some of comics' earliest caped crusaders found themselves mask-to-face with a maddened monkey!

How can I put this delicately…? Oh, forget that, here it is, straight up: Many of these artists could not draw apes. Some of them drew the dumpy-guy-in-a-baggy-gorilla-suit gorilla. Some evoked racial or sexual stereotypes, many blatant. Some pulled off passable swipes from nature photos. But in their defense, the entire comic-book art form was in its infancy then. And as Arthur Adams says, "…in life, you're not really required to know how to draw a gorilla."

Not that it mattered to the average readers of the Great Depression and World War II, the era we now call comics' Golden Age. They were unpretentious, usually poor kids looking for a quick and affordable escape from their reality of hardships. Few could discern between a hack and a master. Toss a snarling beast on that funnybook cover, and Junior would toss down his hard-earned dime—*that's* the law of the jungle.

Hal Foster's *Tarzan* Sunday from April 2, 1933. © 2007 ERB. Courtesy of Heritage Auctions.

TARZAN OF THE APES

The first stop on our jungle-comics safari is Edgar Rice Burroughs' *Tarzan of the Apes*, which first appeared in prose in 1912 and in comics in 1929.

In the first Tarzan story, confrontational king ape Kerchak slaughtered British castaway Lord Greystoke. Protective she-ape Kala, a mother that just lost her baby during a fit of Kerchak's rage, claimed the orphaned human infant as her own. At this pivotal moment, Burroughs' tribe of Great Apes became Tarzan's Smallville—a village raising a child with a great destiny.

Burroughs' apes were as real as any of the story's humans. The author named his principals and assigned them identifiable personalities, and provided them a language and communal rituals. Once Tarzan matured into the role of globetrotting adventurer, his ape family became the great walk-on supporting cast. On comic-book covers and in stories, Tarzan's primate companions were frequently found by the Ape-Man's side (or at his throat, if that's what the editor needed).

Burroughs' *Tarzan of the Apes* was an immediate hit in 1912, but the Jungle Lord's first appearance in comics form did not occur until 17 years later, when classically trained artist Harold (Hal) Foster adapted Burroughs' original tale into a daily (Monday through Saturday) newspaper strip. Distributed by the Metropolitan Newspaper Service, *Tarzan of the Apes* ran for ten weeks during the winter of 1929. Foster declined to resume the strip upon its continuation and was followed by Rex Maxon and later the celebrated Burne Hogarth, although Foster returned in September 1931 to illustrate the *Tarzan* Sunday strips for an outstanding run of nearly six years. Foster and Hogarth, the most famous of all Tarzan artists, each had a unique way of drawing apes: Foster's were often squat and belligerent, where Hogarth, a master of anatomy, rendered lissom, sinewy beasts.

The Ape-Man also made his comic-*book* premiere in 1929 when Foster's dailies were collected in *The Illustrated Tarzan Book*. Throughout most of the Golden Age, Tarzan remained the lord of the collected edition. *Tarzan* strips by Foster, Maxon, Hogarth, and their successors were recycled from the funnypapers to funnybooks in the pages of United Features Syndicate's (formerly Metropolitan Newspaper Service) anthologies *Tip Top Comics* and *Comics on Parade*.

Once Dell Comics began publishing the jungle hero's adventures, new Tarzan material stealthily crept into print, beginning with original spot illos accompanying text pieces. *Four Color Comics* #134 (1947), "Tarzan and the Devil Ogre," was the first all-new Tarzan story produced exclusively for comic books. Its cover and interior artist, Jesse Marsh, remained on board in early 1948 when Dell released *Tarzan* #1—the Ape-Man was at last headlining his own, original comic book.

A glorious Tarzan vs. ape cover by Burne Hogarth, from United Features' *Sparkler Comics #21 (1941)*. © 2007 ERB.

As a Dell comic-book star, Tarzan's adventures, written by Gaylord DuBois and drawn by Marsh, strayed from Burroughs' vision of the character, mirroring instead the Tarzan popularized in the movies. Dell's Tarzan was the treehouse-dwelling father figure, patriarch of a loinclothed nuclear family consisting of his wife Jane; the Korak, Son of Tarzan surrogate Boy (from the films); and a chimp (that's 1.5 children!).

Russ Manning, another of the all-time great Tarzan artists, first drew the character in 1952 in a story intended for a 3-D issue that was shelved. This Manning tale finally saw print in 1954, after the artist had spent over a year drawing *Tarzan*'s popular and long-running backup feature, "Brothers of the Spear." Artists who have worked with or under Manning have remarked of his tremendous respect for animals; this is often evident in Manning's *Tarzan* work, where idyllic scenes with the Ape-Man at peace with his jungle family are common.

Detail from the cover to a Saalfield 1975 Tarzan Coloring Book, with art by Russ Manning.
© 2007 ERB.

JUNGLE FEVER

Nipping at Tarzan's heels were numerous half-naked do-gooders—including Sheena, Queen of the Jungle; Nyoka the Jungle Girl; Wambi the Jungle Boy; Jo-Jo, Congo King; Ka-Zar; Ka'a'nga; Wild Boy; Tiger Girl; and Zegra—encroaching upon the Ape-Man's story terrain, cribbing his wardrobe, and duking it out with his brethren beasts.

Variations on the hero-vs.-ape theme could be found amid this primate proliferation, setting the pace for some of the classic gorilla comics that would appear in the Silver Age. Long before the Gorilla City of Grodd and Solovar, Ka'a'nga fought "Gorilla Hordes" (*Jungle Comics* #14, 1941) and Sheena struggled against both the "Devil Apes" (*Jumbo Comics* vol. 2 #11, 1942) and the "Empire of the Hairy Ones" (*Jumbo Comics* #49, 1943). Sheena also battled a "Super-Ape" in 1940's *Jumbo Comics* #22, almost two decades before Superman editor Mort Weisinger introduced Titano in 1959. And could the eye-patched Gorilla Witch from 1966's *Strange Adventures* #186 have existed without Tiger Girl's tussle with a gorilla in war paint on the cover of 1948's *Fight Comics* #55 paving the way?

The caveman comic, the jungle comic's cousin, had appeared in newspaper syndication since the early 20th century. To the uninitiated the two genres might have appeared indistinguishable, but the rule of telling one from the other is: Jungle heroes fight *apes* (and lions and giant snakes), and caveman heroes fight *dinosaurs*! (You "history" types might argue that humans and dinosaurs did not coexist, but don't go there—I've got a stack of

Ka'a'nga #7's (1951) "Beast-Men of Mombasa" featured this armored gladiator-gorilla. Art by Frank Riddell. © 1951 Fiction House. Courtesy of Heritage Auctions.

comics that say they did.)

Joe Kubert's *Tor: One Million Years Ago*, originally published by St. John in 1953, bridged the caveman and jungle genres with its hero's sidekick: Chee-Chee the monkey. Or monkey ancestor. "Your guess is as good as mine" chuckles Kubert when asked if the prehistoric Chee-Chee is actually a monkey. But Kubert and his then-writing partner Norman Maurer obviously had a monkey in mind when adding this

Meet Tor and Chee-Chee, on the cover of St. John's *1,000,000 Years Ago! #1* (a.k.a. *Tor #1*) (1953). Art by Joe Kubert. © 2007 Joe Kubert.

inquisitive, whimsical companion to the adventures of their caveman. And Maurer knew that a monkey made an effective sidekick—earlier, he scripted stories starring publisher Lev Gleason's Crimebuster, the teenage super-hero with a monkey partner named Squeeks.

Squeeks (see Chapter 3) was one of several apes that evolved into leading roles during the Golden Age. The Gorilla, an ape with a human brain (see Chapter 5), headlined a short-lived backup series in 1941's *Blue Beetle* #9 and 10 from publisher Victor Fox. In 1952, issue #3 of the little-known Avon Periodicals title *White Princess of the Jungle* offered the origin of the Blue Gorilla in a backup story drawn by Everett Raymond Kinstler. When DC Comics' jungle explorer Congo Bill graduated from his long-running backup series into his own title in 1954 (see Chapter 5), Chota the Chimp, pet of Bill's sidekick Janu, was a reliable comic-relief character and was even showcased in stories during *Congo Bill's* brief seven-issue run.

The era of the gorilla-as-star had begun!

© 2007 Marvel Characters, Inc.

MAN-OO THE MIGHTY

Marvel (then using the imprint of Atlas) Comics' *Jungle Action* vol. 1 #1 (1954) was published during an awkward time for the company, when it was stretching to find its niche in a marketplace harassed by content watchdogs and weakened by shifting consumer tastes. Manufactured in the "House of *Borrowed* Ideas," *Jungle Action* parroted three jungle-comic archetypes by introducing Lo-Zar, Lord of the Jungle (a Tarzan clone), Leopard Girl (a Sheena/Tiger Girl copy), and Jungle Boy (Marvel's version of Boy or Korak). Chop through that thicket of triteness and you'll discover the title's fourth feature (of four): Man-Oo the Mighty.

Man-Oo was the first gorilla character to be cover-featured as the star of his own strip (although he was not solo-featured there; *Jungle Action's* covers depicted each of its four stars in single panels). Written by Don Rico and drawn by a revolving door of artists (Paul Hodge, George Tuska, and Syd Shores), the Man-Oo series positioned its star as the guardian of the jungle, sort of Tarzan as a *real* ape. Man-Oo's bestial rage was not tempered by Tarzan's intellect, however, and Man-Oo killed any hunter or animal stupid enough to venture into his neck of the woods. But they had it coming to them, Man-Oo's readers thought. Bad time for such controversial content: The Comics Code was implemented halfway through *Jungle Action's* six-issue run (the Code's seal was so large on issues #4–6, it obliterated the "e" in the logo's "Jungle"), and by the time the book was canceled in 1955, the now-sanitized comics world was no place for a killer-gorilla hero.

Mo Gollub's *Korak* #1 (1964) cover painting, from the
Gold Key issue's back cover. © 2007 ERB.

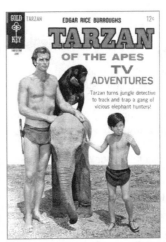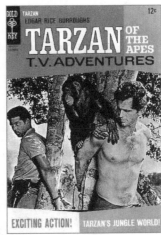

© 2007 ERB.

stuck closer to Burroughs' material, but soon had to "cease and
desist" itself off the racks.

The Burroughs company began to better police its property,
and in 1965 Gold Key made it clear that its Ape-Man was the
real deal by plastering onto the cover of *Tarzan* #155:
"Authentic! Authorized!" They also put a gorilla on the cover—
best to pull out all stops to show who's boss!

THE SHRINKING FOREST

By the mid-1950s, the flurry of Tarzan imitators had mostly
retired, the jungle craze giving way to newer fads such as Cold
War-induced paranoid science fiction (which, as you'll read in
Chapter 4, provided gorillas with new cover opportunities). The
Tarzan comic book in 1962 shifted from Dell to Gold Key Comics
with issue #132 and chugged along reliably there until the early
1970s. (Dell replaced *Tarzan* by creating *Kona, Monarch of
Monster Isle*; 1966's *Kona* #20 featured the series' sole gorilla
cover.) *Tarzan* was one of Gold Key's best illustrated titles,
dignified by Mo Gollub's and George Wilson's naturalistic
painted covers and Manning's attractive interiors.

When Gold Key trotted out its new *Korak, Son of Tarzan*
spin-off in 1964, repurposing "Boy" into the character he was
intended to be, they started the series by pulling out the big guns:
gorillas. Issue #1's gorgeously painted cover by Gollub showed
the junior jungle man imperiled by not one, but *three* gorillas.
And if that weren't enough to drive readers ape, its cover copy
made it clear that Korak's inaugural adventure took him "deep
into fierce gorilla country."

Also in 1964, Charlton Comics, that aggressive little company
out of Derby, Connecticut, released four unauthorized issues of
Jungle Tales of Tarzan at a period when the Tarzan copyright was
vulnerable due to corporate inaction. Written by Charlton
workhorse Joe Gill and drawn by Sam Glanzman, *Jungle Tales*

Sam Glanzman's 2000 recreation of his cover art to Charlton's unauthorized
Jungle Tales of Tarzan #2 (1964). © 2007 ERB. Courtesy of Heritage Auctions.

WHEN JIMMY MET BRUNA

Superman's Pal, Jimmy Olsen #98 (Dec. 1966) included what might very well be the *strangest* jungle comics story ever, "The Bride of Jungle Jimmy!"

Wedding covers seemed to be the purview of *Lois Lane* back during Mort Weisinger's Superman editorial reign, but no get-hitched-to-Superman *Lois* cover could ever top this Curt Swan/George Klein doozy. If you can take your eyes off of the unsettling cover picture of Jimmy marrying a gorilla for a moment, you'll notice that Superman is wearing a witchdoctor's headdress! Wonder what Swan told his kids when they saw *this* one on Daddy's drawing board??

Joe Kubert's cover art to DC's first two *Tarzan* issues, 1972's #207 and 208. © 2007 ERB.

© 2007 DC Comics.

The nine-page story, by Leo Dorfman and Pete Costanza, followed reporters Olsen and Clark Kent on assignment covering the filming of a jungle flick in Africa. The chintzy director paid his native extras in baubles and free movies. During a showing of *King Kong*, the natives' deity, a female gorilla named Bruna, mimicked Kong's snatching of Ann Darrow and grabbed Jimmy as her… >ahem<… prime-mate. To appease the locals, Superman performed a marriage ceremony between Jimmy and Bruna. The newlyweds kissed, but we weren't invited to the honeymoon…

Jimmy tricked Bruna into a quickie divorce by playing for her a movie featuring an ape heaving a human off of a cliff, and Jimmy was hurled into a different type of big plunge. Fortunately, on the final page, Superman was there to catch the falling Olsen—and to spare readers from another page of this monstrosity.

THE SWINGING '70s AND BEYOND

Despite its visual spit and polish, Gold Key's *Tarzan* had grown bland by the '60s. Photo covers featuring Ron Ely (and a chimp!), during the actor's 1966–1969 starring role in TV's *Tarzan*, generated interest only while the show was on the air. Marvel's 1970 release of *Conan the Barbarian* #1, which introduced comics readers to a new kind of uncivilized hero, stole Tarzan's thunder—as well as a gorilla (Thak, the Barbarian's adversary in 1971's *Conan* #11). Tarzan was no longer fresh, and Gold Key lost the license in 1972, *Tarzan* #206 being its last issue.

DC Comics picked up the property, resuming with *Tarzan* #207, cover-dated Apr. 1972. Other than the continued numbering, nothing else about DC's *Tarzan* seemed familiar to Gold Key's readers. Writer/artist/editor Joe Kubert loyally adapted the original Burroughs stories (see the Kubert Q & Ape), his sketchy art style giving the series—and its sometimes ferocious, sometimes frolicking Great Apes—the pulpy feel intended by ERB. Kubert's apes were real, like those in Burroughs' novels.

Kubert's second issue, *Tarzan* #208, was a particular milestone in his ape renderings: The reader could almost smell the sweat (and monkey breath) as Tarzan danced in the Dum-Dum ritual with his fellow "savage revelers," and the Ape-Man's grief over the murder (by a hunter's arrow) of his adopted mother, Kala, was genuine and poignant.

Once Tarzan and Korak were no longer available, Gold Key spun off *Tarzan*'s backup, Brothers of the Spear, into its own book; launched a new series starring a pair of Korak clones, *The Jungle Twins*; and hopped on the *Conan*-inspired savage-swordsman trend with *Tales of Sword and Sorcery Starring Dagar the Invincible*. Each series featured at least one ape cover during its run. *Jungle Twins* clocked in at three.

A big Thak attack on the cover to Marvel's *Conan* #11 (Nov. 1971). Art by Barry (Windsor-) Smith.

© 2007 Conan Properties.

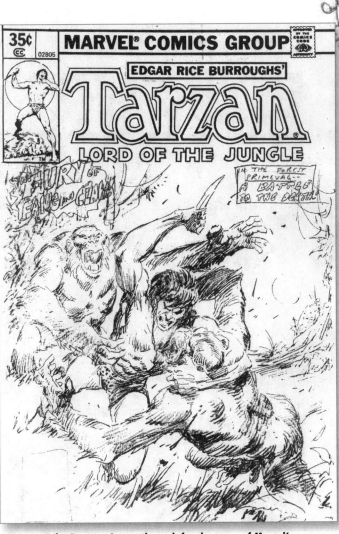

John Buscema's pencil rough for the cover of Marvel's
Tarzan #14 (July 1978). © 2007 ERB. Courtesy of Tom Ziuko.

DC had high hopes for its Kubert *Tarzan*. Carmine Infantino, then-publisher of DC (see the Infantino Q & Ape in Chapter 3), presumed Tarzan's worldwide popularity would make the title a bestseller. When "Warner Bros. had that amusement park in New Jersey, one of the Six Flags, I think, we put two books in there," Infantino recalls. "I thought *Tarzan* would be a natural… and *Superman*. *Superman* outsold *Tarzan*, can you believe it?!"

After its exciting start, DC's *Tarzan* eventually lost its energy once Kubert's busy schedule divorced him from the art chores—first he did layouts over which Rudy Florese and Frank Reyes provided finishes, then he bowed out of the title and it briefly limped along, sometimes running Kubert reprints from earlier issues, until being canceled with #258 in 1977. "It didn't do well," Infantino laments. "We didn't have luck with that character."

Marvel snatched up the property for a 29-issue run beginning with a first issue—not a renumbering of the old series—cover-dated June 1977. Writer/editor Roy Thomas adapted Burroughs stories with John Buscema as *Tarzan*'s penciler. Readers were treated to Buscema's inks over his own pencils in the first two issues, with Tony DeZuniga (and later, other inkers) embellishing his work beginning with the third issue. Especially when inking himself, Buscema's Tarzan was raw and vigorous, and his apes were frenetic and often frightening.

Moon-Boy is the monkey on Devil Dinosaur's back in this two-page spread from *Devil Dinosaur* #1 (1978). Script and pencils by Jack Kirby, inks by Mike Royer. © 2007 Marvel Characters, Inc. Courtesy of Heritage Auctions.

During *Tarzan*'s tenure at the House of Ideas, legendary writer/artist Jack Kirby produced an atypical Marvel series that was weird for even the "King's" fertile imagination: *Devil Dinosaur*, starring a crimson T-Rex and his monkey-like sidekick, "the first human," Moon-Boy. Kirby developed Devil Dinosaur with an animated TV series in mind, which never materialized. The comic book lasted a mere nine issues

Tom Yeates pencils, Al Williamson inks, from the "Tarzan vs. the Moon Men" serial written by Timothy Truman. From Dark Horse Comics' *Edgar Rice Burroughs' Tarzan* #19 (Feb. 1998). © 2007 ERB. Courtesy of Heritage Auctions.

(cover-dated Apr. 1978–Dec. 1978), but nostalgia inspired later creators to bring back both characters upon occasion, especially Moon-Boy.

Marvel's *Tarzan*, like DC's, started off strong but soon meandered and was canceled in 1979. Since then, Tarzan of the Apes has appeared on and off in comics, bringing his Great Apes with him: Marvel produced a two-issue *Tarzan* miniseries in 1984; Malibu published three *Tarzan* miniseries in 1992 and 1993; and Dark Horse Comics obtained the license in 1995, publishing a handful of *Tarzan* series through the early 2000s. Dark Horse's series were often graced by superlative visuals from artists including Tom Yeates, Lee Weeks, and Igor Korde, although it remains to be seen if history will regard any of those as "classic" Tarzan or apes illustrators.

The smattering of jungle comics that have appeared since the 1970s have leaned more toward the caveman/dinosaur genre… although don't shed tears for gorillas—as upcoming chapters show, they've found plenty of employment elsewhere.

GIRL-GRABBING GORILLAS!

TARZAN THROUGH THE YEARS

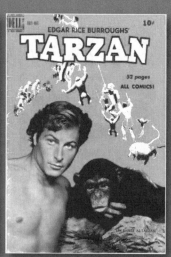

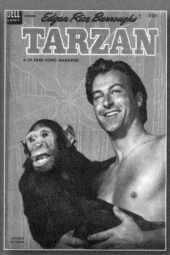

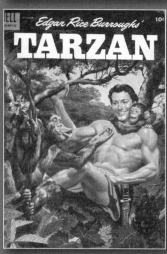

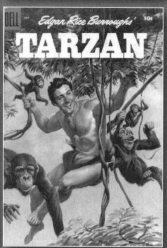

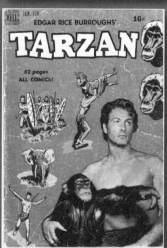

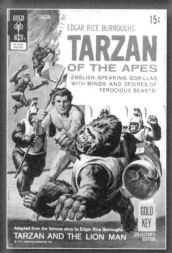

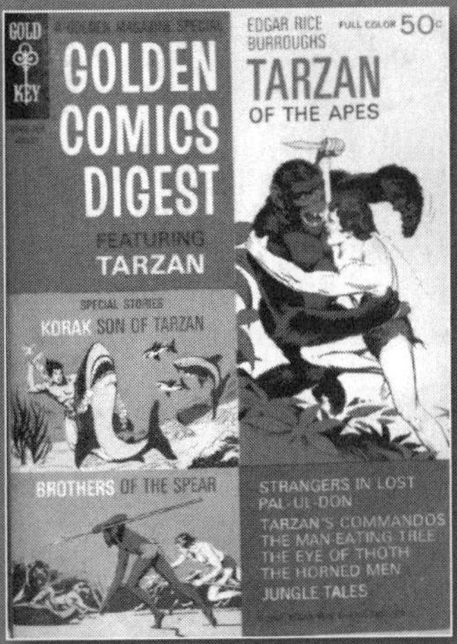
GOLD KEY
GOLDEN COMICS DIGEST
FEATURING TARZAN
EDGAR RICE BURROUGHS
TARZAN OF THE APES
FULL COLOR 50¢
SPECIAL STORIES
KORAK SON OF TARZAN
BROTHERS OF THE SPEAR
STRANGERS IN LOST PAL-UL-DON
TARZAN'S COMMANDOS
THE MAN-EATING TREE
THE EYE OF THOTH
THE HORNED MEN
JUNGLE TALES
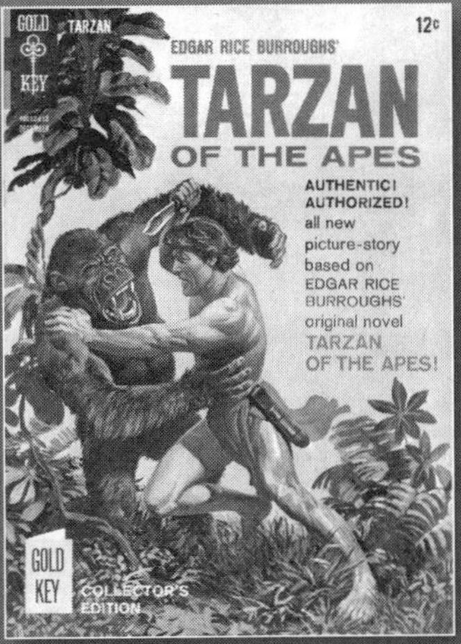
GOLD KEY
TARZAN
12¢
EDGAR RICE BURROUGHS'
TARZAN OF THE APES
AUTHENTIC! AUTHORIZED! all new picture-story based on EDGAR RICE BURROUGHS' original novel TARZAN OF THE APES!
COLLECTOR'S EDITION
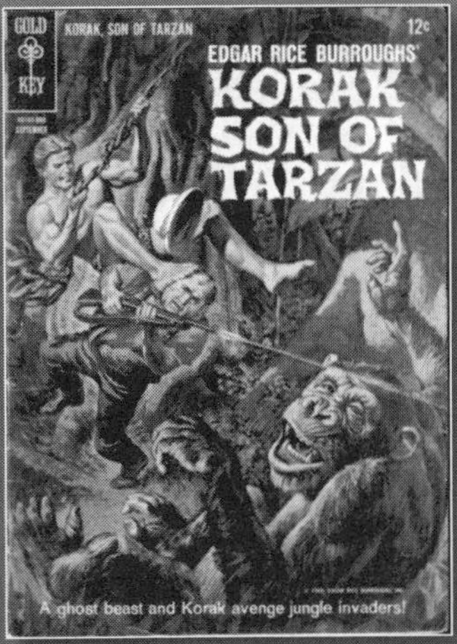
GOLD KEY
KORAK, SON OF TARZAN
12¢
EDGAR RICE BURROUGHS'
KORAK SON OF TARZAN
A ghost beast and Korak avenge jungle invaders!
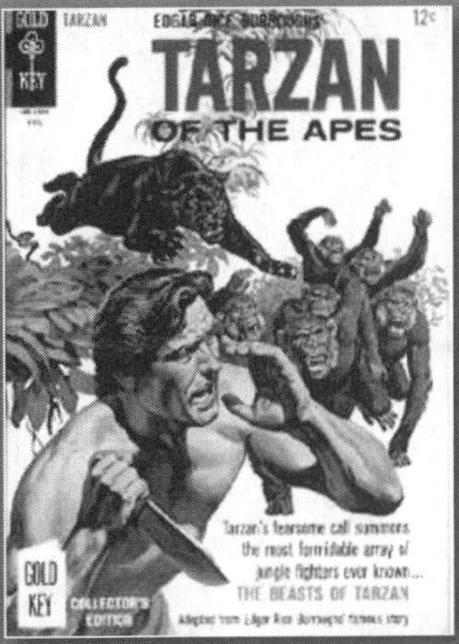
GOLD KEY
TARZAN
12¢
EDGAR RICE BURROUGHS'
TARZAN OF THE APES
Tarzan's fearsome call summons the most formidable array of jungle fighters ever known... THE BEASTS OF TARZAN
COLLECTOR'S EDITION
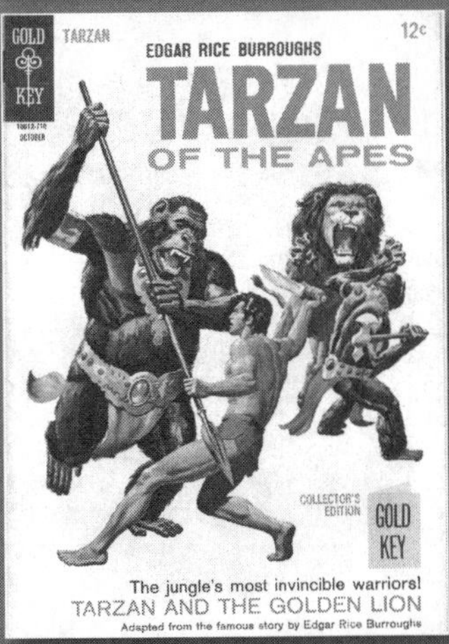
GOLD KEY
TARZAN
12¢
EDGAR RICE BURROUGHS
TARZAN OF THE APES
COLLECTOR'S EDITION
The jungle's most invincible warriors!
TARZAN AND THE GOLDEN LION
Adapted from the famous story by Edgar Rice Burroughs
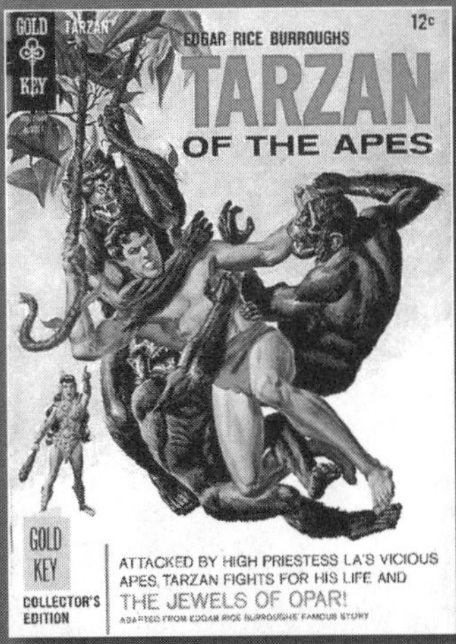
GOLD KEY
TARZAN
12¢
EDGAR RICE BURROUGHS
TARZAN OF THE APES
ATTACKED BY HIGH PRIESTESS LA'S VICIOUS APES, TARZAN FIGHTS FOR HIS LIFE AND THE JEWELS OF OPAR!
COLLECTOR'S EDITION
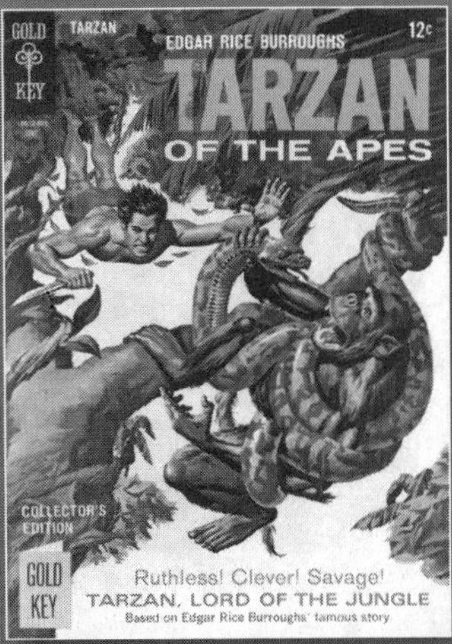
GOLD KEY
TARZAN
12¢
EDGAR RICE BURROUGHS
TARZAN OF THE APES
COLLECTOR'S EDITION
Ruthless! Clever! Savage!
TARZAN, LORD OF THE JUNGLE
Based on Edgar Rice Burroughs' famous story
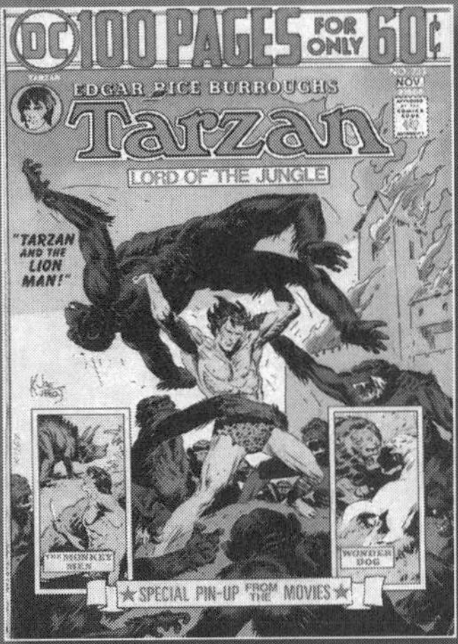
DC 100 PAGES FOR ONLY 60¢
EDGAR RICE BURROUGHS
Tarzan
LORD OF THE JUNGLE
"TARZAN AND THE LION MAN!"
SPECIAL PIN-UP FROM THE MOVIES
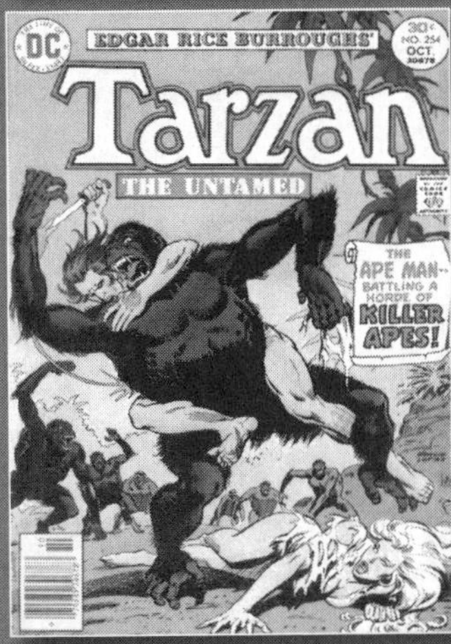
DC
EDGAR RICE BURROUGHS'
NO. 254 OCT.
Tarzan
THE UNTAMED
THE APE MAN-- BATTLING A HORDE OF KILLER APES!
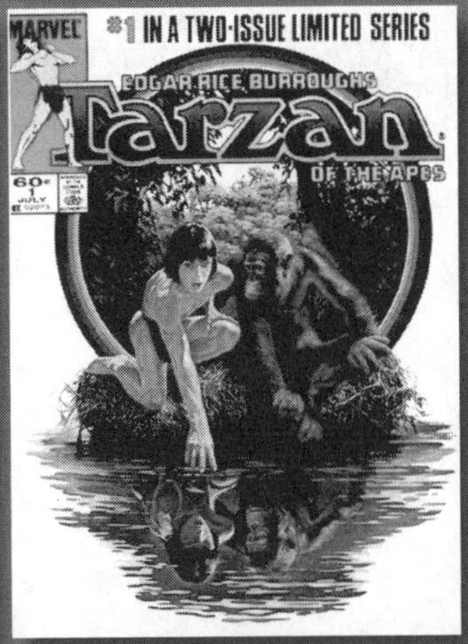
MARVEL
#1 IN A TWO-ISSUE LIMITED SERIES
EDGAR RICE BURROUGHS
Tarzan
OF THE APES
60¢
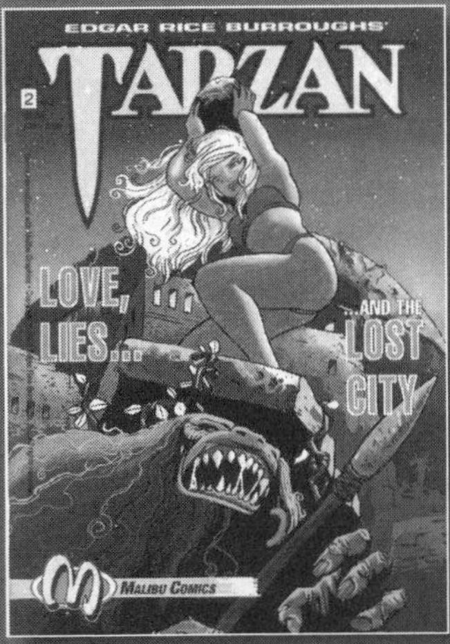
EDGAR RICE BURROUGHS'
TARZAN
LOVE, LIES...
...AND THE LOST CITY
MALIBU COMICS
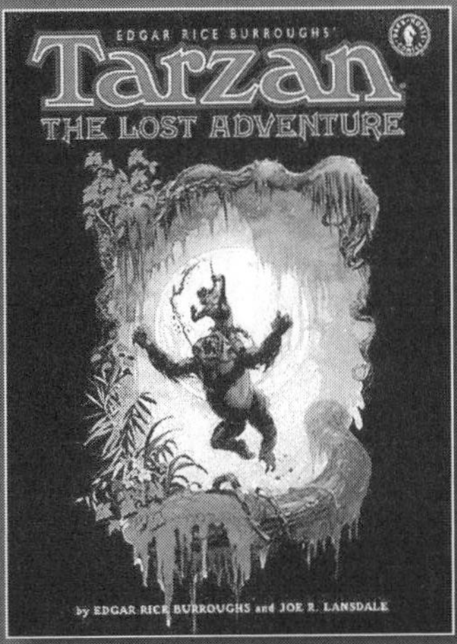
EDGAR RICE BURROUGHS'
Tarzan
THE LOST ADVENTURE
by EDGAR RICE BURROUGHS and JOE R. LANSDALE
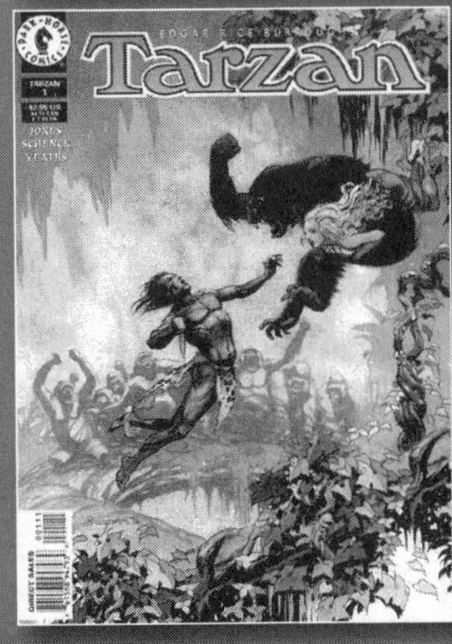
EDGAR RICE BURROUGHS'
Tarzan
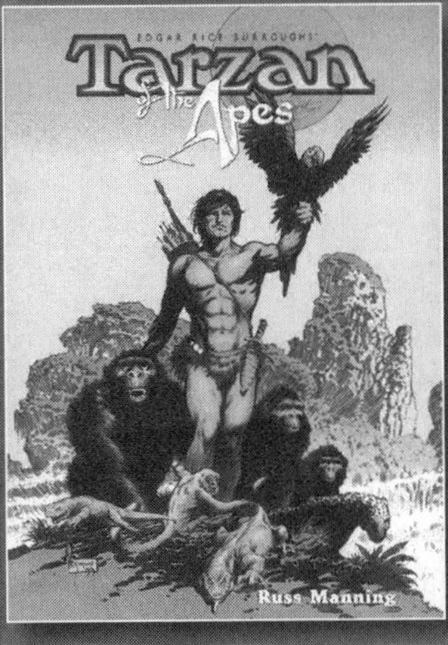
EDGAR RICE BURROUGHS'
Tarzan
of the Apes
Russ Manning
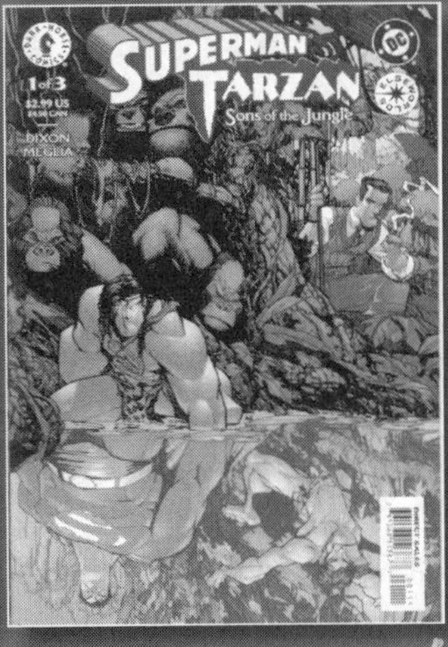
SUPERMAN
TARZAN
Sons of the Jungle
1 of 3
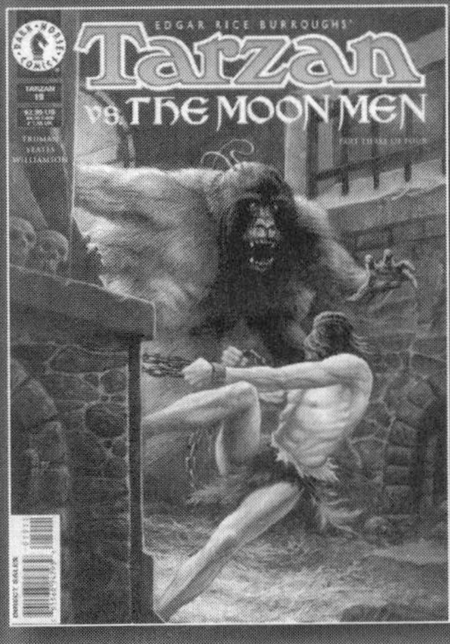
EDGAR RICE BURROUGHS'
Tarzan
VS. THE MOON MEN

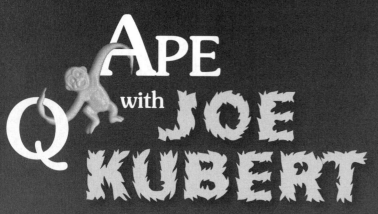

Ape Q with JOE KUBERT

Conducted by telephone on September 13, 2006

SPOTTED AMONG THE APES IN:

Tor, Tarzan, Sgt. Gorilla in *Star Spangled War Stories,*
random DC Comics gorilla covers

OTHER CAREER HIGHLIGHTS:

Flash Comics, co-creator of 3-D comics (1953), Viking Prince,
Silver Age Hawkman, Sgt. Rock, Enemy Ace, *Tales of the
Green Berets* comic strip (1966–1968),
The Joe Kubert School of Cartoon and Graphic Art,
Fax from Sarajevo

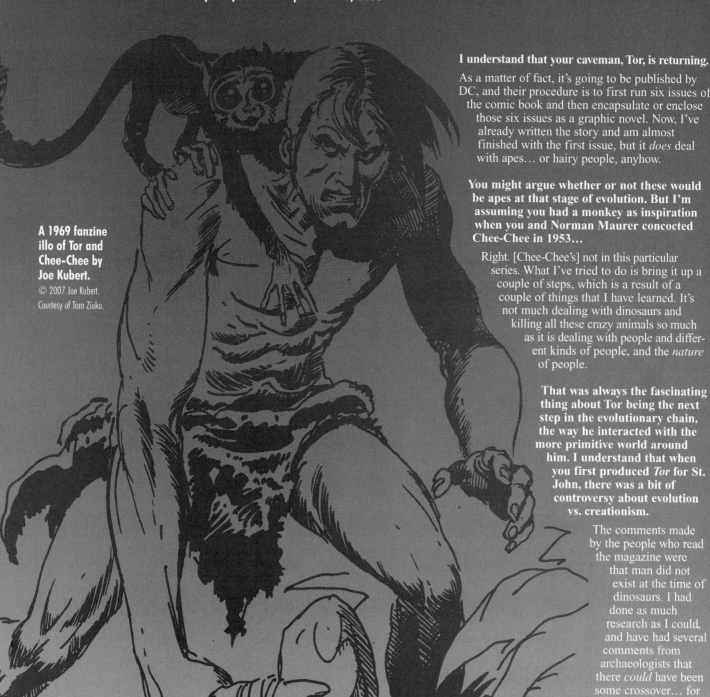

**A 1969 fanzine
illo of Tor and
Chee-Chee by
Joe Kubert.**
© 2007 Joe Kubert.
Courtesy of Tom Ziuko.

I understand that your caveman, Tor, is returning.

As a matter of fact, it's going to be published by
DC, and their procedure is to first run six issues of
the comic book and then encapsulate or enclose
those six issues as a graphic novel. Now, I've
already written the story and am almost
finished with the first issue, but it *does* deal
with apes… or hairy people, anyhow.

**You might argue whether or not these would
be apes at that stage of evolution. But I'm
assuming you had a monkey as inspiration
when you and Norman Maurer concocted
Chee-Chee in 1953…**

Right. [Chee-Chee's] not in this particular
series. What I've tried to do is bring it up a
couple of steps, which is a result of a
couple of things that I have learned. It's
not much dealing with dinosaurs and
killing all these crazy animals so much
as it is dealing with people and different kinds of people, and the *nature*
of people.

**That was always the fascinating
thing about Tor being the next
step in the evolutionary chain,
the way he interacted with the
more primitive world around
him. I understand that when
you first produced *Tor* for St.
John, there was a bit of
controversy about evolution
vs. creationism.**

The comments made
by the people who read
the magazine were
that man did not
exist at the time of
dinosaurs. I had
done as much
research as I could,
and have had several
comments from
archaeologists that
there *could* have been
some crossover… for

example, something that resembles people—not necessarily people who looked like the character of Tor—they could be designated as people and could have possibly existed during the time that dinosaurs were dying out. So that's my answer.

I grew up with *The Flintstones*, so I'm used to a wooly mammoth as a vacuum cleaner, you know. The medium of comics enjoys the suspension of belief... some things have to be taken with a grain of salt.

That was my very optimistic answer! [*laughter*]

So apes are involved in the new *Tor* storyline?

Well, kind of. I sort of stepped off the classic gorilla type and tried to make the crossover, the missing link, where they still resemble apes to a great extent, but are taking on more the look of humans.

Regarding the original material, what do you think Chee-Chee brought to *Tor*?

Well, as you've described, he was a monkey-type second banana, so to speak.

This photo of then-partners Joe Kubert and Norman Maurer was originally published in 1953 in *1,000,000 Years Ago!* #1. On their drawing board is the cover artwork for *Three Stooges* #1 & *1,000,000 Years Ago!* #1.

Good choice of words.

At the time, when I put the story together, I thought it would be great. Tarzan had Cheeta the chimp as buddy and friend, and Chee-Chee was a smaller version of that—a monkey, a likeable monkeylike form, and it made it easy for him to tag along and add a little bit of humor to the story.

The original *King Kong* movie was released during your childhood. For those of us who discovered Kong from reruns or remakes, describe what it was like when this was something *brand new*.

Incredible. As a young person coming into a movie theater, where the screen was so large, especially compared to today, when

you saw this ape appear on the screen, it was shocking—shocking and mesmerizing at the same time. It just drove my imagination into all kinds of directions. All these things—the movie, reading the *Tarzan* stories originally done by Hal Foster—all engendered an interest in me to want to draw these things and other things as well, to at least in some way generate the kind of impact in my drawing that these things created on me.

You've succeeded quite well. As a matter of fact, I've recently reread some of your very first *Tarzan* stories that you produced for DC... there's a timelessness to them, and they hold up very well today.

It was a joy to do it. It was like revisiting my younger years.

When I started *Tarzan*, what I did was go through all the Burroughs books—I think there were 30 or 31 of them that were originally written—and I reread them. I had read them when I was a kid, but I wanted to get back that same flavor that I got when I read them as a kid, which is what I wanted to inject when I did them. Then I read the Foster *Tarzan*s, and those really impressed me. I think those newspaper strips came out in the early '30s, [when] I was four or five years old. I still recall getting the newspaper where I saw the strip for the first time, *The New York Mirror*, in which *Tarzan* took the whole back page of the tabloid paper. I looked forward to that; it only appeared on one day of the week, on Sunday. I just loved it. Foster and his work beyond *Tarzan* was an inspiration to me and I don't know how many [other] guys who came into the business. When I read that as a kid, it was more alive to me than many of the movies I saw afterwards. When I read the stuff that Foster did, I felt that *I* was in that jungle. I felt that absolutely that the Tarzan character was a real, living person. That's what I tried to do. That's why I reread the stuff and got as much of that material as I could. Not to emulate, not to copy what I saw, but to get that certain element that he was able to get into his work. Foster was a master at storytelling and characterization.

I think you've succeeded at that just as well. Both of you have been able to produce a dense, but very alive jungle atmosphere for *Tarzan*.

I thank you for what you're saying.

You're welcome.

When [former DC editorial director] Carmine Infantino was approached by the Burroughs people to do *Tarzan*, you weren't part of the package, is that correct?

There are perhaps two stories. [*laughs*] My

© 2007 Joe Kubert.

© 2007 DC Comics.

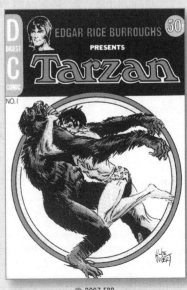

© 2007 ERB.

Early variant covers (with the same interior contents), on *3-D Comics* #2 (the Oct. 1953 and Nov. 1953 editions), a.k.a. *Tor* #2. The Nov. edition's cover is also in 3-D. © 2007 Joe Kubert.

understanding was when Carmine asked me if I was interested in doing *Tarzan*, I was editing half a dozen or more other books at the time—a lot of war books, [it was] perhaps closer to ten books I was editing. When the Tarzan deal came up, as I remember it, Carmine offered it to me if I wanted to do *Tarzan*; he knew of my interest in the Tarzan character. As I remember it, the Burroughs people, having seen my work, wanted me to do it.

Later on, years later, and perhaps I heard it wrong, but later on Carmine told me that the Burroughs people weren't too sure about my doing the Tarzan character until they saw the first few stories that I did. I can't fault Carmine for that, but I doubt that second version a little bit, simply because [publisher] Mike Richardson, up at Dark Horse, had spoken to Danton Burroughs. Mike told me that Burroughs said that he was delighted when he heard that my version of Tarzan was going to be put in the form that Mike Richardson eventually published.

As you know, stories get colored with different perspectives over the years and as our memories falter. We either misremember or have our own spin on things.

This isn't an accusation that Carmine is wrong, you know. I might have very easily misread it. The versions I repeated are the ones I know.

I've been told by Carmine that the Burroughs licensors originally wanted their own, previous *Tarzan* artists on the DC series, but he believed that you were the right person for the job—and that once they saw your work, *they*

agreed. **Whatever the genesis, the end result, of course, is one of the most memorable Tarzan interpretations that lives on today, collected in hardcover by Dark Horse.**

It's very gratifying.

With the affinity you have for the character and to Burroughs and Foster, when *Tarzan* became a reality for you it must have been *extremely* gratifying.

Very, very gratifying. Doing that series was a wonderful, wonderful experience. Very enjoyable to me. The only lousy part of it, Mike, [was that] I had so much other work I had to do. I [eventually] relegated myself to just doing very tight breakdowns, 8½" x 11", that I sent to the Filipino artists who did a wonderful job, but it just wasn't what I felt that I wanted to do myself.

What were some of your biggest challenges in adapting Burroughs stories to comics?

It was a challenge to the extent that some things were strictly prose; or [with stories] that were illustrated before, trying to compare them to a form or forms that were done before was a challenge. I found it easier to do the stories that hadn't been done [in comics form] before. I found it more difficult to do stories that *had* been done, simply because the earlier stories that had been done by Foster were so damn hard [to redo]. [*laughter*] I didn't see that there were many other directions that could have been done to tell the story other than what Foster did.

Your ability to draw apes is amazing… I'm curious to hear what kind of reference you used.

I don't know how many books, *National Geographic*s, and novels [I consulted].

The apes that Foster drew were *his* conceptions of a different kind of gorilla. If you compare what he drew with *Tarzan* in 1931, '32, they weren't true chimpanzees or gorillas… they were something just slightly different from actual living gorillas. I approached it the same way. And the result was my conception based on my references and backgrounds I did. I went down to the zoo, doing sketches, and what I tried to capture were the movements, reactions, the facial characteristics, the variations between different gorillas. I also found chimpanzees very helpful, because their expressions are a heck of lot more elastic and flexible than those of a gorilla. I tried to incorporate all these things when I was doing the gorilla characters.

I've watched a lot of *Animal Planet* television footage of apes recently, particularly of chimpanzees, and I agree with you regarding the overall elasticity and… the "humanness" of their facial features, especially their eyes. There's an emotional connection with the humans they interact with.

Exactly.

Most readers aren't aware that you drew one of DC's earliest gorilla covers, a Hawkman cover for *Flash Comics* #70 (Apr. 1946), featuring a gorilla with boxing gloves…

© 2007 DC Comics.

Oh, God, you just reminded me of this. Yes. That was years ago.

Was that your first professional ape drawing?

I can't recall. I can't say that, but I know it was one of the earliest.

Do you remember Sgt. Gorilla, from Bob Kanigher's story "You Can't Pin a Medal on a Gorilla!" (*Star Spangled War Stories* #126, Apr.–May 1966)?

Vaguely. I don't have any copies of that.

You not only did the cover, but you drew the story, too.

Oh, did I?

Yes, sir, you did indeed. It was about a serviceman who was an entertainer. He had a pet gorilla that was there with the troops—a gorilla in a US Marines uniform. "Sgt. Gorilla" emulated human behavior, and saved the soldiers at the end of the story.

[*laughs*] I don't remember that, not at all.

A gorilla G.I. was a bit far-fetched for the realism of DC's war comics— discounting "The War That Time Forgot" series, maybe. But of course, gorilla covers are a longtime staple at DC.

Well, you know the reason for that?

I'd like to hear it from your perspective!

The way I got it was, [DC editor] Julie Schwartz had discovered that sales increased when there was a gorilla on the cover.

That's what I'd heard, too. I wanted to know if that was a fact… or an urban myth.

I'd spoken to Julie about this many times over the years. I think there were other covers, not many, one or two, when they repeated an illustration and the sales came up a little bit, but especially with the gorilla covers. Then they came out with a whole flurry of gorilla covers… as comic books usually do, if one sells, put out a hundred. Surprise, surprise! A hundred don't sell as well. [*laughter*]

Is there anything else you'd like to add about apes and our fascination with them?

Well, there is a deep connection between what I've seen, and what I've known, and what I've learned about gorillas' behavior that has helped me do what I'm doing, and helped me understand animals in general. The tendency is for us to give apes human qualities simply because they look so much like us. But beyond that, I've tried to understand and see some humanity in the movement and reaction of the gorilla itself. That extends to all animals and this helps people, *me* in particular, to try to understand try to incorporate that with other animals in other drawings. It's helped me with everything in general.

Sans logo and graphics, Kubert's gorilla-loaded cover art to DC's *Tarzan* #249 (May 1976), part 2 of Joe's adaptation of Burroughs' *Tarzan and the Champion*. © 2007 ERB.

Q APE with ANNE TIMMONS

SPOTTED AMONG THE APES IN:

Wild Person in the Woods, *"Talking" Orangutans in Borneo*, *Jane Goodall: Animal Scientist*

OTHER CAREER HIGHLIGHTS:

GoGirl!, *Dignifying Science*

Conducted via email on October 4, 2006

Dr. Galdikas makes a friend on page 14 of *Wild Person in the Woods*. Art by Anne Timmons. (This story was collected in the *Dignifying Science* trade paperback, available at *http://gt-labs.com/dignifying.html*.)

You illustrated two "edu-comics" scripted by Jim Ottaviani, *Wild Person in the Woods* and *"Talking" Orangutans in Borneo*, for the Orangutan Foundation International (*www.orangutan.com*). Would you briefly recap their stories?

Wild Person in the Woods is a story of Biruté Galdikas, who is a leading authority on orangutan

Timmons' artwork to page 13 of *"Talking" Orangutans in Borneo.*

behavior and has studied them in the wild. The story is based on her journals and her work. Her colleague, Dr. Gary Shapiro, worked with her in Borneo. He took the study a step further: Along with helping Galdikas fight poachers and forest fires, he was able to teach one of the orangutans to communicate using sign language. Both stories are told in kind of a day-in-the-life, stretching over several decades.

How did you get those assignments?

I had heard about Jim Ottaviani's comics through a mutual friend, Steve Lieber. He'd told me about a book that Jim was doing on orangutans. I jumped at the chance to work on this because I love to draw animals.

Did you have any interest in orangutans before those projects?

I've been pretty fascinated with all animals. I actually was more familiar with Jane Goodall's work with chimpanzees. I learned that she and Biruté were colleagues and both studied under and worked with anthropologist Louis Leakey.

Speaking of Jane Goodall, I recently inked a Goodall biographical graphic novel [penciled by Cynthia Martin]. This book is published by Capstone Press— more apes! [*Editor's note:* Discover the Jane Goodall book at *www.capstonepress.com.*]

What type of research did you conduct before drawing those stories?

I was fortunate to watch the orangutans at the Portland [Oregon] Zoo and I also observed the orangutans at the San Diego Zoo. I sketched them and took lots of photographs. They make marvelous subjects for drawing because they are very sedentary until it's meal time!

Did you get to meet Dr. Galdikas, the "star" of *Wild Person*?

I have not had the opportunity to meet her, but I heard she really liked the comic. The Orangutan Foundation International (OFI), of which she is the president, purchased most of the first print run of *Wild Person in the Woods.* Jim Ottaviani and I were also approached by OFI to do the other book, *"Talking"*

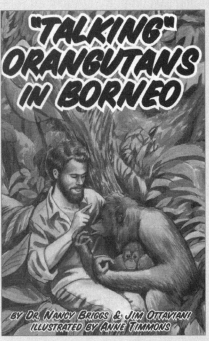

Orangutans in Borneo. Their key interest was to publish the books to help educate people on how they can help save the orangutans.

Dr. Galdikas joins Jane Goodall and the late Dian Fossey as three of the most famous primatologists. Any theories as to why these (and other) women have been drawn to studying apes in their native habitats?

I think some women have more patience with animals. They know that animals are unpredictable, and they go into the research knowing that they may need to sit still for many hours or days before they see any action. I think these women prefer to work alone or in very small groups when they are so devoted to their study. Also, I think some women feel that they can help the animals trust them. Of course, there are men who work with animals. Dr. Shapiro (who I painted for the cover of *"Talking" Orangutans*) has worked with orangutans for a long time.

Conversely, aside from you, the ape-drawing comics community seems to be a boys' club. Why don't female cartoonists like drawing monkeys?

I think female cartoonists would love to draw apes if given the opportunity. Honestly, I learned so much about drawing from drawing these orangutans. It helped me with my drawing because I really studied their movement.

If you had to choose comics' all-time best ape artist, who would it be?

I don't really have a favorite artist. I guess I admire anyone who can draw any ape with accuracy.

Who's your favorite fictional ape?

I would have to say that King Kong is my favorite ape. I like all of the film adaptations. I just like the story. But more than anything I am fascinated by how they make that huge gorilla look so real and show so many emotions.

Most super-heroes have either fought evil apes or been temporarily turned into gorillas. Has this happened to GoGirl?

Not yet. She *has* had her troubles with giant robots, though, in *GoGirl!: Robots Gone Wild* (Dark Horse, 2006)!

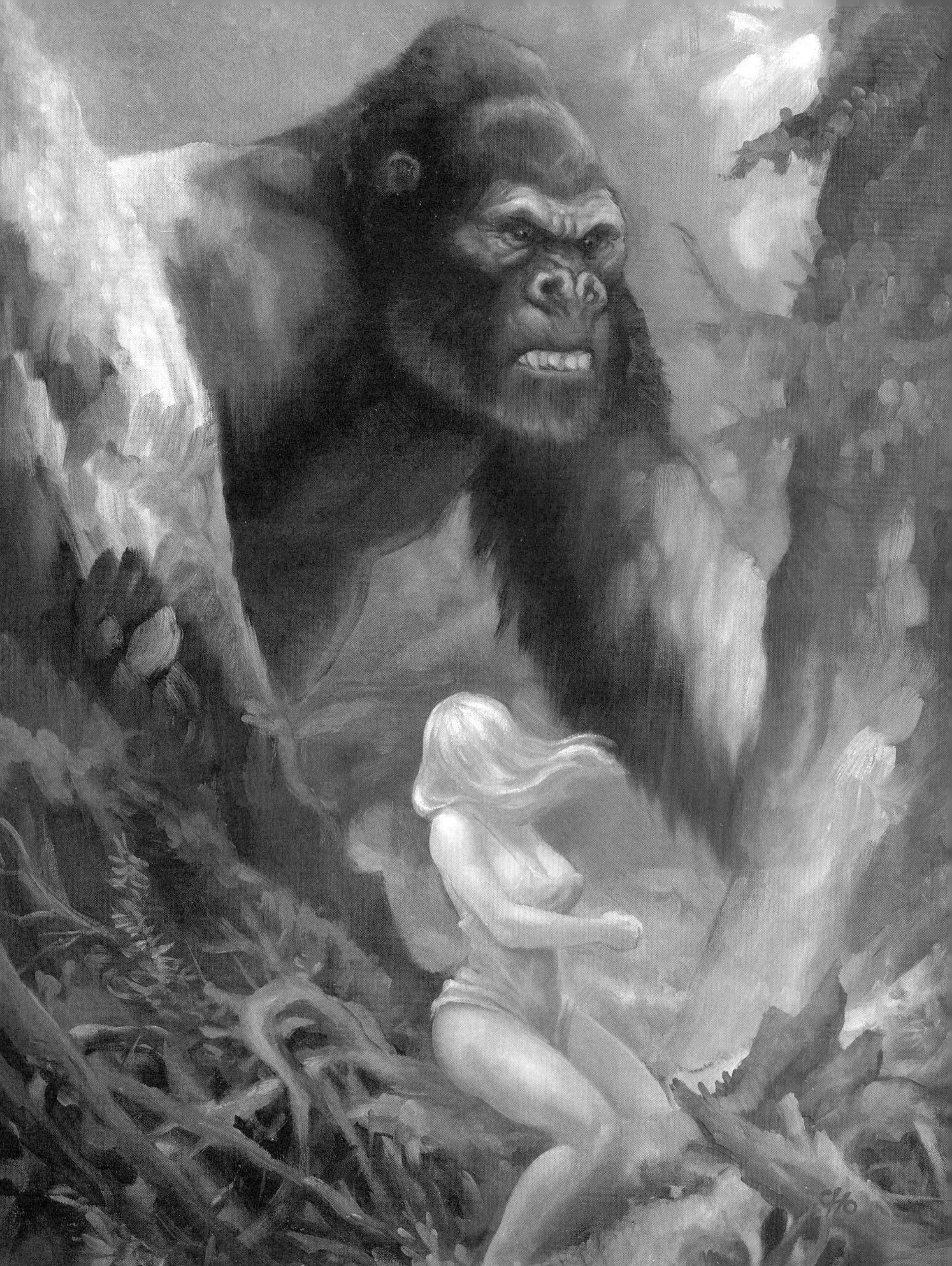

"Encounter." Frank Cho's lush giant ape-meets-girl painting. Courtesy of the artist.

Bright lights, big city... even bigger gorilla. One that's ten times as big as a man!
Eighth Wonder of the World, or most-aped ape? These Kong klones are...

WALKING TALL!

Stop me if you've heard this one: A metro girl pretty enough to turn the Pope's head catches the eye of a jungle giant. This beast won't take no for an answer and keeps reaching out to her. Her boyfriend tries to protect her, even though he's out of his league, leading to a showdown atop the city's most recognizable landmark—

—the *Daily Planet* building.

"More Fantastic Than KING KONG!" roared the cover blurb of *Superman* #127 (Feb. 1959), which introduced the super-sized Super-Ape, Titano. Editor Mort Weisinger so liked that copy that it was recycled in Otto Binder's splash-panel caption of Titano's second appearance, *Superman* #138 (July 1960). (Incidentally, Titano scaled the *Planet* building in his second story, not his first.)

But *more fantastic* than *Kong*? Sorry, Titano, Kong's the King.

The original film version of *King Kong*, directed by Merian C. Cooper and Ernest B. Schoedsack and based upon a story by Cooper and Edgar Wallace, stomped into theaters on March 2, 1933. It starred a very blonde Fay Wray as "golden goddess" Ann Darrow, the movies' most famous damsel in distress, and slick-haired Robert Armstrong as slick-tongued Carl Denham, the go-getting filmmaker whose determination to make the ultimate in jungle pictures nearly wrecks Manhattan. The film's *true* star, however, was pioneering stop-motion animator Willis O'Brien. From King Kong's dinosaur battle in the murky jungles of Skull Island to his tragic last stand on the spire of the Empire State Building, Kong was shocking and completely believable, thanks to O'Brien. Muscling an initial box office of over $10

© 2007 DC Comics.

million (at a cost of $670,000), *King Kong* was a huge hit for the then-suffering RKO Pictures—and a profound inspiration to generations of comic-book artists.

Despite that acclaim, it took three-and-a-half decades for King Kong to become a comic-book star. Although if you weren't a careful reader, you might've *thought* you'd seen him around...

KONGA

King Kong loves New York, but London's calling Konga.

Before he became a Hollywood producer, Herman Cohen (1925–2002) honed his chops as the assistant producer of *Bride of the Gorilla* (1951) and (real title!) *Bela Lugosi Meets a Brooklyn Gorilla* (1952). Could any man be better qualified to executive-produce the next giant-gorilla movie??

Such a monumental task required a partner. Cohen and Aben Kandel had co-written a string of late-'50s teen-horror flicks like

***Konga* movie poster.**
© 1961 Herman Cohen Productions. Courtesy of Heritage Auctions.

Ever hear of "the Black Monkey"? Of *course* you haven't! That's because giant chimpanzees *do not make scary monsters*, as *Boris Karloff Tales of Mystery* #46 (1973) shows. So *never* question why Konga grew from chimp to gorilla…
© 2007 Boris Karloff estate.

I Was a Teenage Werewolf and *How to Make a Monster*. Together they penned *Konga*, directed by John Lemont and released by American International Pictures in March 1961. *Konga* starred Michael Gough—you probably know him as the pre–Michael Caine Alfred of the *Batman* movies—as Dr. Charles Decker, part-time botanist, part-time girl-crazy whackjob. Since

doctors in monster movies are cliché-obliged to create the film's beast, Decker, like a mad Alec Holland, gives a chimpanzee regular injections of his plant-based growth serum. Instead of becoming a bigger chimp, "Konga" sprouts into a full-grown gorilla and becomes Decker's obedient executioner—until stretching for new heights as the Kong-sized leveler of London.

Konga was indeed "…as big as KING KONG!"—it said so on the cover to his first comic book, published by Charlton Comics in 1960, *before* the film's release (a Monarch paperback based on the movie was also issued in 1960). Dick Giordano's *Konga* #1 cover art is the perfect movie teaser: It recreates the movie's climactic battle with its rumbling mega-rilla defying

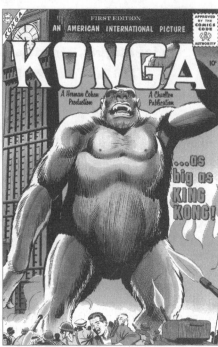

Charlton Comics' *Konga* #1 (June 1960). Cover art by Dick Giordano.
© 1960 Herman Cohen Productions.

All the big guy wants is a buddy! The Steve Ditko-drawn splash page to *Konga* #12 (May 1963).
© 1963 Herman Cohen Productions. Courtesy of Michael Ambrose and *Charlton Spotlight*.

YEEEOOOOOW

soldiers at Big Ben, *Konga*'s Empire State Building proxy. Just look at those Brits run! The next time you'd see this much monkey-mania in London would be during the *Planet of the Apes* craze of the '70s (see Chapter 6).

The movie kicked up enough stir for Charlton to resume publication of *Konga*, its second issue cover-dated Aug. 1961. Since (SPOILER WARNING!) Konga perished at the end of the first issue, Charlton's ongoing *Konga* series introduced a "version 2" of the character, under the tutelage of researchers Sandra and Bob, who were carrying Decker's research into more beneficial directions. But what do you do in a continuity about a monster protagonist? A better question in this case might be, "What *don't* you do?" *Konga* appropriated from current cinema, classic sci-fi, and real-world headlines: Mutant prehistoric beasts, the hydrogen bomb, flying saucers, Communist armies, subterranean cavemen, and giant robots were all enemies of the big brute. You could never predict what Konga would face next.

Nor could you predict how he would be drawn—from cover to cover, issue to issue, Konga might appear potbellied, or barrel-chested, or wiry, or with an abnormally large head. If the artists were working from model sheets, they clearly weren't following them.

Steve Ditko drew many of *Konga*'s stories and some of its covers. Unlike the terrifying Konga in the movie, Ditko's Konga was playful and approachable, an alteration necessary to sustain the beast as a regular character. Overall, Ditko's quirky art style was comfortably suited to the book's eccentricities.

The inexhaustible Joe Gill was *Konga*'s chief writer, which should surprise no one familiar with Charlton's history and Gill's scripting of much of it. His goal with both *Konga* and Charlton's other giant-monster headliner, *Gorgo*, was to make each of the beasts "a sympathetic character," Gill told Jim Amash in an interview for *Charlton Spotlight* #5 (Fall 2006). *Konga* continued until late 1965 for a run of 23 issues, each issue carrying the cover brand (or derivative thereof), "A Herman Cohen Production." The book was retitled *Fantastic Giants* (doubling up with *Gorgo*) for a 24th and final issue in 1966; Charlton also published *Konga* one-shots, the last being a 1968 reprint.

FOLLOWING KONG'S FOOTPRINTS

But long before Konga, other giant gorillas tried their best to steal Kong's thunder. The ape fighting the super-magician Yarko on artist Lou Fine's cover to *Wonder Comics* #2 (1939) is close to Kong-sized, and is cradling a Fay Wray wannabe just to make sure Yarko's young readers didn't miss the Kong reference. Dan Ripoll, a collector of King Kong original art, notes that Fine's "cover image was later swiped by Bob Kane and included in Oct. 1939's *Detective Comics* #31, which has a giant gorilla kidnapping Batman's fiancée."

Thirteen years after *Wonder Comics* #2, Ken Bald's cover to *Forbidden Worlds* #6 (1952) featured a skyscraping simian with girl in hand, fighting warplanes from a highrise. Not only did *King Kong* make the giant gorilla a monster archetype, but its Empire State Building battle was now of equal pop-culture stature.

Throughout the Silver Age, comic books of every stripe—from *Strange Worlds* to *The Dick Van Dyke Show* to *Turok, Son of Stone* to *Blackhawk*—featured giant gorillas on their covers and in stories, bridging comics' first home of gorillas—jungle series—with the

sci-fi series of the 1950s where mutant or intelligent gorillas became commonplace (see Chapter 4). This trend has continued for decades since. There are so many King Kong tributes, take-offs, and rip-offs that a full reckoning would drive the average reader to a rooftop for a maddened rant. Most of them can be found in the accompanying Kong-a-Line Cover Gallery, but some of the King's followers are true standouts…

(above) Lou Fine's cover to *Wonder Comics* #2 (June 1939), and (below) Bob Kane's swipe of Fine's ape from Batman's fifth story in *Detective Comics* #31 (Sept. 1939).

Ken Bald's unabashed Kong pastiche, from *Forbidden Worlds* #6 (1952).

10 BIG APES

YOU CAN LOOK UP TO!

1. TITANO THE SUPER-APE

Joining editor Weisinger and writer Binder on *Superman* #127's "Titano the Super-Ape!" were penciler Wayne Boring and inker Stan Kaye. Just imagine those idea wheels turning in Weisinger's New York office back in '58: *Chimpanzees Cheeta and Zippy are household names, so why don't we turn a chimp into King Kong?* (Herman Cohen was thinking the same thing 3,000 miles away in Hollywood…)

In *Superman* #127's Titano origin story, Titano was born Toto, the "famous intelligent chimp" that had a crush on Lois Lane.

Like Ham the astro-chimp in the real world's headlines, Toto was blasted into orbit, where his ship was whacked by uranium and kryptonite meteors. Returning home, the irradiated Toto mutated into the giant ape Titano, and his newly acquired Kryptonite vision kept Superman from getting too close.

Readers responded positively to Titano, although a few felt twinges of déjà vu: Before *Superman* #127, the character had already been tried out, as "Big Boy," in the *Superman* comic strip.

Weisinger brought back Titano the next year, in *Superman* #138, by the Binder/Boring/Kaye team, even recycling the original "Titano the Super-Ape!" story title for the rematch. Boring originally drew Titano with a chimp's head on giant gorilla body, just like he had done earlier as the artist of sequence of syndicated dailies featuring "Big Boy." For the Super-Ape's second outing, Titano's head was now a gorilla's, making his appearance more Kong-like.

Titano was a semi-regular in Weisinger's Super-titles until the mid-1960s, then returned in 1970 in one of the editor's last *Superman* tales. Writer Martin Pasko brought back Titano in 1978, in *Superman* #323–325. In Pasko's own words (from his March 2006 interview in my book, *The Krypton Companion*), the Super-Ape's return was ill-fated: "We kept forgetting that what you got when you called upon the hyper-realistic and earthbound Curt Swan to draw menacing giant monsters invariably they looked cute and cuddly at best, and at worst, like something that reminded you of an old Toho movie and made you look for the zipper. I seem to recall that the mail suggested that Titano was one Weisingerism that was best relegated to obscurity."

…Which is where Titano resided until *Superman Annual* vol. 2 #1 (1987), when he was reintroduced in Superman's post-*Man of Steel* revised continuity. John Byrne wrote (with co-plotter/penciler Ron Frenz) "Tears for Titano!", the story of a genetically altered laboratory chimp mutated to gigantic proportions by a scientist attempting to create an army of super-soldiers. Frenz's Titano returned to the original chimp-faced interpretation for the character's single appearance. A shapeshifting menace did a messy walk-on "as" Titano in *Superman/Batman* #28 (2006). Outside of comic books, Titano has appeared in Superman TV cartoons in 1966 and 1997.

2. BIZARRO TITANO

By the time 1962 rolled around, Superman's dopey doppelganger, Bizarro No. 1, had populated his backwards Bizarro World with imperfect duplicates of just about every character in the Superman family. Titano got his shot in *Adventure Comics* #295 (Apr. 1962), becoming a raging Bizarro-beast in "The Kookie Super-Ape!" Since the

© 2007 DC Comics.

Bizarro Code is "Us do opposite of all earthly things," Bizarro-Titano *should* have been docile instead of the easy-to-anger big ape written by Jerry Siegel and penciled by John Forte. But logic never applied to a Bizarro story, and besides, Bizarro-Titano's wrestling match with Bizarro-Lois No. 1 ranks as one of the goofiest moments in DC's Silver Age.

3. KINGORILLA

Titano wasn't DC Comics' first attempt to squeeze "King Kong" into its Superman mythos. In *Adventure Comics* #196 (Jan.

© 2007 DC Comics.

1954), Super*boy* ("The Adventures of Superman When He Was a Boy") had a smackdown with the rampaging giant Kingorilla. This story, drawn by John Sikela and possibly written by William Woolfolk (remember, story credits were rare in those days), took teenage Clark (Superboy) Kent and Lana Lang into the African jungle to find Lana's missing parents. It soon blatantly sponged off *King Kong* by having the Langs and Clark held captive by natives as sacrifices to Kingorilla, but seeing Superboy in action against a mammoth ape was a heck of a lot of fun.

4. GORGILLA

Before he co-created the Fantastic Four in 1961, writer/editor Stan Lee had had his fill of scripting the innocuous monster stories that were Marvel Comics' bread and butter during the early '60s. So the assignment to pen "I Discovered Gorgilla! The Monster of Midnight Mountain!" for *Tales to Astonish* #12 (Oct. 1960) went to Stan's brother, Larry Lieber. Like King Kong,

© 2007 Marvel Characters, Inc.

Gorgilla was a giant ape (or missing link, actually, between ape and man) that lived on an island (Borneo) on the highest hilltop (Midnight Mountain), where he was worshipped as a deity by the locals. (He also fought a T-Rex.) Unlike King Kong, Gorgilla was designed by Jack Kirby, who gave him the four fingers and toes so common among Kirby monsters, as well as a tail and a flowing mane of rock-star hair.

Marvel brought Gorgilla back in *Tales to Astonish* #18 (Apr. 1961), this time having him visit New York, where he was cornered atop—no, not the Empire State Building—the Statue of Liberty. (Careful where you sit, Gorgilla. Lots of sharp points up there.)

Gorgilla could have slinked away into limbo like so many of the other Marvel monsters, but after a couple of 1970s reprints (in *Monsters on the Prowl* #9 and *Where Creatures Roam* #5), he got an overhaul. Gorgilla's origin was reprinted, albeit with art and lettering changes, in *Weird Wonder Tales* #21 (Mar. 1977), with the Marvel mystic Dr. Druid substituting as the lead character, replacing Scotty, an anthropologist from the original tale. Gorgilla later appeared as a menace in a few Marvel titles, and reappeared as a monster-fighter in 2005's *Marvel Monsters: Fin Fang Four* #1. No longer your father's "Monster of Midnight Mountain," the retooled—and rehabilitated—Gorgilla has learned to speak, and has been shrunk to human size by super-whiz Mr. Fantastic.

5. *KING COLOSSO*

Americans had lots to worry about during the Revolutionary War: a smallpox epidemic, scurvy, invading redcoats, coonskin hat ringworm… and a giant gorilla. Placed into the pages of *Tomahawk* #86 and 93 (May–June 1963 and July–Aug. 1964, respectively) by editorial decree because of the sales impact of gorilla covers (see Chapter 4), King Colosso lumbered through two adventures with Tomahawk and his Rangers; in the first, Colosso was the typical misunderstood monster, ultimately befriending the Rangers, and in the second, things got even wonkier as he battled a dinosaur found frozen in ice. Both issues are graced by striking cover art by Bob Brown.

And were the very notion of a giant gorilla during the American Revolution not absurd enough, *Tomahawk* writer France Herron trumped his own King Colosso stories with "Double-Cross of the Gorilla-Ranger" in issue #107 (Nov.–Dec. 1966), mixing King Kong with Tonto by introducing Mikora, the giant ape who learns archery from a Native American chieftain named Tanka and assists—and apparently betrays—the Tomahawk team as Gorilla-Ranger.

A DOUBLE-LENGTH BLOCKBUSTER...
The RANGERS VS. KING COLOSSO!
TOMAHAWK
12¢

FANTASTIC FOUR
MARVEL COMICS GROUP
20¢ 137 AUG
THE WORLD'S GREATEST COMIC MAGAZINE!
FANTASTIC FOUR
REED! BEN'S DOWN-- AND NOW THAT CREEP'S GOT MEDUSA!
DON'T GIVE UP, TORCH-- NO MATTER WHAT!
IF WE FALL-- THE WORLD IS FINISHED!
WHERE WALKS WAR-HEAD!

6. *WAR-HEAD*

The one-hit wonder War-Head, seen in *Fantastic Four* #137 (Aug. 1973), is comics' only giant gorilla with a noggin shaped like Sputnik. Does he look familiar to you? He does if you've seen *Robot Monster*, the cheesy 1953 horror flick produced on such a shoestring budget that its bad guy wore a gorilla suit and a space helmet. Gerry Conway's *FF* story, penciled by Big John Buscema, included a reality-warping sequence that enabled the writer to get his movie jollies by bringing to life a Kong-sized version of Robot Monster in the shape of War-Head. And poor Medusa didn't realize that her serving as a stand-in for the Invisible Girl put her first in line for War-Head's gorilla grip!

MOON MONSTERS LAUNCH ATTA
AGAINST EARTH!
HOW CAN SCIENCE MEET THE MENACE of ASTRAL ASSASSINS? New SCIENCE-FICTION THRILLS!
3D
ADVENTURES INTO THE FUTURE in New TRU-3 DIMENSION!
ROBOT MONSTER
RELEASED THRU ASTOR PICTURES CORP.
with GEORGE NADER CLAUDIA BARRETT
Produced by AL ZIMBALIST

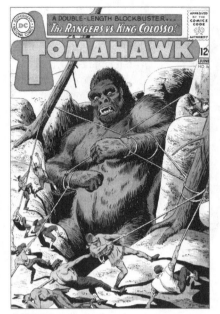

The inspiration for War-Head.
This Robot Monster movie poster went for over $4,000 in a November 2006 Heritage auction (*www.HA.com*).

MARVEL COMICS GROUP 171 JUNE
25¢
THE WORLD'S GREATEST COMIC MAGAZINE!
FANTASTIC FOUR
DON'T TAKE A OUT WITH WE PUNCH--
--SUE'S A DEAD WOMAN!
MIGHTIER THAN KONG! DEADLIER THAN GODZILLA! THIS IS--GORR!
NOT JUST ANOTHER GIANT GORILLA STORY!
YOU'LL GASP AT THE STARTLING SECRET

7. *GORR*

Writer/editor Roy Thomas one-upped comics' other super-sized simians by claiming that his glowing, golden gorilla Gorr was "Mightier Than KONG!" *and* "Deadlier Than GODZILLA!" And this was over a year before Marvel's *Godzilla* monthly…

"Death is a Golden Gorilla!" in *Fantastic Four* #171 (June 1976), by Thomas, pencilers Rich Buckler (pages 1–3) and George Pérez, and inker Joe Sinnott, rose above the standard Kong homage. Thomas affectionately recreated *King Kong*'s climax, from the rampaging Gorr spying (and then grabbing) Ann Darrow-surrogate Sue Richards through a Baxter Building window to the inevitable rooftop conflict with Gorr fending off an aerial assault from the Fantasti-Car. There's a twist ending that I won't spoil here (other than mentioning that this is probably the only *FF* comic to ever have Reed Richards say, "The gorilla talked!").

8. THE GREAT GRAPE APE

With all the destruction and carnage that routinely follows a 40-foot gorilla, how refreshing it was to meet the Grape Ape, Hanna-Barbera's purple, simple-minded Samson who bellowed "Okey dokey!" whenever called upon to help and who punctuated his sentences by saying his name twice ("Grape Ape! Grape Ape!"). Voiced by Bob Holt, Grape Ape and his smooth-talking partner-in-adventure Beegle Beagle, voiced by Marty Ingels, harkened back to the days when comedy duos were showbiz kings. Premiering in September 1975 as ABC's *The Tom and Jerry/Great Ape Show*, *Grape Ape* got a boost from the buzz around the in-production 1976 *King Kong* movie remake…

…enough of a buzz to convince Charlton Comics, which by the mid-'70s had become *the* publisher of TV-and-movie-to-comics-adaptations, to release two issues of *The Great Grape Ape* comic book in the fall of 1976. Written and drawn by Frank Roberge, Charlton's *Grape Ape* series featured accessible, light-hearted stories that pitted "G. A." and Beegle against everything from bank robbers to ghosts to a renegade steam shovel. Once Marvel (of all companies!) picked up the H-B licensing rights in '78, the Grape Ape plodded along in series such as *TV Stars* and *Laff-a-Lympics* (the latter of which was the cartoon equivalent of *The Love Boat*, where moldy H-B characters were gathered *en masse* for whatever combined marquee value they could still muster).

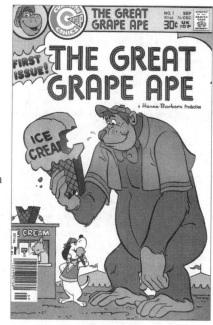

© 2007 Hanna-Barbera.

© 2007 Budd Root.

9. KLYDE

Leave it to a giant gorilla to upstage the voluptuous headliner (and head-lighter) of Bud Root's sexy *Cavewoman* comic. "The most dangerous creature to ever walk the planet, next to man," Klyde is the big, crabby "Kong" of Cavewoman's prehistoric world—although as artist Frank Cho (an occasional *Cavewoman* contributor) observes, size-wise "Klyde is a lot like Mighty Joe Young" (the title star of Merian C. Cooper's 1949 not-as-big-as-Kong ape movie). And size *does* matter to Klyde, or at least to the ape's creator: In *Cavewoman: Reloaded* #4 (2007), a reprint of Klyde's first full appearance from issue #4 of the original *Cavewoman* miniseries of the mid-'90s, Root redrew the Klyde sequences, enlarging the ape.

You'll find no comic book that honors the original *King Kong* more so than *Cavewoman* (self-published by Root's Basement Comics, except for a brief period when published by Caliber). The title star is actually Meriem Cooper (name sound familiar?), who, as a child, was rescued by her sympathetic grandfather, Francis Reicher (actor Frank Reicher played Capt. Englehorn in *King Kong*), from her abusive home. "Gramp" carried Meriem, via time machine (which no Gramp should be without!), into the past, when dinosaurs ruled the Earth. *Cavewoman*'s cast of characters, time-displaced residents of the town of Marshville, Oregon, also includes Meriem's boyfriend Bruce Kabbit (as in Bruce Cabot, *Kong*'s daring Jack Driscoll), whiz kid Will O'Brian, a hermit named Roberto Armstrong, and a couple named Fay and Ray.

10. GORILLA GORILLA

There's nothing quite as exciting as a giant gorilla fighting a giant lizard. Willis O'Brien knew this. So did Toho (if you don't know that Toho's the Godzilla production company, whose movie classics include *King Kong vs. Godzilla*, you do now).

And so does Art Baltazar. Baltazar's *Gorilla Gorilla* is a King Kong-as-super-hero comic that premiered in the Feb. 2004 issue of *Disney Adventures*, that colorful digest magazine you'll find at the grocery check-out racked next to *Reader's Digest*. Its star, a tiny gorilla named Gorilla, has a cell-phone hot-line connection to the president of the United States. Gorilla grows into the super-strong skyscraping simian Gorilla Gorilla in times of national crisis (generally another rampage by that "overgrown reptile" Lizard Lizard, who's secretly Gorilla's roommate Lizard).

© 2007 Walt Disney Productions.

Baltazar keeps the monkey-vs.-lizard concept fresh with a broader rogues' gallery including evil space aliens, Banana Banana, Vanilla Gorilla, Mega-Rilla (a robot gorilla), and Floating Shark. *Gorilla Gorilla*'s art and stories are funny and vibrantly colored, contemporizing the giant gorilla of yesterday for today's attention-span-challenged audience. A trade paperback collection, *Comic Zone vol. 2: Gorilla Gorilla*, was released in 2006.

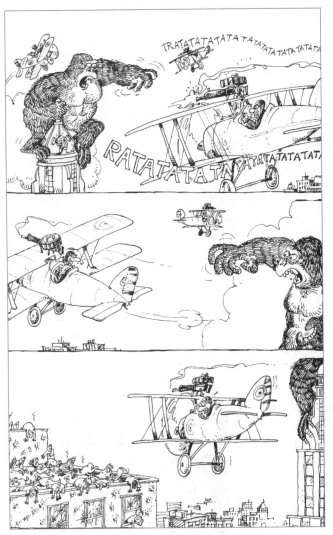

A King Kong takeoff by Sergio Aragonés, from his 2001 Dark Horse Comics miniseries *Actions Speak.*

© 2007 Sergio Aragonés. Courtesy of Dan Ripoll.

KING KONG IN COMICS

"The earliest reference to a character named 'King Kong,'" reveals Kong collector Dan Ripoll, "was in *Black Hood* #14, from Spring 1945; the story has a gangster named King Kong Ross. No giant gorillas, though, unfortunately."

Poor Kong! Comics-writing and -drawing vultures swooped at him from all directions, snatching his look, his shtick, and his very name, a name that satirists loved: He was

From 1968, the splash to Roy Thomas and Marie Severin's Kong send-up, from Marvel's *Not Brand Echh* #11. © 2007 Marvel Characters, Inc. Courtesy of Heritage Auctions.

(left) © 2007 ABC-TV. Characters TM & © their respective copyright holders.

(below) Kong for kids, from *America's Best TV Comics* #1 (1967).

King Kong © 2007 Universal.

"Ping Pong" in *MAD*, "King Konk" in *Not Brand Echh*, "King Klonk" in *Jerry Lewis*, "King Gong" in *Underdog*… and even the truest and bluest of super-folk impersonated the big guy in two red kryptonite stories, "Superboy Goes Ape!" (*Superboy* #142, Oct. 1967) and "When Superman Became King Kong!" (*Superman* #226, May 1970).

Considering those parodies, it's ironic that King Kong's first author-ized comic book was itself a bit of a mockery.

America's Best TV Comics was a Giant published by the American Broadcasting Company (that's ABC-TV, monkey boy) and produced by Marvel Comics in 1967 to promote "An All-Star ABC Animated Power-Packed Line-Up You Just Can't Miss!" It's a collector's curiosity because it contains, under one cover, comic stories starring a scattershot ensemble you'd never expect to see gathered in one place: the Fantastic Four, Casper the Friendly Ghost, Spider-Man, George of the Jungle, Journey to the Center of the Earth, and King Kong. (Add to that mix Batman and Batgirl, who plow through hoodlums in artist George Tuska's comic-drawn ad for ABC's live-action *Batman*.)

Included in *America's Best TV Comics* was an uncredited (perhaps wisely so) ten-page comic-book story based upon the

King Kong animated show of 1966–1969. (Those of you who watched the show as kids now have its theme song stuck in your heads…) TV's *King Kong* was from Rankin/Bass Productions, the folks responsible for those endearing but trippin' stop-motion Christmas specials like *Rudolph the Red-Nosed Reindeer* (1964). Avoiding the sacred ground of Willis O'Brien, who pioneered the same technology then being popularized on TV with *Rudolph*, Rankin/Bass played it safe by producing *King Kong* as a traditional cartoon, farming out the animation to Japan. Imported into R-B's *Kong* was the boy-and-his-giant concept from the Japanese series *Gigantor*, with a dash of *Jonny Quest* added for flavor. This kinder King Kong answered to danger-prone boy Bobby Bond, who moved to Kong's Mondo (not Skull—too scary for Saturday morning!) Island when research-scientist father set up a lab there.

The plot of *America's Best TV Comics'* "King Kong" took the Eighth Wonder of the World to the circus, where he's invited by showman P. T. Bunkum to perform for charity. Kong obediently squatted on a barge towed by an ocean liner to the California circus, and under the Big Top was pimped into parlor tricks like pushing elephants through hoops. When the Big Top's animals escaped, Kong heroically scooped them up—and earned a parade in his honor from a "grateful city."

No, that paragraph wasn't a mistake. King Kong, who once showed dinosaurs that they no longer ruled the Earth and scraped squashed people off his heels, received a parade… *and* a plaque from the mayor. Among the banners celebrating the

beast was one screaming in red letters: "WE LOVE KONG."

"King Kong" was a very juvenile tale for the youngest of readers, with rudimentary artwork. Its biggest weakness, however, was not the fault of the writer or artist. The Rankin/Bass *King Kong* was an early case of identity theft, where the Kong name was appropriated (fully under license) to describe a new character that, at best, only remotely resembled his namesake. This was Kong done wrong.

Kong's comics prospects improved the next year, fortunately. In 1969 the Alberto Giolitti studio adapted the 1933 *King Kong* movie in a Gold Key Comics one-shot first published in 1968 as *Movie Comics* 30036-809 and later re-released in various formats. Italian cartoonist Giolitti (1923–1993), who emigrated to the United States in the late 1940s and over the ensuing decades produced reams of pages of cinema and media comics adaptations for Dell and Gold Key (including *Gunsmoke*, *Star Trek*, and, coincidentally, Gold Key's 1970 adaptation of *Beneath the Planet of the Apes*, as well as *Turok, Son of Stone* and *The Phantom*), fronted a studio of over 50 artists that produced the adaptation.

An undated King Kong pencil study by *Planet of the Apes* artist Tom Sutton. King Kong TM & © 2007 Universal. Courtesy of Heritage Auctions.

Gold Key's *King Kong* was a giant of a comic, a whopping 64 pages, and its stunning painted cover adds to its collectibility. Giolitti and crew steadfastly translated Merian C. Cooper's story, the only diversion from the original being the alteration of some of Kong's bestial enemies.

King Kong #1-6, a 1990–1991 miniseries published by Fantagraphics under its Monster Comics imprint, was another faithful adaptation—but of the 1932 book *King Kong*, Cooper and Edgar Wallace's original tale expanded by Delos W. Lovelace.

Writer/artist Donald Simpson was *Kong*'s architect, and ably delivered a moody atmosphere for Skull Island and its slithering terrors, but the miniseries is best remembered for its covers drawn by superstar artists:

Dave Stevens, Mark Schultz, William Stout, and Schultz inked by Al Williamson.

Dark Horse Comics is, as of this writing, the most recent publisher of *King Kong*. In the mid-'90s, after adapting a string of then-current and classic movies (*Aliens*, *Predator*, *Star Wars*, and *Godzilla*, among others) to comic books, Dark Horse considered but never published a number of *King Kong* projects, including *Rocketeer vs. King Kong* by Dave Stevens, a *Kong* adaptation by Arthur Adams, and Frank Cho's *Tarzan on Skull Island* (a.k.a. *Tarzan vs. King Kong*). The publisher, via its DH Press imprint, finally released its first Kong project in 2004: The illustrated novel *Kong: King of Skull Island* was the authorized sequel to *King Kong*, created and illustrated by Joe DeVito and written by Brad Strickland with John Michlig. *King of Skull Island* ignored the actual film sequel to the original, 1933's *Son of Kong*. In late 2005 and early 2006, Dark Horse published a three-issue adaptation of the Peter Jackson-directed *King Kong*, written by Christian Gossett and drawn by Dustin Weaver.

A boatload of Kongs! Colossal gorilla sailors roil the sea in this George Evans cover for *Weird War Tales* #85 (Mar. 1980).
© 2007 DC Comics. Courtesy of Dan Ripoll.

(left) Rejected cover for Dark Horse's 2005 *King Kong* adaptation. Dave Dorman pencils.
King Kong © 2007 Universal. Courtesy of Dan Ripoll.

Says artist Bruce Timm of this jungle girl vs. giant ape illustration: "This is an unpublished prelim for a Tigress pin-up I did for Mike Hoffman. The final published version is more obviously her, and this one seems less 'Tigress-specific' to me and more 'generic jungle girl.'"

Tigress © 2007 Mike Hoffman. Art © 2007 Bruce Timm. Courtesy of Anthony Snyder.

KONG-A LINE: THE APE THAT WOULD BE KING

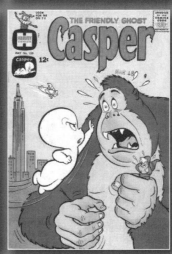

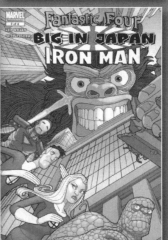

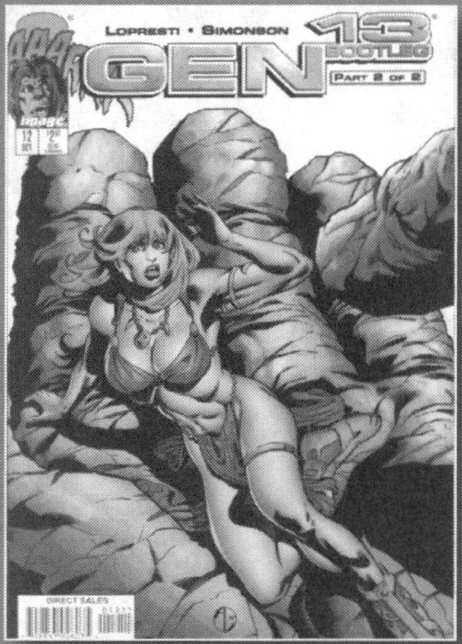

LOPRESTI • SIMONSON
GEN 13 BOOTLEG
PART 2 OF 2
DIRECT SALES

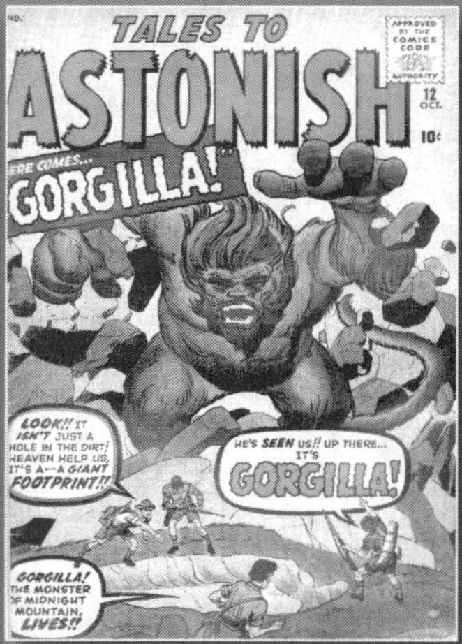

TALES TO ASTONISH
12 OCT.
10¢
GORGILLA!
LOOK!! IT ISN'T JUST A HOLE IN THE DIRT! HEAVEN HELP US, IT'S A-- A GIANT FOOTPRINT!!
HE'S SEEN US!! UP THERE... IT'S GORGILLA!
GORGILLA! THE MONSTER OF MIDNIGHT MOUNTAIN, LIVES!!

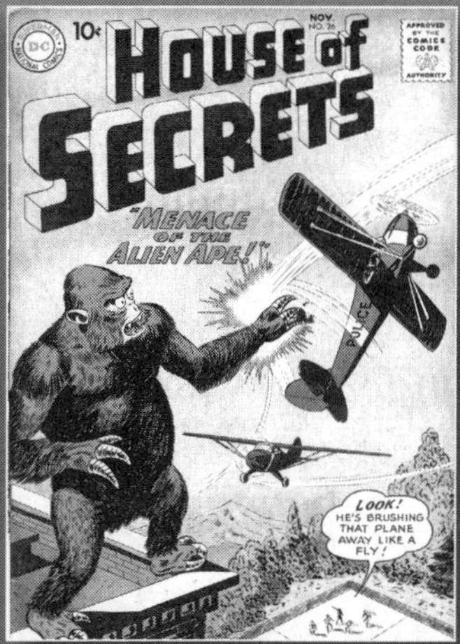

10¢
HOUSE of SECRETS
"MENACE OF THE ALIEN APE!"
LOOK! HE'S BRUSHING THAT PLANE AWAY LIKE A FLY!

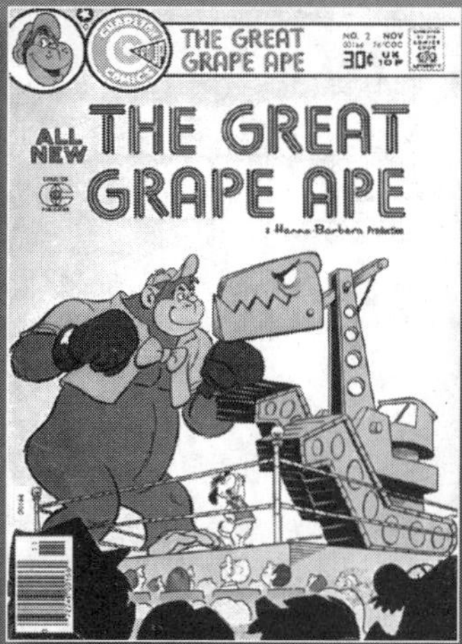

THE GREAT GRAPE APE
30¢
ALL NEW THE GREAT GRAPE APE
a Hanna-Barbera Production

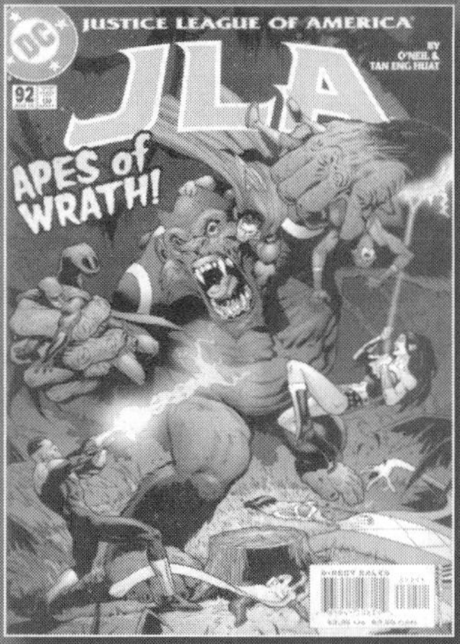

JUSTICE LEAGUE OF AMERICA
JLA
92
APES of WRATH!
DIRECT SALES

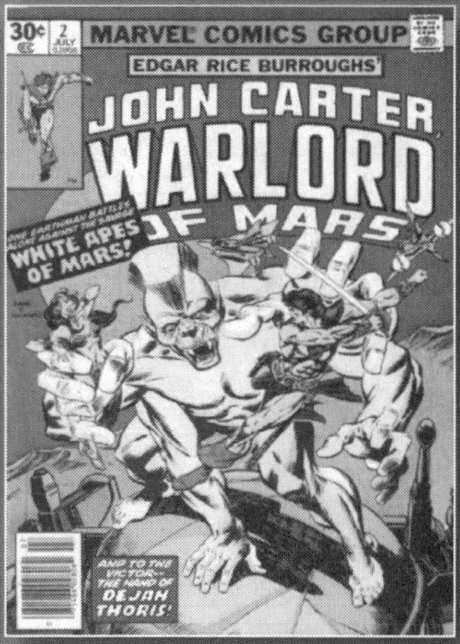

30¢
2 JULY
MARVEL COMICS GROUP
EDGAR RICE BURROUGHS'
JOHN CARTER WARLORD OF MARS
WHITE APES OF MARS!
AND TO THE VICTOR-- THE HAND OF DEJAH THORIS!

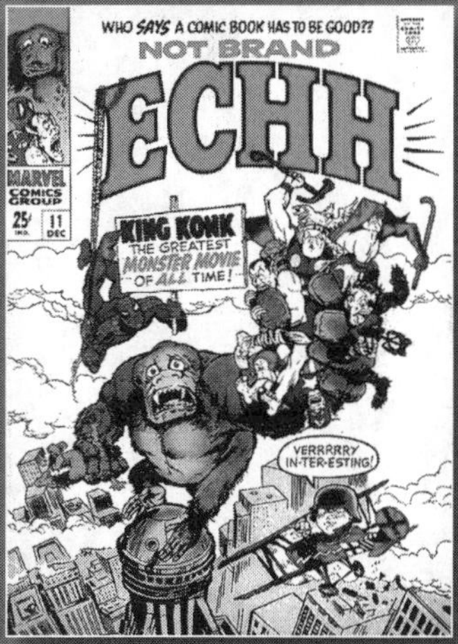

WHO SAYS A COMIC BOOK HAS TO BE GOOD??
NOT BRAND ECHH
MARVEL COMICS GROUP
25¢
11 DEC
KING KONK THE GREATEST MONSTER MOVIE OF ALL TIME!
VERRRRRY IN-TER-ESTING!

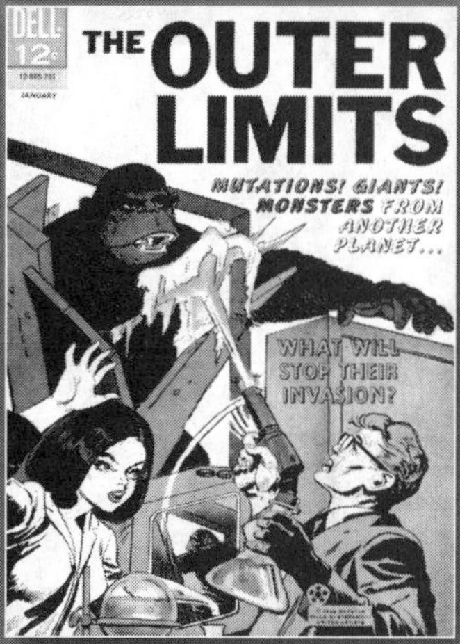

DELL 12¢
JANUARY
THE OUTER LIMITS
MUTATIONS! GIANTS! MONSTERS FROM ANOTHER PLANET...
WHAT WILL STOP THEIR INVASION?

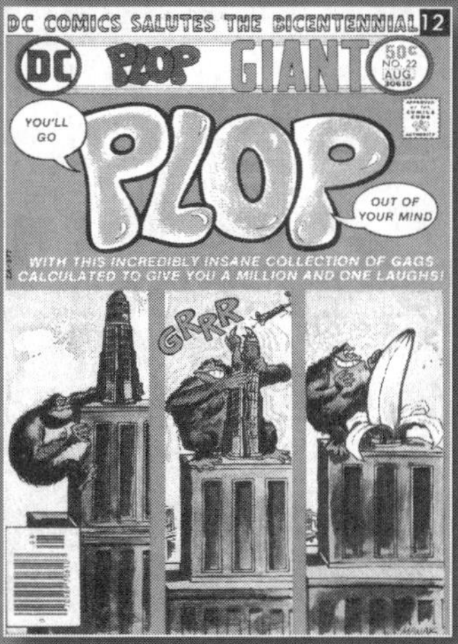

DC COMICS SALUTES THE BICENTENNIAL
12
DC PLOP GIANT
50¢ AUG.
YOU'LL GO
PLOP
OUT OF YOUR MIND
WITH THIS INCREDIBLY INSANE COLLECTION OF GAGS CALCULATED TO GIVE YOU A MILLION AND ONE LAUGHS!
GRRR

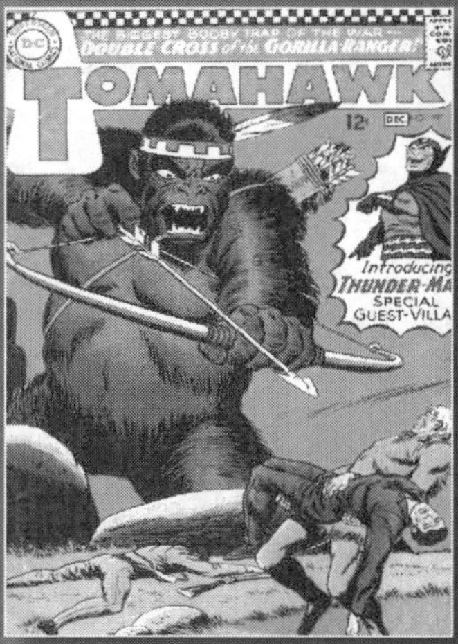

THE BIGGEST BOOBY TRAP OF THE WAR-- DOUBLE CROSS of the GORILLA RANGER!
TOMAHAWK
12¢
Introducing
SPECIAL

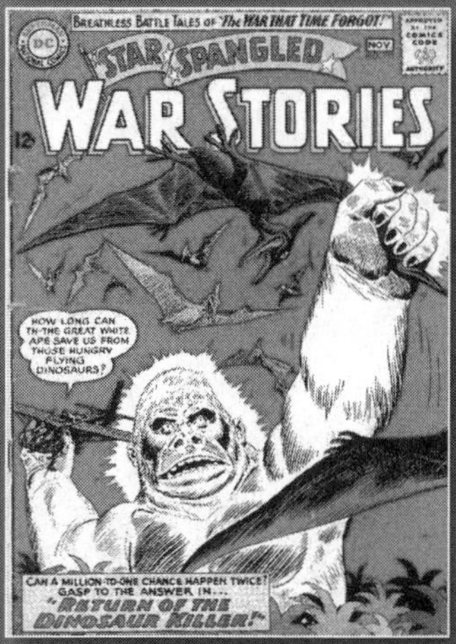

BREATHLESS BATTLE TALES OF THE WAR THAT TIME FORGOT!
STAR SPANGLED WAR STORIES
12¢
HOW LONG CAN THE GREAT WHITE APE SAVE US FROM THOSE HUNGRY FLYING DINOSAURS?
CAN A MILLION-TO-ONE CHANCE HAPPEN TWICE? GASP TO THE ANSWER IN... "RETURN OF THE DINOSAUR KILLER!"

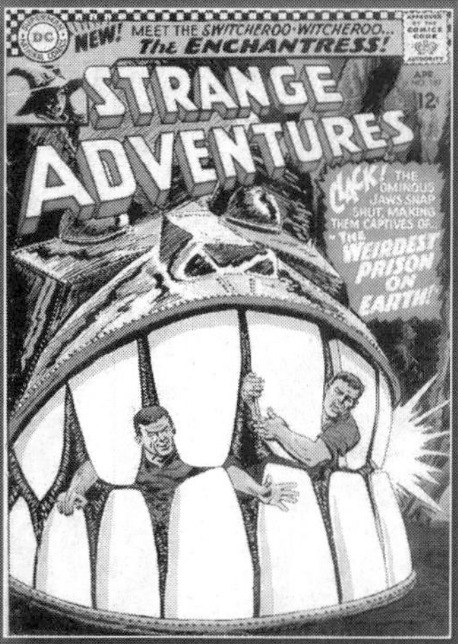

NEW! MEET THE SWITCHEROO-WITCHEROO... THE ENCHANTRESS!
STRANGE ADVENTURES
12¢
CLACK! THE OMINOUS JAWS SNAP SHUT, MAKING THEM CAPTIVES OF THE WEIRDEST PRISON ON EARTH!

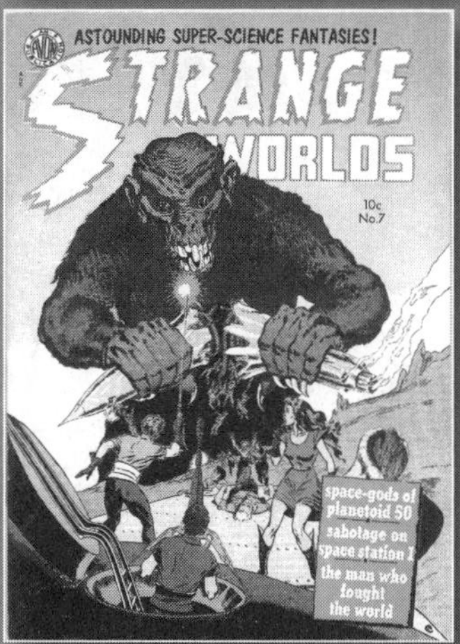

ASTOUNDING SUPER-SCIENCE FANTASIES!
STRANGE WORLDS
10c No.7
space-gods of planetoid 50
sabotage on space station 1
the man who fought the world

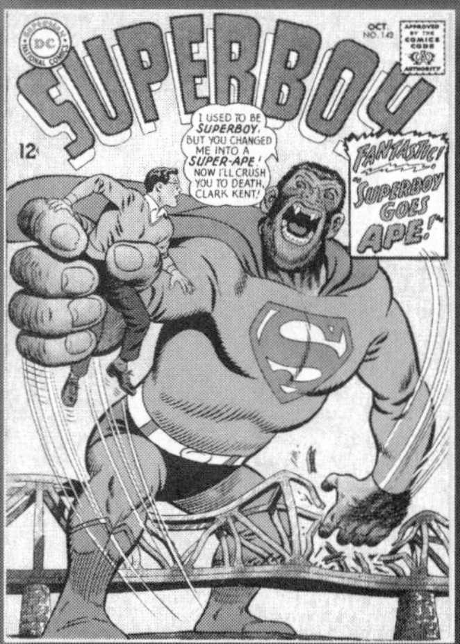

SUPERBOY
12¢
I USED TO BE SUPERBOY, BUT YOU CHANGED ME INTO A SUPER-APE! NOW I'LL CRUSH YOU TO DEATH, CLARK KENT!
FANTASTIC! SUPERBOY GOES APE!

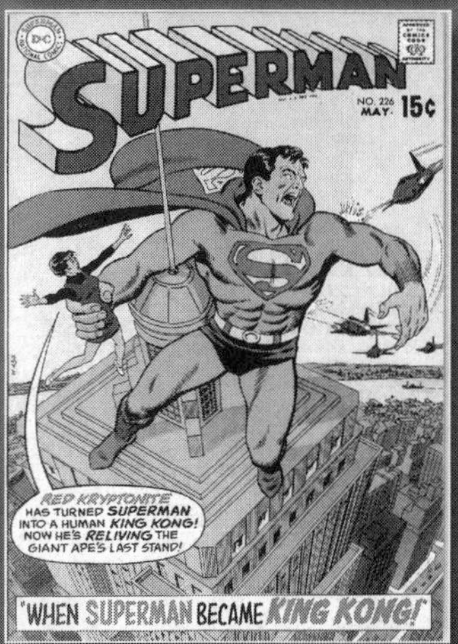

SUPERMAN
NO. 226 MAY
15¢
RED KRYPTONITE HAS TURNED SUPERMAN INTO A HUMAN KING KONG! NOW HE'S RELIVING THE GIANT APE'S LAST STAND!
"WHEN SUPERMAN BECAME KING KONG!"

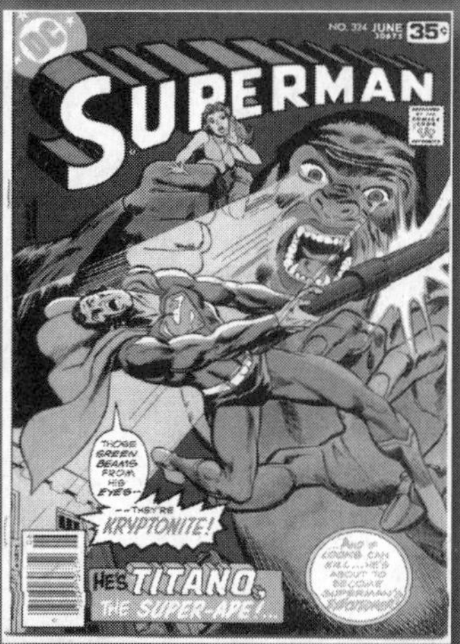

DC
NO. 334 JUNE
35¢
SUPERMAN
THOSE GREEN BEAMS FROM HIS EYES-- THEY'RE KRYPTONITE!
HE'S TITANO, THE SUPER-APE!...

APE Q with ARTHUR ADAMS

Conducted by telephone on November 1, 2006

SPOTTED AMONG THE APES IN:

Monkeyman and O'Brien,
covers for "JLApe" crossover in 1999 DC Comics Annuals,
drawing gorillas (and Godzillas) every darn chance he gets

OTHER CAREER HIGHLIGHTS:

*Longshot, X-Men, Gumby, Fantastic Four, Godzilla,
Creature from the Black Lagoon,*
Jonni Future in *Tom Strong's Terrific Tales*

Art's 2005 recreation of the *FF* cover introducing golden gorilla Gorr. Fantastic Four © 2007 Marvel Characters, Inc. Courtesy of *Modern Masters*.

Art Adams' baggy-suited giant gorilla as seen in *King Kong vs. Godzilla*, from Random House's *The Official Godzilla Compendium* (1998).
© 2007 Universal. Courtesy of *Modern Masters*.

Do you remember your very first ape drawing?

No. [*laughter*]

One of two answers you could have given me.

Sadly, it's true.

As a kid, which did you see first: the *King Kong* movie in reruns or the *King Kong* Saturday morning cartoon?

The *King Kong* movie first.

Really?

It must have been early on, because it had such a big influence on the rest of my life. I'm guessing I must have been three or four or five… I don't have a clear memory of when, I've just seen it many, many times, for as long as I can remember. When they put back in some of the scenes cut out of *King Kong*, in the early '70s, one of our local horror-show hosts [showed it]. I must've been nine or ten. That's my most clear memory of seeing the repaired *King Kong*. Not to mention *King Kong vs. Godzilla*!

I'm sure, as a small child, you saw the Saturday morning *King Kong* cartoon.

Of course!

Kong was a little sanitized there.

But he was "ten times as big as a man"! [*laughter*]

Did they ever measure him?

I don't think he was ten times taller, but ten times heavier. [*laughter*]

With the average American gaining weight, I don't think that's the case anymore.

Ouch!

Which of the *King Kong* movie remakes do you think is most watchable? Or is it blasphemy to even pose such a question?

I think the Peter Jackson one; I haven't re-watched it since seeing it in the theater. I thought it was too long; it's interesting because they're putting out an *extended* version now! [*laughs*] If you have a weekend available….

I like to think that I liked the Dino DeLaurentis remake, but really the only good thing that came out of that was two Frank Frazetta paintings!

Well, Jeff Bridges had cool hair… and it introduced Jessica Lange!

The last page of the Monkeyman and O'Brien adventure "Trapped in the Lair of the Shrewmanoid," originally published in a 1994 *Dark Horse Insider* promo 'zine.

© 2007 Arthur Adams. Courtesy of Heritage Auctions.

Yeah… I'll go with that, sure! I'm trying to think of who the artists were for those poster for that movie. They were iconic illustrations. [***Editor's note:*** The 1976 *King Kong* teaser poster, with Kong perched atop the two World Trade Center towers, was illustrated by John Berkey.]

You did *Godzilla* and *Creature from the Black Lagoon* comics for Dark Horse. Why wasn't there a *King Kong*?

Well, we talked about that. For the latest remake, the rights were a horrible mess. Dark Horse couldn't find a way to get the rights to do it. Someone held rights for music, someone for the movie, someone for the story, and were ready to sue each other whenever anyone wanted to do anything with it.

"People, can't we just get along?"

It was funny, because both Frank Cho and

I wanted to do adaptations of *King Kong* and we were talking, "Maybe we can get Dark Horse to get the rights right now, and you'll do one and I'll do one, and people can just pick! Or buy both!" [*laughs*]

I'm sure you're aware that Frank Cho proposed *Tarzan on Skull Island*, with Tarzan fighting Kong, which I thought was a no-brainer for a hit!

Yeah, it would've been better than *Predator vs. King Kong*. Or, actually, now that I think of it, it would've been better than *Alien vs. King Kong*. Um, maybe *King Kong vs. the Queen Alien*....

[*laughs*] Are you the grandchild of Willis O'Brien?

You'd be surprised how many times I have been asked that question!

How many times?

None. [*laughter*] Actually, I suspect that's not the case.

The name Willis O'Brien might not mean anything to some people reading this interview, so tell us, who was Willis O'Brien?

Well, he's the stop-motion inventor, the genius who did stop-motion animation for the original *King Kong*. I think Ray Harryhausen helped him with *Mighty Joe Young*, *The Lost World*, and several other early classics.

Didn't he also do uncredited work on one of my childhood favorites, *The Valley of Gwangi* (1969)?

Harryhausen?

No, O'Brien.

Well, I think he did some of the story, but he didn't do any work on it; I think he was dead by that time. Harryhausen carried on after, and the story is quite different from O'Brien's original story.

So, in *Monkeyman and O'Brien*, the name "Ann Darrow O'Brien" is a combination of Fay Wray's character from *King Kong*, Ann Darrow, and the last name of the *King Kong* animator.

That is correct.

But where'd you come up with Monkeyman's name, "Axwell Tiberius"?

Well, I think my ex-girlfriend came up with that name. I couldn't for the life of me think of a name. It was going to be called "Tool and Dy," and all I know is I wanted a gorilla and a hot chick. Tom Orzechowski suggested Tool and Dy, because he thought it would be a good name. I tried to use it, but it didn't work.

While I was working it up, Mike Mignola was coming up with Hellboy and we talked about our characters. And I kept referring to [Axwell] as "that monkeyman fellow." So Mike said, "Well, why don't you just call him 'Monkeyman'?" Okay, fine. But I think my ex came up with the Tiberius. I was thinking about "Maxwell," but she thought it would be better to have a name that wasn't quite so... human? Not that I know anyone named Maxwell, but who knows?

And the name "Axwell" has "ax" in it, always a plus for a comics character. [*laughter*]

Did Monkeyman and O'Brien evolve after your original vision, or did they come out the way they are?

The way they are. I think I remembered that Monkeyman was going to have more guns. And one so big that he would ride around on it. I just felt like drawing guns.

What's unique about *Monkeyman and O'Brien* is your twist on the brain/brawn dynamic, with the ape being the "mind" and the woman being the "muscle." Was that how you first saw the characters?

When I made it up, I thought about what I loved most about a child, and I loved *King Kong*, and you can't have King Kong without Fay Wray, so there you go. So I thought I couldn't have him be a savage beast, and she has to do something besides screaming, so she'll be a technical whiz, kind of a nerd, but she has to be able to stand up to various things that a giant ape-man can be coming across, so she has to be strong.

I was already wanting him

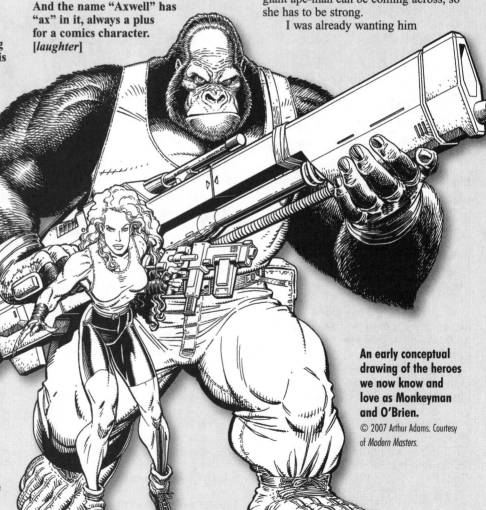

An early conceptual drawing of the heroes we now know and love as Monkeyman and O'Brien.

© 2007 Arthur Adams. Courtesy of *Modern Masters*.

Adams' pencil art to the splash from *Monkeyman and O'Brien* #2 (1996). © 2007 Arthur Adams. Courtesy of *Modern Masters*.

to be really smart because I like characters like Sherlock Holmes. The reason I have trouble writing characters is because I come up with characters smarter than me! [*laughter*] It was more difficult than I thought it would be.

And after I'd sketched them out, I was real proud of myself for the first hour. Then I thought, *Awww*... I realized I'd made up Angel and the Ape.

Kind of, but not really.

Well, they're not the same, but they are a gorilla and a blonde chick!

I interviewed [Angel and the Ape co-creator] Bob Oksner for this book—and he told me it was his first-ever interview about Angel and the Ape.

That is crazy! He just did some really

great work, and I know that there are a lot of people who really like that stuff. I really don't know why DC couldn't get a good grip on Angel and the Ape.

Had you ever done any comics writing before *Monkeyman and O'Brien*?

Not officially. I would occasionally write balloons with Chris Claremont, funny lines, and he'd egg me on. He said, "I'm not funny. Art, would you write the funny lines?"

Did you find that writing your own stories was easier or harder than you'd expected?

I was always prepared for it to be difficult, but once I started, I found that it wasn't all that difficult. If it was easy, I thought I must be doing something wrong.

I find that my characterization is pretty good, with weird little moments. When I did *Monkeyman and O'Brien/Gen 13*, I liked writing for the characters Freefall and Grunge. I found them to be fun to write for because I had a pretty clear idea [of their voices], and could hear them in my head pretty clearly.

I've never been keen on my plotting… I don't think I'm particularly good at coming up with stories. I don't think I can do it on a monthly basis… otherwise I'd have to have something to rip off! [*laughter*]

Don't we have Erik Larsen to thank for *Monkeyman and O'Brien*?

Yes. He wanted both me and Mr. Mignola to come up with something for Image Comics. And without that, I may never have come up with Monkeyman and O'Brien, and Mike may never have come up with Hellboy.

How would reality as we know it have differed if *Monkeyman and O'Brien* had ended up at Image instead of Dark Horse?

Well, I probably would done about as much work, or less, and made a whole lot more money. I'd probably be living in the south of France somewhere after drawing one issue of *Monkeyman*. [*laughs*]

I know you love toys, so where are the Monkeyman and O'Brien action figures?

Well, believe it or not, there is a company involved in putting out some toys. A sample is supposed to be shown at one of the toy shows coming up, to see if retailers will be willing to buy them. So we're waiting to see how that goes.

What little Monkeyman and O'Brien merchandise *does* exist includes a shot glass and a Zippo® lighter. Are there any other vices your characters are available to endorse?

I was trying to get a roach holder, but they wouldn't go for that, as well as a Monkeyman bong. Dark Horse thought that wouldn't fly.

Wouldn't make it into red states?

It wouldn't make it into a lot of places!

One of the apes you drew before Monkeyman was Gorilla Grodd, for me, as DC's *Who's Who* editor in the early '90s. You realize you were my go-to guy for Grodd.

That was fun. And they finally did an action figure of him based on that drawing.

Let's talk about "JLApe." You got to draw the Justice Leaguers as gorillas!

Funny! People at conventions will ask for a drawing, and sometimes I'll draw Batman as a gorilla. Makes perfect sense, doesn't it?

You know that old Sheldon Moldoff cover with Bat-Ape… (*Batman* #114, Mar. 1958)?

Sure, absolutely. I wanted to have a Monkeyman and O'Brien crossover with Batman, where Batman is in trouble and naturally, Monkeyman fills in for him—

That's probably more believable than Alfred subbing for him in the old *Batman* TV show!

—some long adventure with Monkeyman dressed as Batman. He'd take off his mask in a crowd of people who knew him. They'd say, "It's you!" They couldn't tell that he weighed ten times as much as Batman!

Were any of the Justice Leaguers tougher to do as gorillas?

Wonder Woman was difficult.

She *has* been a gorilla before (in *Wonder Woman* #170, May 1967).

Yes, she has been a gorilla before! She's so beautiful, she makes a great gorilla. I just did a takeoff of that for a pin-up for *Ghost*. I did it awhile ago, but it just got printed.

But even though she's a gorilla, because she's still Wonder Woman, there's an inclination to make her pretty. But then I said, "What the hell am I thinking? She's a gorilla!" Then, I just drew a female gorilla.

That worked pretty well.

It wasn't my favorite cover of the bunch, but it came out pretty well.

What *was* your favorite JLApe cover?

I liked the first one, the *Aquaman* one, and the *Flash* one. I think they all came

out okay. I tried to give Superman the gorilla the old S-spit curl, but it didn't really work out. They were all fine… I thought it was funny that the Martian Manhunter gorilla was hairless.

Who came up with that project?

I really don't know. I got hired to do those covers by [editor] Dan Raspler when he was at DC, and don't know who came up with it. It was one of those things where I wasn't really keen on the insides of the books. The *Green Lantern* one was pretty good, but I thought [the JLApe Annuals] were drawn by people who didn't really know how to draw gorillas. But in life, you're not really required to know how to draw a gorilla. It was kind of a joke on the cover and they cruised through how many pages they had. I thought it could've been a little more fun than it was.

What's your favorite gorilla cover drawn by someone else?

Bill Stout did a real nice cover for a King Kong adaptation about a decade ago.

By Fantagraphics. Don Simpson did the interiors.

Yeah, that's it. There are two covers by Bill Stout, I think I liked the Tyrannosaurus one better than the Kong one. Dave Stevens drew one and it was very nice. Don't make me pick a favorite gorilla!!

So I can't ask you about your favorite comic-book ape?

I don't want to pick the favorite, because then I'll have to pick the least favorite, and I don't want to get stuck with that!

So let me ask you instead, if you had to choose comics' all-time best ape artist, who is it?

In comics, that is *too* hard.

Let me rephrase the question: Who are some of your favorite ape artists?

Frank Cho does interesting creatures. I'll stick with Frank right now. And Frazetta's drawn some damn fine gorillas, as would be expected.

Anything else to add about apes?

I'm glad I don't own one!

(right) **Arthur Adams' 1999 *Wonder Woman Annual* JLApe cover.** © 2007 DC Comics. Courtesy of John Bamber and Jason Harris.

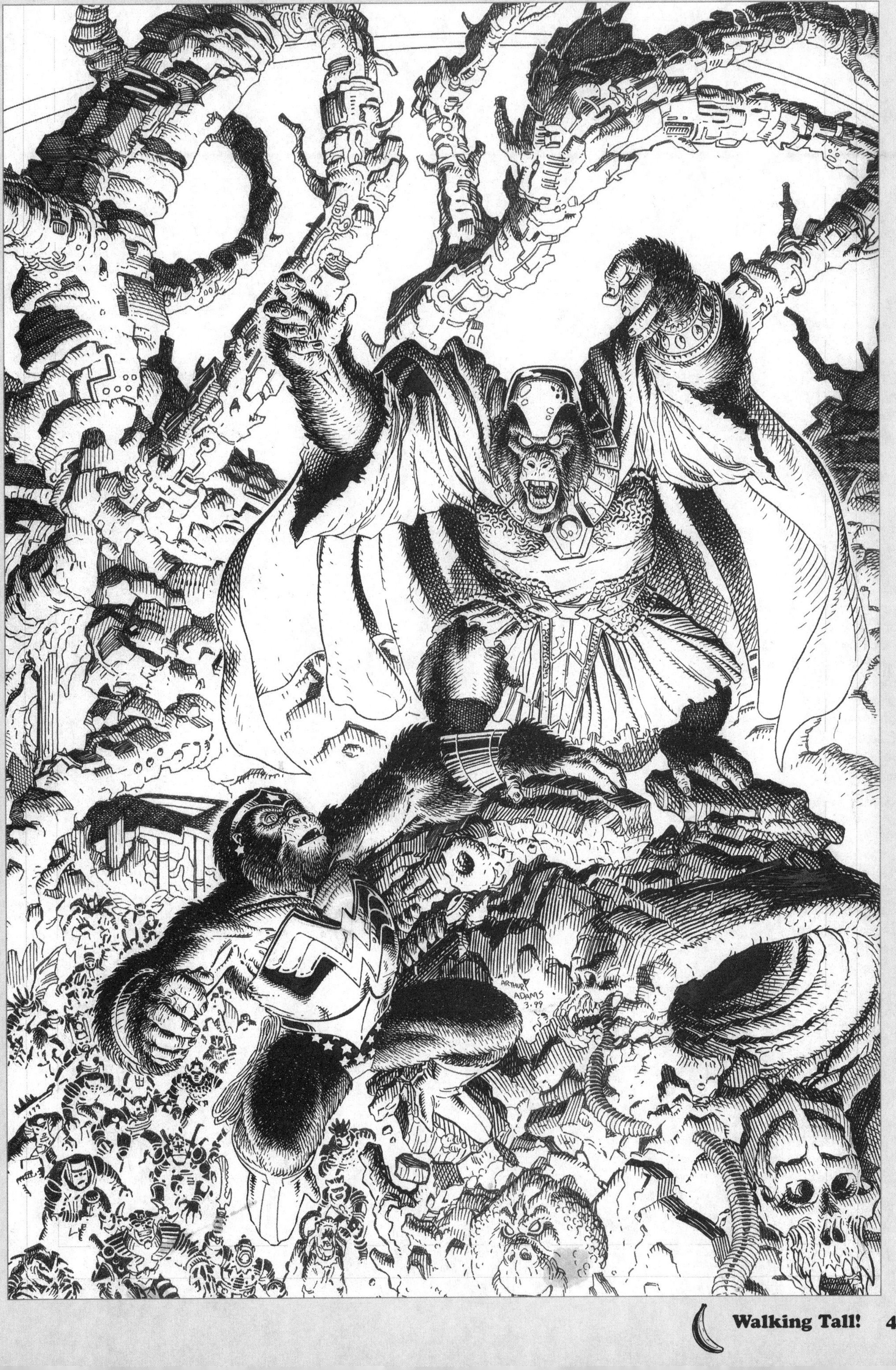
ARTHUR
ADAMS
3.99

APE Q with FRANK CHO

Conducted by telephone on October 31, 2006

SPOTTED AMONG THE APES IN:

"Monkey Boy" self-caricatures, "Bride of the Beastman" in ***Titanic Tales*** (Insight Studios), apes sketches and covers for Edgar Rice Burroughs, fanzines and sketchbooks

OTHER CAREER HIGHLIGHTS:

Liberty Meadows, Shanna, the She-Devil, New Avengers, Mighty Avengers

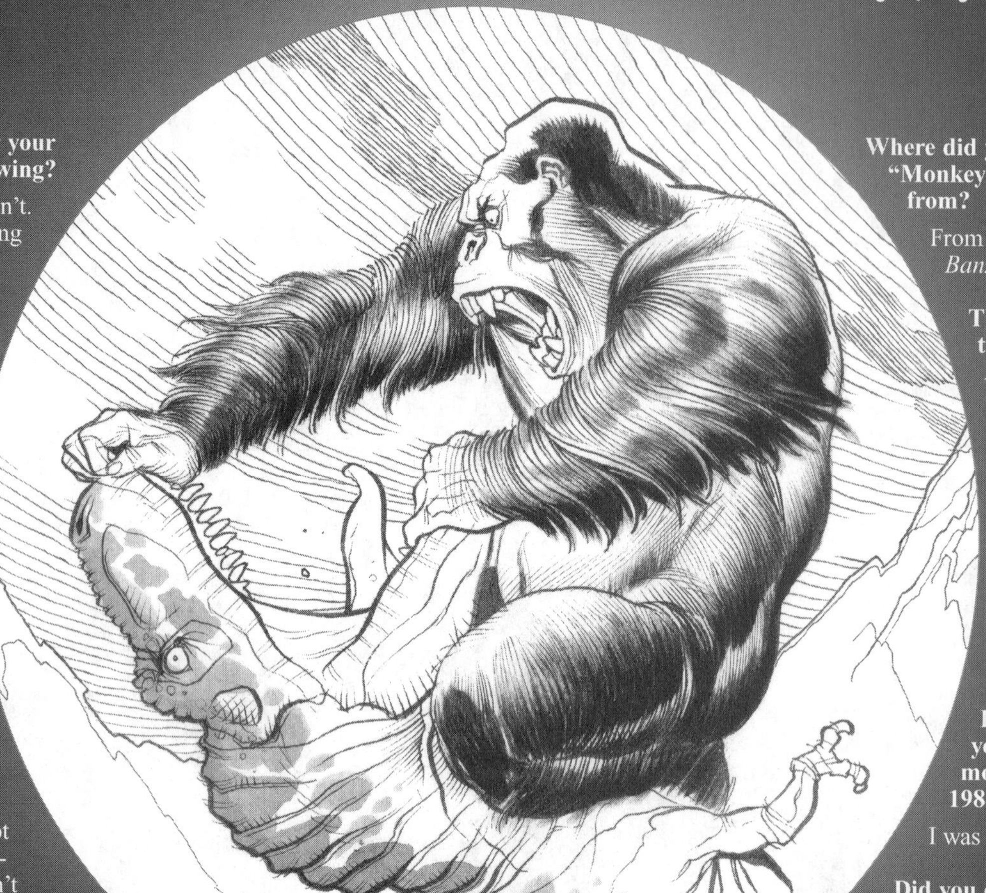

Dino learns it's not smart to mouth off to King Kong. Illustration by and courtesy of Frank Cho. King Kong TM & © 2007 Universal.

Do you remember your very first ape drawing?

No… actually, I don't. I remember watching *King Kong*, the original [Willis] O'Brien *King Kong,* when I was little. It was around first grade.

Were you disappointed in the 2005 *King Kong* remake, the Peter Jackson one?

I wasn't. I'm one of the few people who liked it. I've talked with a lot of hardcore *King Kong* fans, and a lot of them were disappointed. But I wasn't one of them. I liked it. I thought the whole Ann Darrow character being a stage actress, and performing slapsticks to gain Kong's affections, were the missing pieces from the original O'Brien *Kong*.

Ever see the 1976 *King Kong*, the one with Rick Baker in the gorilla suit?

I think I saw it roughly around the same time as the original. Me being a kid, I liked *both* of them! But it was pretty bad. I don't know why I enjoyed that as a kid… there was a certain charm to it, but it was basically a guy in a gorilla suit, you know? But as a kid, I thought it was a really cool movie. Whattaya know, you're a little kid in the first grade?

So, when you were a gullible little kid, were you disappointed to discover that spider monkeys couldn't shoot webs out of their hands?

[*laughs*]

Where did your nickname "Monkey Boy" come from?

From *Buckaroo Banzai*.

That's what I thought—*The Adventures of Buckaroo Banzai* (1984).

It was John Lithgow's character: **"Laugh all you want, monkey boy! Your over-thruster's sh*t!"** [*laughter*]

How old were you when that movie came out in 1984?

I was in middle school.

Did you call yourself "Monkey Boy," or did someone else call you that?

You know that age—you and your friends insult each other constantly, and "Monkey Boy" was one of them. It didn't *really* catch on until I was in college. It's the same thing in college, where you insult each other like crazy, and "Monkey Boy" made us all laugh! [*laughs*] So I just put it into the strip.

In *Liberty Meadows* you draw yourself as Monkey Boy Cho, a chimp, but there aren't any apes in the regular cast. Why not?

Because *I* was the monkey?

[*laughs*] So one monkey is enough…

You did a *Planet of the Apes* takeoff on the cover of *Small Press Expo 97*.

That was awhile ago.

Are you equally fascinated with *Planet of the Apes* the way you were with *King Kong*?

Yes, the original *Planet of the Apes* with Chuck Heston. And yeah, it was one of the movies you see as a kid where it really disturbs you.

It disturbs adults, too.

Yeah, it kinda creeped me out, you know? I like the first one, and I also liked the third one, where the two monkey characters go into our time and have the baby. The female switched her baby with the circus chimp and threw chimp's baby into the water, and the real baby is in the care of the circus performer. I thought that movie was heart-wrenching.

I know you've been fascinated with and have drawn a lot of Edgar Rice Burroughs' characters. What sparked that interest?

Oddly enough, I discovered the movies first. My intro to *Tarzan* was through Johnny Weissmuller. Again, when I was a kid, I was a TV and movie junkie. Every Saturday at noon there was a *Tarzan* movie on in Maryland. Me and my brothers would watch all the *Tarzan* movies. It was one of the coolest things I'd seen. [Tarzan's] treehouse started it all. He had a waterfall for a refrigerator and cool wooden elevators.

Did you build a treehouse after that?

I tried to! That kinda started it all. Then I went through all the *Tarzan* movies and saw Gordon Scott, one of the better Tarzans. Better than Johnny. Each of them had a different charm. After [seeing] the movies, I read the books, and they were completely different! I didn't

Frank's model sheets for Level 5's 2007 Monkey Boy statue.
Art © 2007 Frank Cho. Courtesy of Frank Cho.

really like the books until college, and I reread the books and then something clicked—I went through half the *Tarzan* series. After a while, it started repeating itself. And then I went through the [*John Carter of*] *Mars* series, which, oddly enough, I liked better. That was my introduction to the world of Burroughs.

Let's talk about the *Tarzan vs. King Kong* comic that you pitched to Dark Horse. When did you pitch it and why didn't it go anywhere?

Oh. Wow. From Frank Cho's *Bride of the Beastman*, written by Allan Gross.
Art © 2007 Frank Cho. Bride of the Beastman TM & © 2007 Allan Gross and
Frank Cho. Courtesy of Ray Cuthbert.

FOR AL GROSS,
A TERRIFIC WRITER AND MONKEY BOY,

4-10-99

©1998

I think it was '96. You'll have to ask Al Gross; he was the writer, I was just the artist. He's a good friend of mine; he's another big Burroughs fan. We met through the Burroughs fan club, the National Panthans, Maryland and Virginia chapter, that we belong to. Turned out he was already a comic writer, and so he and I both loved Tarzan and King Kong, and he had a really good story. Dark Horse rejected it, I think, because they already had another King Kong story in the works. I think Dave Stevens was working on a King Kong story.

Take that, ya big ape! Tarzan strikes!
Tarzan TM & © 2007 ERB. Courtesy of Frank Cho.

King Kong sketches.
King Kong TM & © 2007 Universal. Courtesy of Frank Cho.

Dark Horse did a number of Tarzan crossovers—with Batman, Superman, and Predator, as well as crossovers other Burroughs characters. Mixing Tarzan with King Kong would've been an attention grabber.

I never really talked to Dark Horse. Al did, and they told him that Dave Stevens was toying with a *Rocketeer vs. King Kong* and didn't want to put another one into the pipe.

**Unfortunately, ten years later, neither happened.
        Didn't you pitch another *Tarzan* miniseries to Dark Horse?**

I tried out as the regular artist for their *Tarzan* [monthly] book. I did a bunch of submissions, and ultimately they chose another guy over me… which in hindsight, I agree with their decision. I went back and looked [at my art] with a fresh eye—the work was okay, but not that good.

Is *Tarzan* still something you would want to do someday?

Yeah, I'd like to take a shot eventually at *Tarzan*, where I'd write it and draw myself.

Well, you did work with Al Gross on a story "in the grand tradition of Burroughs," *Bride of the Beastman*.

That was for *Titantic Tales*.

Tell me a little about the story.

Bride of the Beastman was a funny thing. It was actually a pulp story, or novelette. By then, I had tons of Burroughs-related drawings [I'd done] around. Al basically wrote the story around my illustrations. It happened kind of backwards. He took some of my better drawings and did the story, and then I did half-a-dozen new pieces to fill in the gaps. If you read the whole *Bride of the Beastman*, it's an homage to Tarzan and Pellucidar.

Now that you're drawing Marvel's *Mighty Avengers*, any chance we'll see Man-Ape or Gorilla Man there?

No. Oddly enough, I've only been getting a lot of *female* characters to draw instead. [*laughs*]

**I'm sure. [*laughs*]
        Who's your favorite comic-book ape?**
The Klyde character in

Cavewoman is one of my favorite ape characters. Budd Root did a fantastic job on *Cavewoman*, and Klyde, Cavewoman's giant gorilla friend, is a lot like *Mighty Joe Young*, which I think I saw—the original one—before I saw *King Kong*. I think it was the first Ray Harryhausen movie. [*Editor's note:* Harryhausen was the special effects "first technician" on *Mighty Joe Young* (1949), working from "technical creator" Willis O'Brien's designs.] That movie had such charm and emotion, and Budd Root does a great job of capturing that and the whole O'Brien foggy, misty jungle. Budd also writes very likeable characters and [a likeable] gorilla personality.

You're an artist who's able to graphically capture apes' personalities. Is there a single reason why you like to draw apes?

They're fun to draw! [*laughter*] They're a grotesque, funny-looking human-man-thing.

If you had to choose the all-time best ape artist, who would it be?

Toss-up between Arthur Adams and Budd Root.

Because…?

They both have a natural flair for drawing apes, with the right amount of caricature, which makes them so alive and energetic.

Any other favorite ape artists?

Mark Schultz. He did a bunch of *King Kong* covers.

For Fantagraphics' *Kong* adaptation. But most people would think of Mark Schultz as a dinosaur artist, don't you think?

I think he did something else that's gorilla-related. He is a brilliant artist. That man is scary! My stuff is crap after looking at his stuff. He and Adam Hughes are the two litmus tests for art, because those two guys are incredible.

Anything you want to mention about drawing apes?

Why I like apes … I guess it's the whole sense of primal… primal *romance* about the apes, and the whole jungle and half-naked women theme.

And by "romance" you mean…?

The landscape and the sense of mystery, freedom and innocence. The whole primal connection.

A 2002 Kong study by Frank Cho. King Kong TM & © 2007 Universal.

Lions, and tigers, and flying monkeys, oh, my!
The Wizard of Oz's most wicked of witches and friends, in a commissioned illustration by **Adam Hughes**. Wizard of Oz © 2007 MGM

MONKEY BUSINESS!

You know you've said it, at least once in your life, while at the zoo or surfing past *Animal Planet* or watching an old *Tarzan* movie:

"Awww, look at the cute little monkey…"

Is there anyone among you who can resist chuckling at a playful chimpanzee or monkey, especially one dressed like a "little man" in a tux or a sailor's suit? Actors from Ronald Reagan to Donna Douglas to Clint Eastwood to David Schwimmer have taken a backseat to their simian co-stars. Show us the monkeys! We *love* 'em!

Cartoonists and comics publishers have long realized the magnetism of merry monkeys. One of the earliest examples of a monkey comic book is artist F. R. Morgan's proto-comic *The Mischievous Monks of Crocodile Isle*. Released in 1908 by Chicago's J. I. Austen Co., this 12-page publication featured a collection of black-and-white and color comic strips starring a pair of intrepid primates.

In the late 1930s comic books metamorphosed from comic-strip reprint volumes to periodicals containing all-new material. During comics' Golden Age gorillas were, with few exceptions, chained to the pages of jungle titles—but chimps and monkeys ran amok throughout the entire comic-book landscape. Every few months readers could count on a monkey cover from some publisher, and with the medium's wide range of genres—including circus and teenage humor—there was ample room for such monkeyshines.

As we learned in Chapter 1, movie-star chimp Cheeta found a welcome home in *Tarzan* comics, and Chota the Chimp was a regular in *Congo Bill*. Simian sidekicks weren't limited to the

The Three Monkeyteers duck the Black Hood's manic motorcycling on Bob Montana's cover to MLJ's (Archie) *Top-Notch Laugh Comics* **#31 (Dec. 1942).**

© 2007 Archie Publications. Courtesy of Heritage Auctions.

wild: Costumed crimefighters Midnight and Crimebuster had monkey partners—Gabby and Squeeks, respectively—and junior sleuth Terry Vance was aided by a monkey named Dr. Watson.

One of the more popular comics genres of the day was "funny animals," anthropomorphic adventures featuring characters as famous as Mickey Mouse and as obscure as Puffy Pig (one of the stars of Timely/Marvel's *Funny Frolics* title). Throughout the Golden Age, most publishers created their "house" monkey solo star (or monkey duo). Among them: Spunky the Monkey (appearing in *Animal Crackers*), Jocko and Socko (*America's Biggest Comics Book*), Morty Monk and Buck Baboon (*Funny Frolics*), Sherlock the Monk (*Fawcett's Funny Animals*), and Chips the Chimp (*Kid Zoo Comics*). By the 1950s short-lived titles like *Monkey and the Bear* and *Bingo, the Monkey Doodle Boy* starred silly simians. Their adventures were routinely slapstick, and—as evidenced by their eventual slip into the chasm of limbo—utterly forgettable.

Not all of these depictions of monkeys were humorous. Monkey brain surgery was the cover subject of 1953's *Weird Mysteries* #5, published before the implementation of the content watchdogs the Comics Code Authority. Readers of EC's crime comics knew that "monkey" was slang for a drug habit, with several graphic stories revealing the horrors of addicts with a "monkey on their backs."

Straddling the line between humor and adventure was Bobo, a.k.a. Detective Chimp, the John Broome/Carmine Infantino co-creation that debuted in DC Comics' *The Adventures of Rex the Wonder Dog* #4 (Aug. 1952) and ran as that series' backup until late 1959. Detective Chimp was the last of the monkey stars of the Golden Age—and only in a book about apes in comics would Bobo be deemed a "star," since he was a secondary character in a secondary title.

In the 1950s "cute little monkeys" ducked for cover as gorillas stormed into sci-fi and super-hero comic titles (see Chapter 4). Gabby was good 'n' gone and Spunky sputtered out of print. Superman editor Mort Weisinger and his writers kept alive the monkey-as-sidekick: the android arch-foe Brainiac was accompanied in his interstellar malice by a space-monkey named Koko, and joining the growing family of Kryptonian survivors was the impetuous super-powered monkey Beppo.

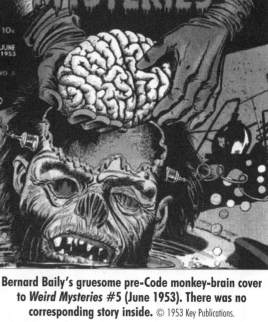

Bernard Baily's gruesome pre-Code monkey-brain cover to *Weird Mysteries* #5 (June 1953). There was no corresponding story inside. © 1953 Key Publications.

An inventive monkey stars in artist Otto Messmer's "Jungle Bungle," published in 1951 in *Felix the Cat* #24.
© 1951 Toby Press. Courtesy of Heritage Auctions.

Overall, however, the Silver Age signaled bad times for monkeys in comics. Outside of the random Gold Key Comics adaptation of a chimp-starring film (*The Monkey's Uncle*) or TV show (*The Hathaways*), monkeys were seldom seen. Even Koko and Beppo disappeared. These once-famous creatures that had earlier scampered across the newsstands were forced into subservience as laugh-getters for anemic kiddie comics, occasionally hamming it up to muster a chuckle in the musty adventures of Jerry Lewis or Mutt and Jeff or Little Dot. In the 1970s TV tie-in titles offered a glimmer of hope for monkey fans. The Saturday-morning live-action program *Lancelot Link, Secret Chimp* inspired a Gold Key title that ran eight issues, and through most of the '70s Gleek, the pet of the Wonder Twins, appeared in a DC spin-off of the TV toon *Super Friends*.

Still don't believe in the genetic link between chimp and man? Here's your proof: from 1953's *Rags Rabbit* #14. © 1953 Harvey Comics.

Monkey ski, monkey do! And a shirtless Mutt and Jeff, too! Ew! From 1965's *Mutt and Jeff New Jokes #3*. Art by Al Smith.
© 1965 Harvey Comics.

Before you criticize Jor-El for using Beppo for space tests, remember, NASA did the same thing: Here are astro-apes Able the squirrel monkey in May 1959 and Ham the chimp in January 1961.
Public domain photos © NASA.

The television appearances of real-life health-food guru Euell Gibbons inspired Scott Shaw!'s independent-comics parody You-All Gibbon. And during the mid-'70s *Planet of the Apes* became a worldwide phenomenon, as well as a Marvel Comics series (see Chapter 6). But by and large, monkeys in comic books had been relegated to M.I.A. status.

Their prospects worsened during the 1980s, the era of world-obliterating crises, dystopian near-futures, bloodthirsty anti-heroes, and super-hero "deconstructions." Scott McCloud's celebrated series *Zot!*, from Eclipse Comics, included among its cast Butch, a teen devolved into a monkey (see Chapter 5), and gorillas continued to score appearances as super-villains. But monkeys were seen infrequently in comics—and when they did pop up, it was rarely for a laugh. A notable example is writer Grant Morrison's DC/Vertigo series *Animal Man*: This "Man with Animal Powers" (see Chapter 5) often crusaded against the abuse of animals, and Brian Bolland's gut-churning cover to 1989's *Animal Man #17*, portraying a mistreated monkey, is a standout of the series.

In the early 1990s the comic-book market experienced an unprecedented boom, as publishers courted misguided speculators by spewing out a barrage of noise-making events, gimmick covers, and variant editions (collect 'em all!). Buyers (most of whom weren't readers) soon got wise and defected *en masse,* and the market hemorrhaged consumers, retailers, and professionals. Some naysayers predicted the end of the comics biz! During this gloomy period, comic-book readers had, sadly, lost the ability to laugh—or, at least, laugh at *comics*. There was no room amid this bleakness for a chimp in a deerstalker's hat. Poor, poor monkeys!

Yet dark is always followed by light. By the mid-1990s a new generation of comic-book creators—writers and artists who had grown up with the Bobos, Beppos, and Blips of yesteryear—began introducing monkeys into their series, or in some cases, producing series about monkeys. The comics readers still left standing after the speculation boom began to realize that reading an entertaining comic book was a more rewarding prospect than hoarding 100 copies of a comic with a foil logo. By the 2000s monkeys had once again returned to their former glory, as stars (*Sock Monkey*, *Banana Sunday*) and as co-stars (*The Way of the Rat*, *Y: The Last Man*). Even Detective Chimp was snatched from obscurity and elevated to stardom! And so, with a toothy grin, *Comics Gone Ape!* proudly salutes comics' most memorable monkeys in…

You probably know that Greg Evigan starred as a trucker—with a chimp partner—in NBC-TV's *B.J. and the Bear* (1979–1981). You probably *don't* know that Gold Key Comics planned a tie-in that never saw print! Here's a peek, with art by the Vince Colletta studio.
© 1979 Universal. Courtesy of Heritage Auctions.

YOUR HANDY-DANDY, A-to-Z
BARREL OF MONKEYS!

© 2007 Brian K. Vaughan and Pia Guerra.

AMPERSAND

Everybody wants a piece of Ampersand, the crotchety Capuchin monkey, and his owner, Yorick Brown, in Brian K. Vaughan and Pia Guerra's DC/Vertigo series *Y: The Last Man*. Yorick and Ampersand are Earth's two remaining mammals possessing a Y chromosome after a plague (a "gendercide") has eradicated all other males. Every man's fantasy? Not by a long shot, as scientists, radical feminists, and sinister sisters keep the boys on the run. While often merely along for the ride (on Yorick's shoulder), the feisty Ampersand was the catalyst for the "Girl on Girl" story arc in issues #32–36 when his abduction led Yorick and his allies on a rescue mission. Since its launch in 2002, *Y* has been frequently graced by painted covers spotlighting Ampersand, by artists including J.G. Jones and Massimo Carnevale.

© 2007 Root Nibot and Colleen Coover.

BANANA SUNDAY

Chuck, an erudite orangutan; Knobby, a romanticizing spider monkey; and Go-Go, a lovable but ravenous pint-sized gorilla; are the talking apes in *Banana Sunday*, a four-issue black-and-white miniseries published in 2005 by Oni Press. Written by Root Nibot (actually, Paul Tobin) and drawn by his wife Colleen Coover, the series centers around a teenage girl named Kirby Steinberg (examine that name closely, comics buffs!), whose father, a primatologist, bestowed upon the trio of monkeys "accelerated learning abilities." Part coming-of-age story and part subtle homage to the world of comics, *Banana Sunday* follows Kirby's and the apes' struggles through high school, as Kirby enrolls the monkeys there to further their education. Tobin's scripts are smartly paced and explore a range of issues from peer acceptance to sexual identity, and Coover's charming middle-of-the-road cartooning style is accessible to both the manga and Archie Comics crowds.

BEPPO THE SUPER-MONKEY

"Monkey see, monkey do"? Imagine the wackiness that ensued when a monkey with the powers of Superbaby (and a miniature Super-suit, to boot) imitated the Babe of Steel's super-feats! Writer Otto Binder, artist George Papp, and editor Mort Weisinger imagined just that in "The Super-Monkey from Krypton!" in *Superboy* #76 (Oct. 1959). Beppo, a Kryptonian ape, was one of Jor-El's guinea pigs as the scientist toiled to perfect a spaceship to escape Krypton's tick-tock toward obliteration. The rascally monkey ended up on Earth by stowing away in baby Kal-El's rocket, and made a handful of appearances in Superman-related titles throughout the 1960s.

Barrel of Monkeys TM & © 2007 Milton-Bradley.

BEPPO WAS AN EXPERIMENTAL ANIMAL OWNED BY SUPERBOY'S FATHER, JOR-EL. WHEN THE BOY OF STEEL, THEN A BABY, WAS SENT TO EARTH TO ESCAPE THE DESTRUCTION OF THE PLANET KRYPTON, LITTLE BEPPO STOWED AWAY IN HIS ROCKET. LIKE SUPERBOY, THE MONKEY GAINED SUPER-POWERS UNDER EARTH'S YELLOW SUN.

© 2007 DC Comics.

Most Silver Age readers best remember Beppo as one of the Legion of Super-Pets (along with Krypto the Super-Dog, Streaky the Super-Cat, Comet the Super-Horse, and later, the shapeshifting splotch of goo named Proty). Though long retired from the pages of comics, in the mid-2000s the Silver Age Beppo the Super-Monkey was immortalized as a plush doll and an action figure by DC's toy-manufacturing wing, DC Direct. Beppo has a counterpart in contemporary DC continuity: Beppo the Super-Chimp, the non-Kryptonian cohort of Metropolis performer Crackers the Clown; this Beppo debuted in *Action Comics* #668 (Aug. 1991).

Some readers who saw *Superboy* #76's cover might've felt a twinge of déjà vu, and understandably so: Beppo was a retread of Bongo, a red-caped, red-briefed (or was that a diaper?) chimp that appeared in the title almost five years earlier in the story "Public Chimp Number One!" in *Superboy* #38 (Jan. 1955). In that tale, Bongo was a Zippy-like (keep reading) TV star-turned-*Superboy* buffoon. Writer Grant Morrison and artist Frank Quietly kept alive the tradition of apes in capes in *All Star Superman* #5 (Sept. 2006) by introducing Leopold, Lex Luthor's pet baboon (in a Superman costume).

© 2007 DC Comics.

BLIP

Second banana? Try *third* in Blip's case, since this monkey is the sidekick to two sidekicks.

When TV toon-titans Bill Hanna and Joe Barbera introduced Space Ghost in during the super-hero-frenzied year of 1966 (on the CBS show *Space Ghost and Dino Boy*, featuring character designs by the awesome Alex Toth), Blip, the pet to teen sidekicks Jan and Jace, was there to provide the impish-but-adorable factor crucial to so many H-B cartoons. He also pulled Space Ghost's and the kids' fannies out of the fire—*many* times—by sneaking, while invisible (via his inviso-power belt), past the villain of the episode and either freeing the heroes or retrieving Space Ghost's stolen power bands. Plus, he was a cute little monkey wearing a cute little super-hero costume—including a *mask*! There weren't many masked monkeys running around in 1966!

Blip was window dressing in the few Space Ghost comic-

book appearances that followed the show's launch, starting with Gold Key Comics' 1967 *Space Ghost* one-shot drawn by Dan Spiegle. He finally made it to the cover of a comic on 1987's *Space Ghost* #1, written by Mark Evanier, drawn by Steve Rude and Willie Blyberg, and published by Comico. Evanier and Rude's one-shot recreated the feel of the animated series, with an invisible Blip adding a most-valuable-primate assist to the heroes. Once Space Ghost became a TV talk-show host on *Space Ghost Coast to Coast*, poor Blip was forgotten… until DC Comics' *Cartoon Network Presents* #8 (Mar. 1998), when the monkey enlisted other H-B apes (Magilla Gorilla, Igoo, Dial M for Monkey, and So-So) for a Space Ghost-and-company rescue mission.

… AS OUR WARNING SENSORS ARE PROVING! WE ARE WITHIN RANGE OF BUZZARD'S SHIP!

This is one of only three panels featuring Blip from this 5-page Space Ghost tale by Mark Evanier and Alex Toth. From Marvel Comics' late-1970s Hanna-Barbera line.

© 2007 Hanna-Barbera. Courtesy of Jerry Ordway.

VOOTIE! VOOTIE!

© 2007 DC Comics.

BONZO THE MARVEL MONKEY

Back in the '50s DC Comics, publisher of Superman, successfully sued Fawcett Comics, publisher of Captain Marvel, and the "copycat" Cap was forced into retirement. Once DC acquired publishing rights for Captain Marvel in the '70s, the publisher copied its own Beppo the Super-Monkey by introducing Bonzo the Marvel Monkey in *Shazam!* vol. 1 #9 (Jan. 1974). "The Day Captain Marvel Went Ape!", by Elliot S! Maggin and C. C. Beck, featured the chimpanzee Bonzo, star of his own TV show, who by a quirk of fate got super-powers (and an adorable li'l Captain Marvel suit) when Billy Batson, Cap's youthful alter ego, said his powers-inducing magic word "Shazam!"

CHIGGER THE FRONTIER CHIMP

Who could resist an Indian-fightin' chimp in buckskin? Apparently readers of DC Comics' Revolutionary War series *Tomahawk* could, since "The Fabulous Frontier Chimp" known as Chigger made only one appearance (in issue #61, Mar.–Apr. 1959), whereas Tomahawk's Kong rip-off King Colosso managed two (three, if you count the Gorilla Ranger). A trained circus chimp on the lam in the American wild, Chigger, dressed like a good little frontier scout, helped emancipate Tomahawk and his partner Dan Hunter from the renegade Native American Running Pine, and saved the day by stirring up a horse stampede!

© 2007 DC Comics.

CHIM-CHIM

Not only were the boy-and-his-monkey team of Spritle and Chim Chim inseparable, this diminutive duo even dressed alike in matching driving suits. Made famous on the cartoon *Speed Racer*, an early anime import to the US, produced in Japan under the title *Mach Go Go*, Spritle itched to be part of big brother Speed Racer's high-octane action. With Chim Chim by his side, Spritle had an annoying (to Speed) habit of stowing away in the trunk of the race car Mach 5. Chim Chim and the rest of the Mach 5's pit crew were adapted to comic books by Now Comics in various *Speed Racer* series between 1987 and 1994, and by DC's WildStorm imprint in 1999.

THE NEW ADVENTURES OF
SPEED RACER
FIRST COLLECTORS' ISSUE
THE FUTURE IS NOW

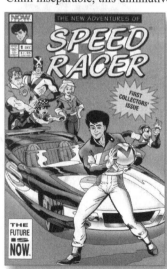

© 2007 Speed Racer Enterprises.

CHOLLY THE CHIMP

Nazi spies do *not* like meddlesome chimps! At least that's what Jack Kirby and Joe Simon believed when they teamed Andre, Brooklyn, Jan, and Alfie—their kid gang of war mascots collectively known as the Boy Commandos—with an ape in "The Triumph of Cholly the Chimp" in *Detective Comics* #83 (Jan. 1944). Cholly was a rambunctious runaway chimpanzee that purloined Axis espionage plans and made monkeys out of the agents on his trail. He is not to be confused with another DC Comics chimp with the same name—that Cholly, from a Leonard Starr-drawn horror tale in *House of Mystery* #55 (Oct. 1956), was a vindictive performing chimp that creepily fingered the killer of his trainer.

DETECTIVE CHIMP

Detective Chimp, the monkey Sherlock Holmes in a deerstalker's cap, might very well be the most famous comic-book ape you've never read—until *Days of Vengeance*, that is.

Brian Bolland cover art to *The Helmet of Fate: Detective Chimp* #1 (Jan. 2007). © 2007 DC Comics.

Detective Chimp's original stories—42 in all!—appeared as the backup series in the relatively obscure title *The Adventures of Rex the Wonder Dog*, DC Comics' answer to TV's popular *Lassie* program. It all started in *Rex* #4 (July–Aug. 1952) when writer John Broome and penciler Carmine Infantino (with inker Frank Giacoia) invited readers to "Meet Detective Chimp." In this tale, Fred Thorpe, an animal trainer, introduced his highly intelligent chimpanzee Bobo to his friend Edward Case, the sheriff of Oscaloosa County, Florida. Thorpe got whacked and the perceptive Bobo ferreted out clues that led Sheriff Chase to the killer. Case solved! And thus began the adventures of Bobo, the simian sleuth/sheriff's sidekick.

As the series progressed, the sidekick dynamic shifted, with Bobo clearly facing front as the star, and the friendly Sheriff

Chase playing second banana to him. While Chase and others in the series realized that Bobo was very bright, readers were privy to the little fella's very thoughts (via thought balloons), where Bobo "spoke" perfect English.

Detective Chimp's adventures ran the gamut of plots and locales: "Monkeyshines at the Wax Museum," "Riddle of the Riverside Raceway," "Case of the Runaway Ostrich," "Death Walks the High Wire," "Bobo Rides a Flying Saucer," "Bobo's New York Adventure," and "Bobo—Sleuth on Skis" were among his tales.

"The character was charming, quite charming," remarks Carmine Infantino of his all-time favorite comic-book feature. While Detective Chimp is most identified with Infantino, both Alex Kotzky and Irwin Hasen also drew several of Bobo's tales.

Curiously, throughout Detective Chimp's 42 appearances in *Rex the Wonder Dog*, not once did Bobo appear on the cover—even in a blurb or headshot. His first cover appearance came in 1968 on *DC Special* #1, an "All-Infantino Issue," but Bobo's grinning puss was just one of a crowd of floating heads surrounding the artist, shown at his drawing board. (Actually, this was Bobo's *second* cover appearance, the first being on the cover of a 1959 British *Superboy Annual* featuring a Detective Chimp reprint.) Detective Chimp also snuck onto the covers of a couple of 100-page editions of DC's *Tarzan* when some of his stories were reprinted there in the 1970s.

Bobo returned in an all-new tale, "Whatever Happened to Rex the Wonder Dog?", the backup in *DC Comics Presents* #35 (July 1981), where he received the ability to speak. Would being a talking chimp now afford Bobo his shot at super-stardom? Not by a long shot. After a 1985 *Crisis on Infinite Earths* cameo (nothing to write home about—every DC character imaginable was crammed into that maxi-series), Detective Chimp returned (making it onto the cover!) in *Secret Origins* vol. 2 #40 (May 1989), where writer Andy Helfer (with Rusty Wells) and artist Mark Badger collaborated on his origin, "IF U CN RD THS." It was revealed that Bobo had once swallowed two microscopically sized extraterrestrial simians, Y-Nad and K-Ram (or Andy and Mark, an inside joke), and in a *Fantastic Voyage*-like effort, the aliens traveled to and amped up Detective Chimp's brain.

Still, Detective Chimp remained one of DC's bargain basement characters. As one of the "Bureau of Amplified Animals," he played a small role in 1999's JLApe crossover (see

© 2007 Cartoon Network.

Chapter 4). It took writer Bill Willingham, fishing for offbeat characters for his supernatural team Shadowpact, to resurrect Detective Chimp in the 2005 miniseries *Day of Vengeance* (a prelude to DC's *Infinite Crisis* crossover). A *Shadowpact* monthly series written by Willingham followed in 2006, leading to a Jan. 2007 release that at one time would have seemed unlikely: a *Detective Chimp* one-shot! Part of an interconnected series of specials, *The Helmet of Fate: Detective Chimp* #1 finally made the "World's Greatest Simian Sleuth" a "major" star.

DIAL M FOR MONKEY

Ever wonder what lab animals do when the scientists are off the clock? In the world of the Cartoon Network's *Dexter's Laboratory* (1996–2003), boy genius Dexter's lab monkey, named "Monkey" (a popular name for primates…), moonlights as… Monkey, a super-hero telepathically summoned into action by the fetching Agent Honeydew.

Dial M for Monkey was a backup segment during *Dexter's* earlier years. It borrowed liberally from comic books, from its title (a la DC's "Dial H for Hero", which itself borrowed from the play-turned-Hitchcock thriller *Dial M for Murder*) to Monkey's heroic transformation (he powered up by coupling his fists over his head, as Rick Jones used to do in the 1970s to become Marvel's Captain Marvel). DC Comics gave Monkey two shots at comic-book stardom in the title *Cartoon Network Presents*: Issue #4 (Nov. 1997) solo-starred Dial M for Monkey, and four issues later, Monkey was one of "Magilla's Guerillas," the team of Hanna-Barberapes that united to aid Space Ghost.

DR. WATSON

Dr. Watson was one of comics' earliest monkey sidekicks, the assistant to Terry Vance, Boy Detective, the high-tech (for the Golden Age) "Schoolboy Sleuth" who used a variety of self-designed sophisticated gadgets, including his detectoscope, to solve crimes. According to the feature's artist, Bob Oksner, Terry Vance was "a play on Philo Vance, who was a very popular detective in hardcover books back in those days." "Those days" for Terry were the early 1940s: This little-known Marvel Comics character and his monkey sidekick premiered in *Marvel Mystery Comics* #10 (Aug. 1940) and stuck around, with the "eek"-ing and "ook"-ing Dr. Watson, through issue #57 (July 1944), followed by a swan song in *Mystic Comics* #2 (Fall 1944).

© 2007 Marvel Characters, Inc.

DRUNKEN MONKEY

A beer-guzzling lout obtains a weapon of unfathomable power and becomes, believe it or not, a super-hero! Yes, that's the plot to the (thankfully!) aborted treatment for the *Green Lantern*

© 2007 Rich Stahnke.

movie starring roly-poly wild-child Jack Black, but it's also the premise of the writer/artist Rich Stahnke's *Furious Fist of the Drunken Monkey*, a pair of mid-2000s miniseries published first by Imperium Comics and then by Silent Devil, Inc. Stahnke's comic stars party animal Chip, a talking chimpanzee living among humans (and strippers) in Bigg City.

Booted from a burger-joint job in the original miniseries, Chip stumbled across the crash of an alien spaceship and scavenged a ring from its dead pilot—not to use it to become a hero, as Hal Jordan did when encountering dying Green Lantern Abin Sur, but to pawn it. Once he tried on the ring, however, it transformed into a shimmering power gauntlet, and the lethargic Chip was dragged into battles with bad guys like the Gene Gnome and Doctor Neanderthal. Chip's sidekick is Al, an acerbic talking toad, who sometimes acts as a voice of reason to the addled monkey. *Drunken Monkey* is filled with sly takeoffs of everything from *Star Wars* to Rob Liefeld-like armored heroes, but Chip's slow course to self-discovery moves the concept beyond pure parody.

GABBY

Gabby, talking-monkey sidekick to the Golden Age masked man Midnight, has a demanding boss to thank for his creation. Cartoonist and *Plastic Man* creator Jack Cole was mandated by Quality Comics to concoct a knockoff of Will Eisner's *The Spirit*—the legendary newspaper-comic supplement also published in comic-book form by Quality—as a security measure in case Eisner, who owned his creation and controlled its exposure, didn't make

© 2007 Hanna-Barbera.

it back from his tour of duty in World War II. Cole's Spirit-look-alike Midnight premiered in *Smash Comics* #18 (Jan. 1941). Sentient simian Gabby was on hand for comedy relief, much like Cole's other, more famous sidekick, Plastic Man's partner Woozy Winks. (Cole apparently liked polka dots: both Woozy and Gabby wore 'em!)

GLEEK

Gleek likes to stick his tail where it isn't wanted—by coiling it around captive super-villains. The blue-furred, bucktoothed monkey from the planet Exxor has, as a super-power, an elongat-ing tail (it also serves as a makeshift helicopter or spring). As the pet of Zan and Jayna, the shapeshifting Wonder Twins, Gleek joined the siblings as super-heroes-in-training during the third season of ABC-TV's 1970s Saturday-morning version of DC's Justice League of America, *Super Friends*, booting out Marvin, Wendy, and Wonder Dog, who previously held those sidekick roles.

Gleek joined the Twins in comic books in 1977 in issue #7 of DC's *Super Friends*, remaining in print there throughout the rest of the title's 47-issue run (the series was cancelled by DC in 1981). Having previously drawn the malleable heroes Metamorpho and Plastic Man, *Super Friends* artist Ramona Fradon was no stranger to elasticizing, comical characters, and her whimsical rendition of Gleek (originally designed for TV by Alex Toth) was absolutely endearing.

JITTER THE MONKEY

Accident-prone chimp Jitter was one of comics' earliest monkey luminaries, starring in a 1936–1943 comic strip by cartoonist Arthur Poinier. Poinier's *Jitter* strips ran for years in Eastern Color's legendary *Famous Funnies*, a comic book ware-housing some of the newspapers' most popular cartoons of the day (reprinted in color) as well as original comics produced for the title. Jitter often appeared on the *Famous Funnies* covers, a testament to his popularity since he bumped big-name series like Buck Rogers for that honor. Poinier discon-tinued *Jitter* in 1943 when he enlisted in the military.

© 2007 DC Comics.

What a *klutz*, that chimp! A mid-1930s *Jitter the Monkey* comic strip by Arthur Poinier.

© 1936 A. A. Kelleher. Courtesy of Heritage Auctions.

KOKO

Even a heartless android needs someone to talk to when traversing the void of the cosmos. For Superman's enemy Brainiac, that "someone" was Koko, the antennaed space-monkey, but their one-sided conversations consisted of Brainiac's boasts about his hobby of shrinking intergalactic metropolises and collecting them in bottles ("An oxygen supply keeps the tiny people alive! Aren't they cute, Koko?"). Koko accompanied Brainiac in his very first adventure (in Otto Binder and Al Plastino's "The Super-Duel in Space," in *Action Comics* #242, July 1958), and was occasionally seen on Brainiac's shoulder in later appearances, but as writers made Brainiac more sinister, the little fella darted off into limbo. The creative team of Alex Ross, Jim Krueger, and Doug Braithwaite didn't forget Koko, though—in Dec. 2005's second issue of the miniseries *Justice*, the monkey was at Brainiac's side when the android performed a bloody brain dissection on JLAer Aquaman (whether or not this was a Koko-suggested retribution for that nasty monkey-brain cover to *Weird Mysteries* #5 remains to be seen).

LANCELOT LINK, SECRET CHIMP

© 1971 SBM Productions.

"It's more fun than a barrel of people!" blurbed the cover to Gold Key Comics' second issue (of eight) of *Lancelot Link, Secret Chimp*, based upon the live-action Saturday-morning kids' farce running from 1970 through 1972 on ABC-TV. Lance and his lady Mata Hairi were the prime operatives of A.P.E. (the Agency to Prevent Evil), the organization sworn to protect the world from the machinations of the insidious chimp cartel CHUMP (Criminal Headquarters for Underworld Master Plan). As with many of Gold Key's adaptations, the photo covers (Chimps in trench-coats! Chimps shooting pool!) are more memorable than the lackluster interior stories.

MAAKIES

Uncle Gabby, a disorderly alcoholic monkey, and his pal Drinky Crow are the stars of Tony Millionaire's alternative comic strip *Maakies*, which premiered in 1994 and continues in print as of this writing. According to Millionaire, a monkey and crow "seemed to be two [creatures] who would be perfect as alcoholic animals." Routinely set in an nautical environment, *Maakies* has been reprinted in several collected editions and has been adapted to animation. (See the Millionaire Q & Ape in this chapter.)

© 2007 Tony Millionaire.

MISTER MONSTER

The obscure "Mister Monster," in Gold Key's *Boris Karloff Tales of Mystery* #91 (May 1979), may have slipped under the radar of even the most dedicated apes enthusiasts. Its hair-raising painted cover by an uncredited artist, with its floating head of a demonic-

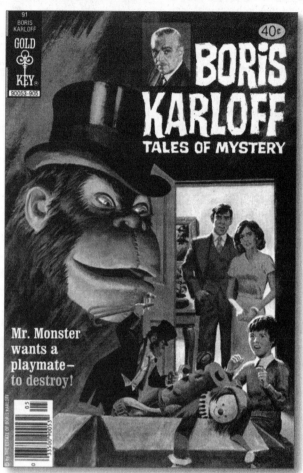

© 2007 Boris Karloff estate.

looking stuffed (look at the detailed lip stitching!) chimp under-scoring the horrific spectacle of toy-beating, suggests two things: 1) that the story's also-uncredited writer was inspired by the recently released Anthony Hopkins movie chiller *Magic* (1978), featuring a murderous ventriloquist's dummy, and 2) that the accompanying story inside would be a nightmare-inducer. Well, we'll give you number 1, but unfortunately, "Mister Monster," drawn by Frank Bolle, didn't live up to its cover potential.

This six-pager began with doting daddy Richard Harrison buying for his hyper-imaginative son Billy a hand-carved chimp doll in a tux and top hat. Dad should've guessed there was trouble in store, since his purchase was made from a street-vendor gypsy who boasted of this "Mister Monster's" magic. Dumb dad!

Billy's unbridled imagination imbued the chimp doll with "life," and it proceeded to use its magic cane to pulverize the boy's other toys. (SPOILER WARNING) Here's where the story went awry: Billy quickly depowered Mister Monster by refusing to believe in the doll any longer. Cop out! Billy was a self-absorbed little brat! He could have at least given readers a couple of pages of siccing Mister Monster on some schoolyard enemy…

Still, the cover *is* a keeper.

MITCH THE MONKEY

British kid-TV pioneer Gerry Anderson's "Supermarionation" process mixed model spacecrafts and sets with… well, dang freaky-looking puppets as "humans." Except in Mitch's case. Mitch was a puppet *monkey*, the pet of ten-year-old Jimmy Gibson. Jimmy and Mitch were the frequent companions of Mike Mercury, test pilot of Supercar, a vehicle that could travel on land, underwater, or through the skies and through space.

Anderson's *Supercar* (1961–1962) was syndicated on America in the early '60s and enjoyed a spate of licensing, including four comic-book issues produced by Gold Key from late 1962 through the summer of 1963. The series' painted covers wonderfully evoked the surreal atmosphere of the TV show, but the line-art interiors, by artist Ray Osrin, felt mundane when compared to the unusual source material.

Fueled by nostalgia, the Texas-based Misc!MAYHEM released the all-new *Supercar* #0 (Feb. 2003), drawn by its publisher, Kez Wilson. Mitch was solo-spotlighted in a black-and-white one-page comic tale by Michael Hawkins, guest-starring *Speed Racer*'s Spritle and Chim Chim. *Supercar* was intended to launch a full line of Anderson-inspired comic books, but poor sales parked "the marvel of the ages" in the limbo garage.

MOJO JOJO

"I wasn't born a super-villain chimp with an oversized brain, you know. Evil geniuses are made, not born."

Mojo Jojo, the most popular of the rogues' gallery of the Cartoon Network's *Powerpuff Girls* (1998–2004), played a role in his own

© 2007 Cartoon Network.

Mitch the Monkey rides center-front in Supercar. Original Ray Osrin art to the inside back cover of *Supercar* #3 (1963).
© 2007 Carlton International Media Limited. Courtesy of Heritage Auctions.

"making." He was originally Jojo, the lab monkey of Professor Utonium. Jojo's antics caused "Chemical X" to spill into the scientist's concoction of "sugar, spice, and everything nice." The mix went *boom!*, creating moppet super-heroines Blossom, Buttercup, and Bubbles… and transmogrifying Jojo into the malicious monkey with a penchant for rambling monologues, Mojo Jojo.

Since 2000 the Powerpuff Girls have starred in their own DC Comics title (and in other Cartoon Network-related series), with Mojo Jojo regularly appearing (hey, he's a monkey super-villain—with its apes-in-comics history, how could DC resist?). While his comic-book appearances sometimes lack the verve of the animated episodes, Mojo Jojo is always a welcome addition to any issue of *Powerpuff Girls*.

MONKEY IN A WAGON VS. LEMUR ON A BIG WHEEL

Writer Ken Lillie-Paetz once described his co-creation *Monkey in a Wagon vs. Lemur on a Big Wheel* as "the ultimate battle for primate supremacy" (and you thought that was *Conquest of the Planet of the Apes*). His comic, illustrated by co-creator Chris Moreno, stars, as you might guess from its title, a monkey in a wagon (yes, a little red wagon) who does *not* get along with a Big Wheel-peddling lemur. Their conflict, sort of like a

© 2007 Ken Lillie-Paetz and Chris Moreno.

deranged *Spy vs. Spy*, remains fresh through constantly changing settings and scenarios and through the creators' sharp wit. *Monkey vs. Lemur* began to build its cult audience in the 2003 *Even More Fund* anthology, a benefit comic for the Comic Book Legal Defense Fund, and has sped into one-shots published in 2005 and 2006.

MONKEYTOWN

An all-monkey team of super-heroes—Monkey "A," Monkey Green, Monkey Giant, Monkey Gun-Boy, and Super Professor Monkey—protect their city in *Monkeytown*, Scott McCloud's madcap online comic (*www.scottmccloud.com/comics/mi/mi-17/mi-17.html*). Their arch-foe is Monkey Head, a "giant floating monkey head with deadly mental powers." There's no end of fun in McCloud's strip, which is packed with monkey-spun takeoffs of super-hero comics' greatest clichés, from ubiquitous super-

Take that, ya walking tin can! From James Kochalka's *Monkey vs. Robot and the Crystal of Power* (2003). © 2007 James Kochalka.

characters (including Cowboy Monkey, Flaming Tail Monkey, and Robot President Monkey) to mindless mutant minions (like Monkey Caveman, Big Fat Monkey, and Rotten Stinking Monkey) to giant robotic apes (Mechanical Monster Monkey).

MONKEY VS. ROBOT

Apes and automatons do *not* get along! Their enmity, a clash of yesterday vs. tomorrow, was first depicted in comic books on the cover of *Smash Comics* #1 (Aug. 1939), featuring Bozo the Robot (in funnybooks' first-ever robot cover) tangling with a gorilla—but no one does primal fury vs. technological wizardry like cartoonist James Kochalka.

The plots for Kochalka's graphic novels *Monkey vs. Robot* (Top Shelf, 2000) and *Monkey vs. Robot and the Crystal of Power* (2003) are simple—at face value, they're stories about two forces of equal determination whacking the crap out of each other. What kid or comics fan wouldn't love *that*? But that simplicity, like Kochalka's unpretentious, thick-lined art style, is deceptive, as the *Monkey vs. Robot* series is really about the resolve of man (or his primeval cousin)

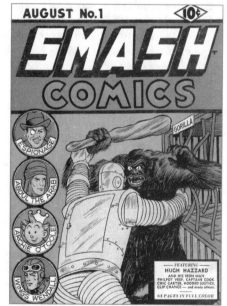

Long before *Monkey vs. Robot* came comics' first robot cover, Quality's *Smash Comics* #1 (Aug. 1939), with its Bozo the Robot vs. gorilla fight. © 1939 Quality Comics.

to protect his territory, no matter the odds. If ever a graphic-novel series screamed "all ages," it's *Monkey vs. Robot*.

MY MONKEY'S NAME IS JENNIFER

Don't let that darling blue dress fool you—no one could ever call Jennifer a "cute little monkey." Nor should you call Jennifer a "she." Jennifer is a male chimpanzee, given a girl's name by his owner Kaitlin, who also bedecks him in a dress… no wonder this primate is p.o'd!

A Huey Lewis first encounter in Ken Knudtsen's "Talking with Jennifer." From the inside front cover of *My Monkey's Name is Jennifer* #5 (Nov. 2002). © 2007 Ken Knudtsen.

My Monkey's Name is Jennifer is Ken Knudtsen's eccentric six-issue 2002 miniseries (also collected in a trade paperback) published by Slave Labor Graphics. Jennifer is, by his own admission (revealed to the reader in askew captions containing stream-of-consciousness harangues), a bad monkey. And a violent one. *My Monkey's Name is Jennifer* pits the psychotic simian against Kaitlin's abusive parents, an evil scientist, pirates, and transvestite ninjas. Knudtsen's jumpy, sketchy art style is reminiscent of Ted McKeever's, and is perfect for what might be one of the most disconcerted but hilarious comic books ever produced.

PO PO

The simian sensei Po Po, an accomplished martial artist and intellectual, appeared in the kung-fu comic *Way of the Rat*, published from 2002–2004 by CrossGen, the aggressive Florida-based publishing house that premiered in early 2000 and, unfortunately, collapsed in the mid-2000s. The bane of Po Po's existence was Boon Sai Hong, a vacuous reformed thief-turned-hero to whom the ape served as mentor. Boon routinely rejected or ignored Po Po's wisdom, which was enough to drive a monkey to drink—which Po Po was notorious for doing. *Way of the Rat* was distinguished by the sharp scripting of Chuck Dixon and expertly

© 2007 CrossGen.

choreographed fight scenes by penciler Jeff Johnson. Twelve of the series' 24 issues are available in trade-paperback format.

RUDY IN HOLLYWOOD

Rudy in Hollywood was a syndicated newspaper strip by William Overgard that ran from 1983 to 1985. It followed the exploits of Rudy the talking chimp, once the toast of the town, monkeying for a comeback in Tinseltown by working the comedy circuit. The lighthearted strip was a departure for Overgard, better known as the cartoonist of the adventures of square-jawed, rough-and-tumble tough guys *Steve Roper and Mike Nomad*. In 1984 Holt, Rinehart, and Winston published a trade-paperback collection of *Rudy* strips.

© 2007 William Overgard estate.

SOCK MONKEY

Sock Monkey, Tony Millionaire's series of comic books and children's books, stars a gentler, more poetic version of the monkey Uncle Gabby from *Maakies*. Uncle Gabby, here an actual stuffed sock monkey that comes to life, is paired with a fellow ambulatory toy, button-eyed Mr. Crow, a softer (but still quite brash)

© 2007 Tony Millionaire.

counterpart to *Maakies*' Drinky Crow. (See the Tony Millionaire Q & Ape in this chapter.)

SO-SO

© 2007 Hanna-Barbera.

So-So is the monkey chum of Peter Potamus, the pith-helmeted purple hippo commanding a hot-air balloon that travels through time. They were first seen in 1964 in the Hanna-Barbera-produced syndicated show *Peter Potamus and His Magic Flying Balloon*, a poor man's version of Mr. Peabody and Sherman, with the duo

visiting significant historical events. Gold Key Comics promptly released a *Peter Potamus* tie-in one-shot (Jan. 1965). Peter and So-So returned to comics in the 1970s when Charlton and Marvel published H-B-related titles, but So-So's coolest comics appearance was his role as one of "Magilla's Guerrillas" in DC's *Cartoon Network Presents* #8 (Mar. 1998).

Lev Gleason Publications sponsored a contest on the back cover of *Squeeks* #1 (Oct. 1953) awarding a free, live monkey to the lucky winner! Wonder how they shipped the prize…?

© 1953 Lev Gleason Publications.

SQUEEKS

Sorry, Robin the Boy Wonder, but super-hero sidekick Squeeks earned a spin-off title decades before you got yours!

Squeeks was a monkey liberated from a wicked organ grinder by Crimebuster, the Charles Biro-created "America's Number One Boy Hero" that was first seen in publisher Lev Gleason's *Boy Comics* #3 (Apr. 1942). In addition to providing frequent assists to Crimebuster in his battles against the metal-mouthed meanie Iron Jaw, lovable li'l Squeeks also provided a wealth of comedy relief. As you might guess, he took his name from his frequent vocalization of "Squeek! Squeek!"

When funny-animal comics hit their popularity peak in the mid-1950s, Gleason launched a solo *Squeeks* series, beginning with a first issue cover-dated Oct. 1953 and running for five issues. Readers of *Squeeks* expecting the same edgy super-hero action from *Boy Comics* were no doubt surprised, but hopefully entertained, by Squeeks' solo adventures, run-of-the-mill antics with lots of comical critters.

SUPER-MONKEYS

Apparently, one Super-Monkey (Beppo) wasn't enough for DC Comics, since the publisher introduced an entire isle of them a few years later! Aerial ace Blackhawk and his high-flying team ventured to "The Island of Super-Monkeys" in *Blackhawk* #184 (May 1963), where they encountered intelligent and belligerent monkeys afforded sentience by a meteor (one of comics' most durable clichés). Things looked bleak as the Super-Monkeys held several of the Blackhawk team as hostages, but once their fearless leader obliterated the meteor, the apes regressed to their original state.

TYLOT

Tylot, a monkey-like alien, became a Green Lantern for a day in the 1981 miniseries *Tales of the Green Lantern Corps*. Not bad for a dead monkey. Yes, dead—Tylot was originally an undead warrior dispatched by GL enemy Krona, but had a change of heart (not that it was still beating) and saved one of the inter-galactic heroes. As a thank-you, Tylot was given a power ring and redeemed himself as a Green Lantern before perishing once and for all.

YOU-ALL GIBBON

Back in the '60s and '70s, naturalist Euell Gibbons became a household name from his numerous TV appearances hawking healthy foods and Post Grape Nuts cereal ("Ever eat a pine tree? Many parts are edible."). Gibbons' ubiquity (he even appeared on *The Sonny and Cher Show*!) made him an easy target for workplace watercooler mockery, but cartoonist Scott Shaw! lampooned him in *print*. Shaw!'s You-All Gibbon, the "Junk-Food Monkey" (a.k.a. the "Ape with the Ape-tite"), first appeared in Star*Reach Publications' offbeat funny-animal anthology *Quack* #1 (July 1976) and stuck around for the series' first three issues. Ironically, Gibbon outlasted the real deal, as Gibbons died in the mid-'70s. Shaw! gave readers one last taste of You-All Gibbon the Pacific Comics one-shot *Wild Animals* #1 (Dec. 1982).

ZIPPY THE CHIMP

Zippy was a real-life performing chimpanzee that was a staple on live and recorded kid's television shows of the 1950s. His popularity inspired a wave of merchandising (check eBay if you don't believe me) including, in 1957, two issues of his own comic book, published by Pines.

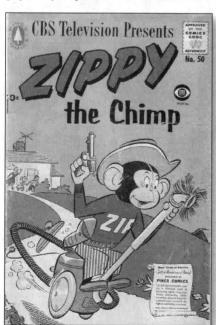

© 1957 CBS-TV.

Imagine a chimp replacing Jerry Mathers on *Leave it to Beaver*, or Jay North on *Dennis the Menace*, and you'll get a pretty good idea of the tone of Zippy's series. Drawn by cartoonist Gene Fawcette, Pines' *CBS TV Presents Zippy the Chimp* #50 and 51 (published during those irritating days when comics houses would rename titles but retain their numbering) was set in whitebread suburbia, on 13 Hectic Street ("just west of Pandemonium Avenue"), where Zippy was the foster "child" of flat-topped Lee and curly-locked Carol Edwards and their squeaky-clean moppets Buddy and Pixie. Naturally, Zippy was mischievous (what did the Edwards expect, trying to domesticate a chimp?) and provided the series with "an explosion" of comical chaos.

THE ORGAN TRAIL

Patsy Walker #8 (Timely, 1945) © 2007 Marvel Characters, Inc.

Zoo Funnies #5 (Charlton, 1946) © 1946 Charlton Comics.

Real Screen Comics #64 (DC, 1953) © 2007 DC Comics.

House of Mystery #58 (DC, 1957) © 2007 DC Comics.

Porky Pig #81 (Dell, 1962) © 2007 Warner Bros.

Bugs Bunny #227 (Whitman, 1981) © 2007 Warner Bros.

MO' MONKEYS, MO' MONKEYS, MO' MONKEYS!

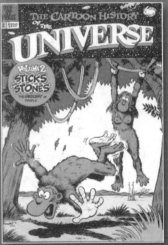

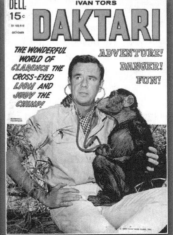

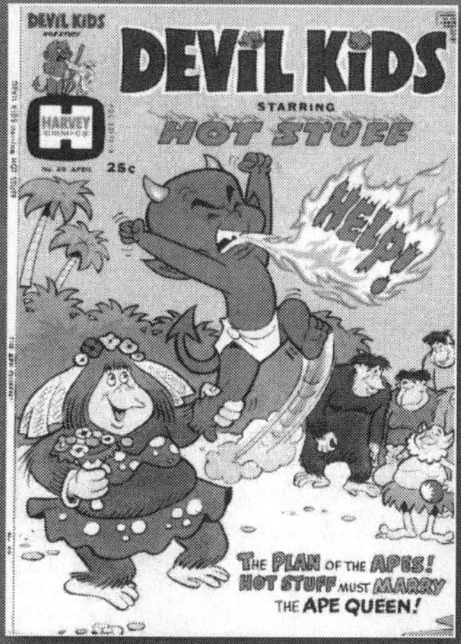
DEVIL KIDS
STARRING
HOT STUFF
25¢
HELP!
THE PLAN OF THE APES! HOT STUFF MUST MARRY THE APE QUEEN!
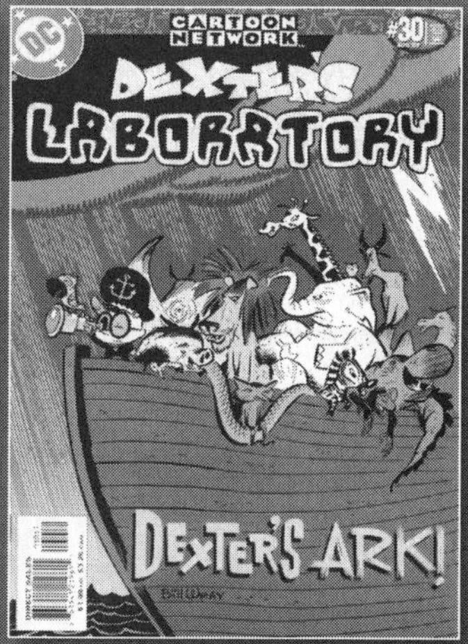
CARTOON NETWORK
#30
DEXTER'S LABORATORY
DEXTER'S ARK!
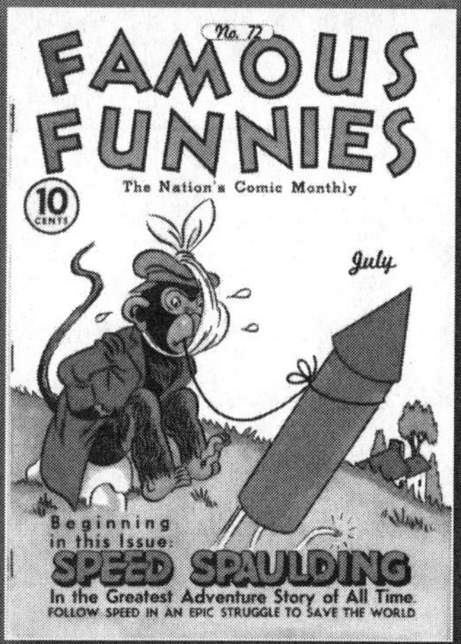
No. 72
FAMOUS FUNNIES
10 CENTS
The Nation's Comic Monthly
July
Beginning in this Issue:
SPEED SPAULDING
In the Greatest Adventure Story of All Time.
FOLLOW SPEED IN AN EPIC STRUGGLE TO SAVE THE WORLD
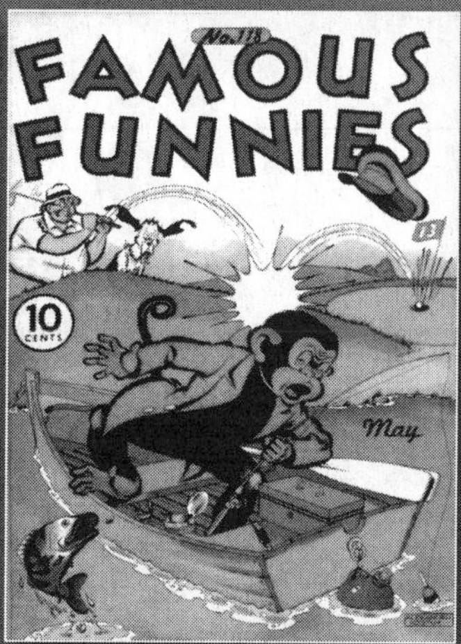
FAMOUS FUNNIES
10 CENTS
May
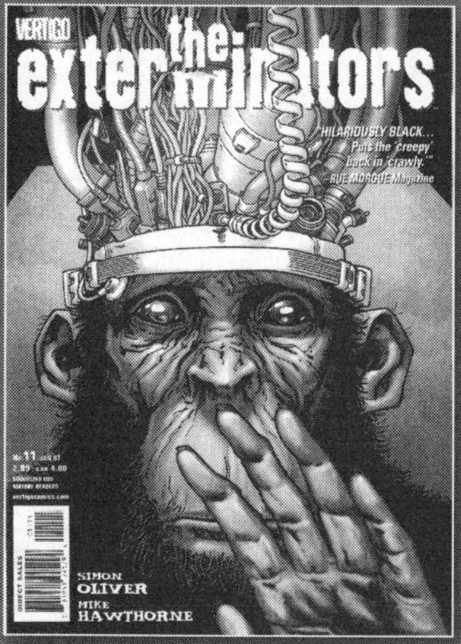
VERTIGO
the exterminators
SIMON OLIVER
MIKE HAWTHORNE
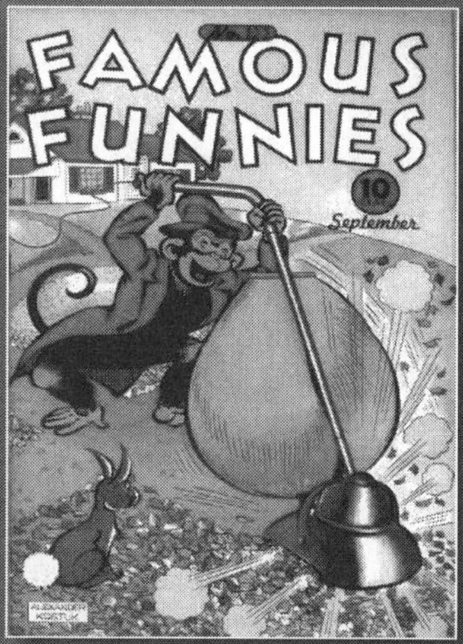
FAMOUS FUNNIES
10
September
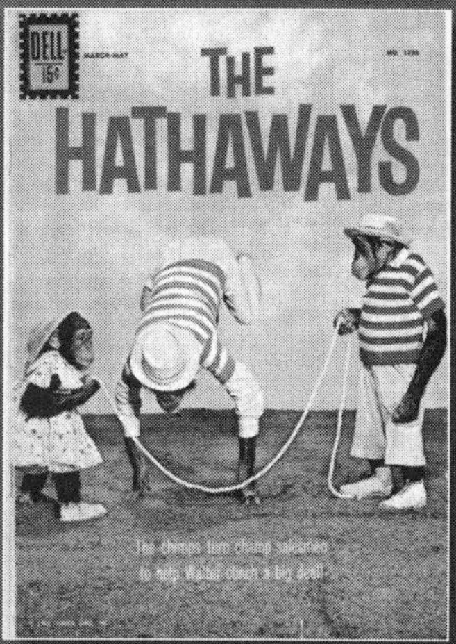
DELL
15¢
THE HATHAWAYS
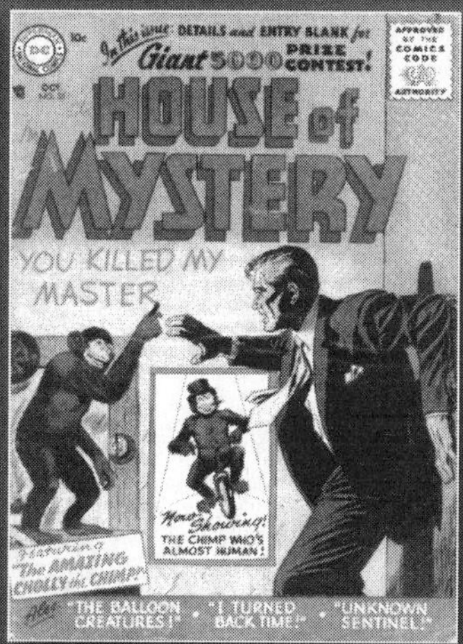
10¢
Giant 5000 PRIZE CONTEST!
HOUSE of MYSTERY
YOU KILLED MY MASTER
THE CHIMP WHO'S ALMOST HUMAN!
"The AMAZING CHOLLY the CHIMP!"
"THE BALLOON CREATURES!" • "I TURNED BACK TIME!" • "UNKNOWN SENTINEL!"
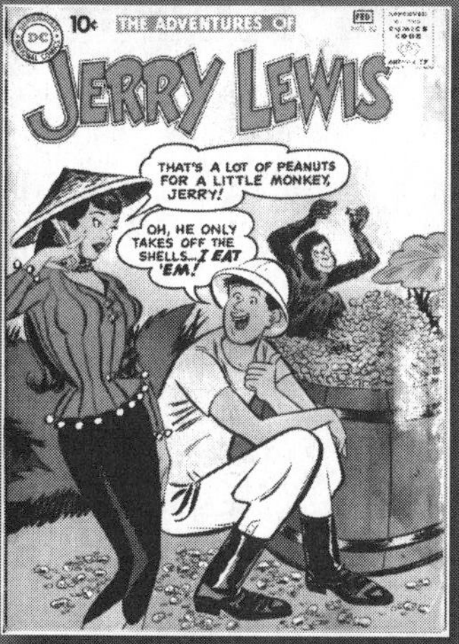
10¢
THE ADVENTURES OF
JERRY LEWIS
THAT'S A LOT OF PEANUTS FOR A LITTLE MONKEY, JERRY!
OH, HE ONLY TAKES OFF THE SHELLS... I EAT 'EM!
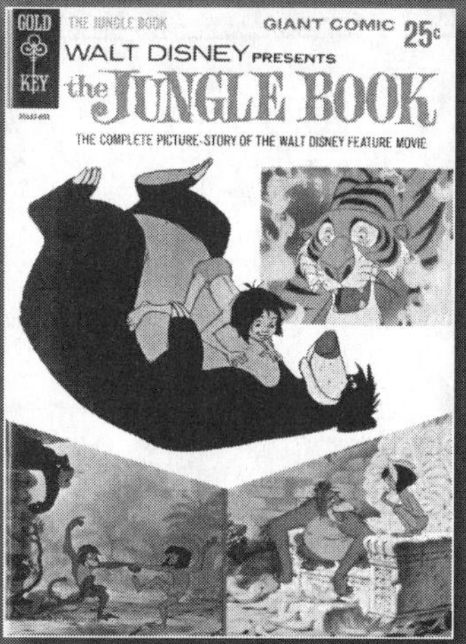
GOLD KEY
THE JUNGLE BOOK
GIANT COMIC
25¢
WALT DISNEY PRESENTS
the JUNGLE BOOK
THE COMPLETE PICTURE-STORY OF THE WALT DISNEY FEATURE MOVIE
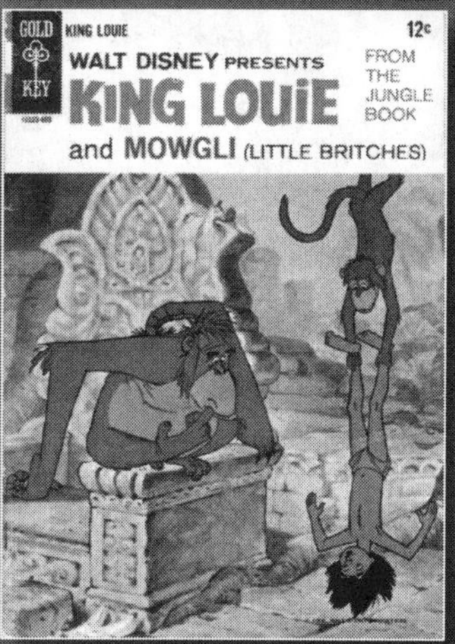
GOLD KEY
KING LOUIE
12¢
WALT DISNEY PRESENTS
KING LOUIE
FROM THE JUNGLE BOOK
and MOWGLI (LITTLE BRITCHES)
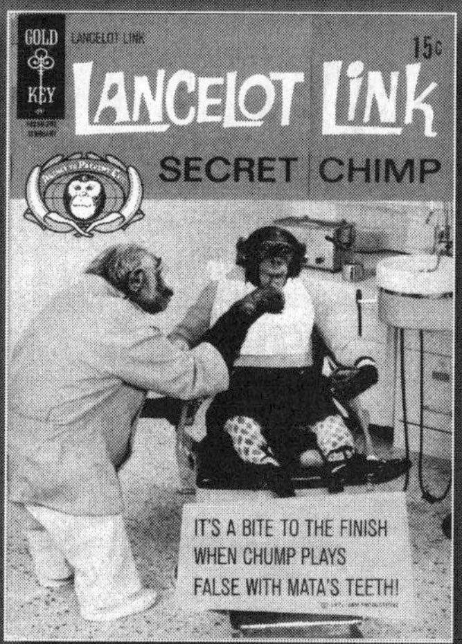
GOLD KEY
LANCELOT LINK
15¢
LANCELOT LINK
SECRET CHIMP
IT'S A BITE TO THE FINISH WHEN CHUMP PLAYS FALSE WITH MATA'S TEETH!
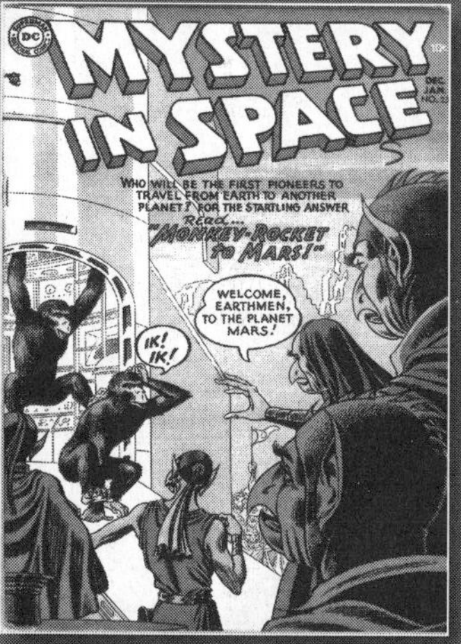
MYSTERY IN SPACE
WHO WILL BE THE FIRST PIONEERS TO TRAVEL FROM EARTH TO ANOTHER PLANET? FOR THE STARTLING ANSWER READ... "MONKEY-ROCKET TO MARS!"
WELCOME, EARTHMEN, TO THE PLANET MARS!
IK! IK!
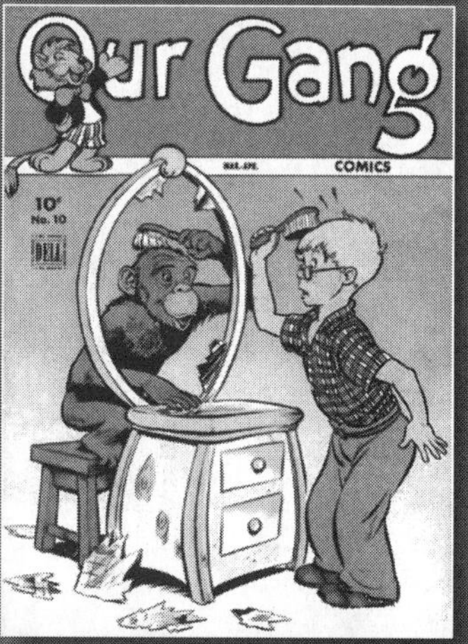
Our Gang
COMICS
10¢
No. 10
DELL
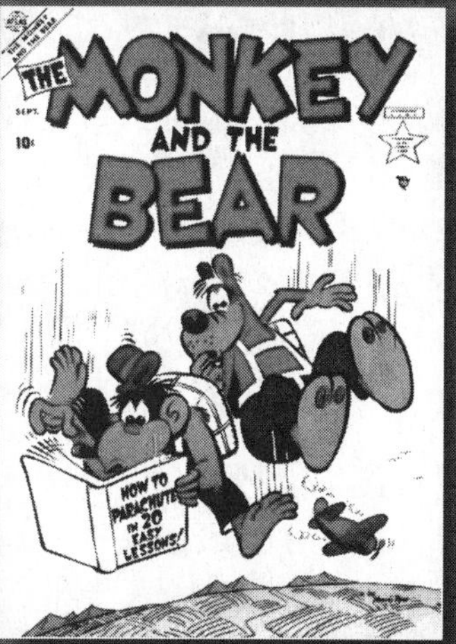
THE MONKEY AND THE BEAR
10¢
HOW TO PARACHUTE IN 20 EASY LESSONS!
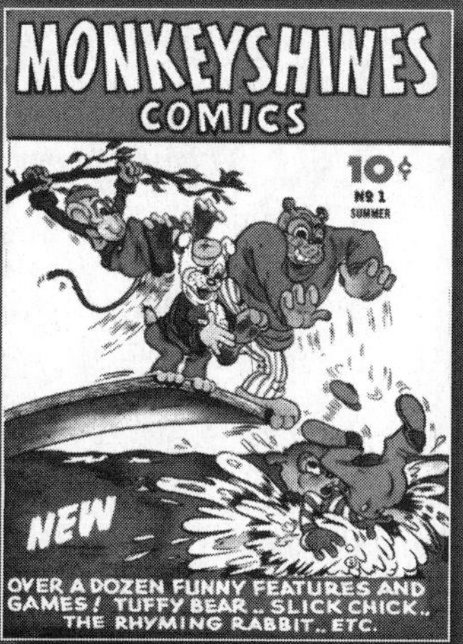
MONKEYSHINES COMICS
10¢
No 1
SUMMER
NEW
OVER A DOZEN FUNNY FEATURES AND GAMES! TUFFY BEAR.. SLICK CHICK.. THE RHYMING RABBIT.. ETC.

APE Q with CARMINE INFANTINO

Conducted by telephone on October 4, 2006

Special thanks to Jim Amash for helping to arrange this interview.

Two rare Detective Chimp cover appearances, drawn by Infantino: *DC Special #1* (Nov.–Dec. 1968) and *The Amazing World of DC Comics #1* (July 1974). © 2007 DC Comics.

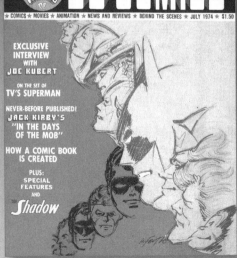

SPOTTED AMONG THE APES IN:

Detective Chimp series in *The Adventures of Rex the Wonder Dog,* Gorilla Grodd in *The Flash,* bringing *Tarzan* to DC Comics

OTHER CAREER HIGHLIGHTS:

Golden and Silver Age Flash, Adam Strange, the 1964 "New Look" *Batman,* the Elongated Man, former DC Comics editorial director and publisher, *Star Wars, Spider-Woman, Batman* newspaper strip

With writer John Broome, you co-created Detective Chimp in *The Adventures of Rex the Wonder Dog #4* (July–Aug. 1952). Was the idea of a chimp running a detective agency John's or editor Julie Schwartz's?

The writer's. Absolutely. John was brilliant at this. I thought his scripts were fantastic, although I do believe he also created Gorilla Grodd, too. Am I correct?

You are correct.

I thought so, because I had one hell of a time, a fun time with that. It was his fascination [with apes] that did it, but I had an awful lot of fun with that.

Had you ever drawn apes before this?

When we did Detective Chimp, I checked out a couple of library books about apes. I figured before I drew them, I'd better learn how to draw them. While I was there, I started reading about apes, which I loved, too, all of a sudden. So a little later, John was writing the stories about Gorilla Grodd and the city… remember the city?

Gorilla City, of course. Through Gorilla City and a lot of your other stories, you were known for your detailed architecture.

I think you could call me a "frustrated architect." [*laughter*]

You never moonlighted as an architect on the side, did you?

I wanted to be one, desperately, as a kid, but financially we couldn't do it. It cost too much for school, and with the Depression my folks didn't have the money, so I did the best I could. If I had an opportunity to draw buildings, I went at it with a vengeance!

You drew Detective Chimp's first two stories, then the strip was penciled by Alex Kotzky or Irwin Hasen for several issues before you returned. Do you remember why you didn't do those issues?

I don't remember that. You mean I stopped and then came back to it?

Yes, sir. Most readers who remember Detective Chimp unequivocally think of you.

That's funny. I don't remember why I stopped and came back to it. You're sure? I don't remember *not* doing it. I thought I was the only who did it. Isn't that crazy…?

Maybe Julie thought the series might not have legs, so he assigned you something else for a while.

That's very possible…

After you returned to Detective Chimp, you began inking your own pencils on the strip. Was that your request or Julie's idea?

I know what happened…. I wanted to ink—that was my thing. Julie Schwartz did not like my inking. [DC's] inking style was a very smooth style of inking and I wasn't a part of that group. I wasn't allowed to take a stand. They demanded I learn how to ink or "go to Hell." But I insisted, so they gave me the chimp and the Elongated Man [to pencil *and* ink]. [*laughter*]

Are you aware that Detective Chimp is back in comics?

He is? Tell me—did they castrate him like all the other characters?

[*laughs*] He's in a book called *Shadowpact*, with other weird characters like Ragman. Back when you did him, he was charming, and was a very smart animal. Now Detective Chimp's able to fully reason and speak, and he's

sort of a wiseguy.

He's different now from the way I handled him? They made him brighter? Is the sheriff still there?

I'm not sure if he's in the new series. That's one of the appealing things about the original Detective Chimp stories: Sheriff Chase, the human, was the second banana to Bobo the chimp. That was an interesting dynamic—sort of like the Star-Spangled Kid and Stripesy, adding a twist to the traditional hero/sidekick dynamic.

Right. I had a lot of fun with that. John did, too.

Original cover art to *Flash* #313 (Nov. 1982), penciled by Carmine Infantino and inked by Mike DeCarlo. © 2007 DC Comics. Courtesy of Heritage Auctions.

Do you remember any specific stories?

I enjoyed the relationship between him and the sheriff, you know. The sheriff was elderly—not elderly, but in his forties, fifties. We never talked about his family. I talked to John about that: Did the sheriff have a family? Wife, kids, what? And [John] talked about maybe getting involved with that sooner or later, but it never happened. Then they moved me from the chimp, to Adam Strange, to Batman; they kept moving me around.

I doubt that Detective Chimp was a big moneymaker.

Yeah, the publisher was paying me good

money and wanted me to do other things. He told Julie "not to waste him on that damn thing." So they kept putting me on the highest priorities. I guess it was a compliment, but I didn't enjoy being moved around.

You've previously stated that Detective Chimp was one of your favorite series ever.

It was, absolutely.

Why was that?

The character was charming, quite charming, and I loved John's writing. That was one of the great pluses for me there.

Were you and John Broome good friends?

No, John didn't have many friends. Very quiet guy, a man of few words. I came in the office every once in awhile, and if he saw me, we'd talk for awhile. We would discuss things about the chimp, and then he talked to me about Gorilla City. So I said, "John, I want to see it. I can't picture it the way you can." So when I got the script, I loved it.

Did you think Grodd was going to be a flash-in-the-pan character?

Yes, but he struck a chord because there were a lot of letters, so we did a lot of material.

One of your covers gave me nightmares as a kid: *Flash* #172 (Aug. 1967), "Grodd Puts the Squeeze on the Flash!", with Grodd holding the Flash's empty costume.

That one did very well, by the way.

One of the lawyers I had—remember, I had a lawsuit going against DC—one of the lawyers asked me a favor: He wanted a recreation of that cover. He, too, remembered it from when he was a child. Isn't that funny?

It's a classic.

You know how we worked, Julie and I? I used to create covers and characters, and then he would write stories around them. We did that, too, with Grodd, the one with the uniform.

What was the first issue with Grodd?

Flash #106 (Apr.–May 1959).

What was the cover?

Flash vs. the Pied Piper. It took a few Grodd stories for him to make it to the cover.

Right, right. We did him inside first, and I remember I enjoyed doing him and then began putting him on the covers.

You were very good at creating covers that asked the reader a question.

Let me explain one particular time. Julie and I had a little game going, and I tried to stump him! Do remember the one with the Trickster running off the cliff in mid-air? And the Flash was skidding to a stop?

I do (*Flash* #113, June–July 1960)!

I went to him and said, "Solve this." And he would! He'd solve everything I did. He'd get really mad, but he'd solve everything.

And then one day I said, "I'll fix him. I'll create a cover that this guy cannot fix." I did "The Flash of Two Worlds" (*Flash* #123, Sept. 1961). Two Flashes, and this girder falling down. And I threw it on his desk and I said, "Here, solve this one."

And by the time I got home, he had it solved! [*laughter*]

You said that John Broome approached you about Grodd. What kind of challenge did you have about drawing a whole city of gorillas that could be taken seriously?

I didn't fool around. I studied, I had a couple of books about gorillas. I worked on it for a couple of weeks… I didn't just pop it out. Get all the angles I wanted, all the motion I wanted. Once I had it under control, then I would begin it.

You did it very realistically.

Well, I had to, otherwise it would be a joke.

Was there any consideration to clothe Grodd and all the gorillas, in uniforms? Despite their intellect, they've always been unclothed.

Of course, always unclothed. They were so superior, that clothes didn't mean anything to them. That was the reasoning for that.

Of course, Schwartz talked to me about that: "Do you want to add clothes?" He asked me, "What about a futuristic uniform?" I didn't think it would work. I thought it would be outlandish to have

this uniform. I felt that the naked apes against this ugly little city really worked, you know?

It sure did!

What types of tricks did you develop to help the reader distinguish between Grodd, Solivar, and the other apes of Gorilla City?

I didn't fool around. I studied,

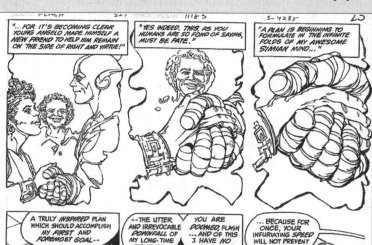

Grodd, the monologuing monkey. A page from *Flash* #327 (Nov. 1983), penciled and autographed by Infantino and inked by Dennis Jensen, over a Cary Bates script. © 2007 DC Comics. Courtesy of Marty Golia.

Solivar, I gave him the white hair along the side, do you remember that? He had grey streaks there and another streak in his body. But, I wanted the grey streaks on the side to make him appear older and wiser.

You also drew gorillas playing pro baseball in one of the earliest Strange Sports Stories (in *The Brave and the*

Bold* #49, Aug.–Sept. 1963).*

I enjoyed that very much.

What was your reaction to drawing gorilla baseball players?

Irwin Donenfeld, who was publisher at the time, was a fan of all kind of sports. He kept pushing a sports book, so they came up with idea of Strange Sports, and Julie called me in the office in and gave me the script. I said, "Julie, I gotta find a different way to draw this because it can't look like any of the other books." So I came up with idea of using the captions and the silhouettes, remember?

Yes, I do.

So for a baseball scene, the bat will be back and he makes a swing in the next panel, so you really get to feel the motion. And it seemed to work, I think. The book didn't sell, by the way, which was unfortunate. I think it was a very different-looking book.

Oh, it was. It was interesting, pretty outlandish, but in a fun way… lots of fun. I wasn't much of a sports fan in the '70s when those stories were reprinted, but they attracted my eye. Your art had a lot to do with that.

Do you remember the one with empty baseball uniforms?

Yeah, that was a great one, and the very first Strange Sports issue (*Brave and Bold* #45, Dec. 1962–Jan. 1963). Julie had empty uniforms on a few other covers, too.

He did?

Sure did. There was an *Atom* cover that Gil Kane drew and a Mike Sekowsky *Justice League* cover with empty uniforms.

I guess it worked!

The return of a successful theme.

Well, the *sports* theme didn't really sell. We tried for while, we tried really hard. I thought it was a good-looking book, but you can't please everybody.

Gorilla covers on DC titles was a successful theme. Why do you think these were so popular?

I don't know why; I think it's connected to Grodd.

There are a lot of unusual ones, like one I mentioned to Joe Kubert that he had forgotten: an issue of *Star Spangled War* with Sgt. Gorilla.

A gorilla was in *that*? How did a gorilla get in the war?

He was the sidekick of a soldier who had been in the circus. They put a uniform on the gorilla for laughs.

Crazy. Was that during my tenure [as DC cover art director, his job before being appointed editorial director], or after?

It was in 1966, before your tenure. Bob Kanigher wrote it.

I don't mean to insult him, but [Kanigher] was a little strange. He had wild ideas, but wrote some perfect books for them, like *Metal Men* and… what was the one with the German aviator?

Enemy Ace.

That book would not sell.

It's developed a cult following.

I don't doubt it. And Joe [Kubert] did a beautiful job on it.

I have to give you a credit for something that happened during the late '60s and early '70s, during your time in DC's top chair: You were experimenting with a lot of different types of titles.

I wanted to do that.

Some were a little ahead of their time, like *Angel and the Ape*.

I loved that thing. Funny concept!

***Bat Lash*, too.**

I plotted that one, you know, and it had that genius Nick Cardy drawing it! I thought he was the best of the best. In fact, when Neal Adams left DC—remember, he got mad because they wouldn't let him create his own covers, and he went to Marvel—I had Nick there to do covers. This is very weird, but Stan Lee called me up and said, "How come the covers that Neal did for you are better than the covers he did for me?" I said, "'Cause I wouldn't let him create them; *I* created them!" [*laughter*] "Oh, *now* I know why." I think [Neal] came back to us.

Carmine, there's one other ape thing you did that was out of the ordinary: designs for a TV show called *Big Top*… a circus show.

Oh, yes, that *was* for a TV show. Where did you see this?

In the fanzine DC produced during the '70s, *The Amazing World of DC Comics*.

What happened was, I drew some roughs for that, and there was a guy named Allen Ducovny… we called him Duke. He wanted to do be creative about *Big Top*. He came to me, and I did the drawings, and he couldn't sell it, you know. I didn't know the drawings existed anymore.

They were printed back in 1975 in *Amazing World of DC Comics* #8.

I don't recall that. There's a lot I don't recall anymore. Isn't that funny?

Well, you know, you *have* drawn a lot of pages and made a lot of decisions.

You know, I have no desire to draw anymore.

Not at all, huh?

I lost every bit of desire. I am a firm believer that you reach a peak. And you become redundant after that. That was the concern for me and I said, "The party's over."

Well, for comics readers, it was one helluva party! [*laughter*]
    I have one more ape question: If you had to choose your all-time favorite ape artist, who would that be?

I think Joe Kubert would be the best. More realistic. Joe is the guy! When you think Tarzan, he's the one I think of.
    When DC was about to do *Tarzan*, the Tarzan people, the whole family, who was that…?

Burroughs.

Burroughs, that family, when they said they wanted [art] samples, I said, "Hell, no, you're not getting samples. I show it to you when it's done. You can't question this. If you do, the whole deal is over."

They had another artist in mind at first, right?

I think it was… who was that guy… Manning? The Russ Manning era. And Manning was upset, but I couldn't see anyone else but Joe [drawing *Tarzan*]. I thought Joe was the better man. Manning was good, don't misunderstand, but Joe was great. He did a brilliant job. That was a good call.

Although Marvel published *Tarzan* a few years after DC, most people remember the Joe Kubert *Tarzan* more.

Who did that?

John Buscema was the primary *Tarzan* artist.

Well, John was a terrific artist. I was a fan of his.

Did you know him personally?

I met John in Italy when I got an award. There's a comic organization there and they called me in, and *that's* where I first met John. Isn't that crazy, after all those years?

APE Q with TONY MILLIONAIRE

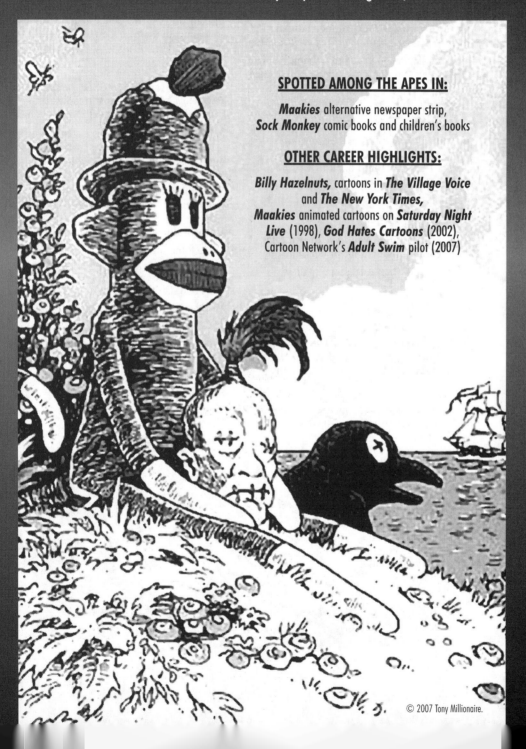

Conducted by telephone on August 30, 2006

SPOTTED AMONG THE APES IN:

Maakies alternative newspaper strip,
Sock Monkey comic books and children's books

OTHER CAREER HIGHLIGHTS:

Billy Hazelnuts, cartoons in *The Village Voice*
and *The New York Times,*
Maakies animated cartoons on *Saturday Night
Live* (1998), *God Hates Cartoons* (2002),
Cartoon Network's *Adult Swim* pilot (2007)

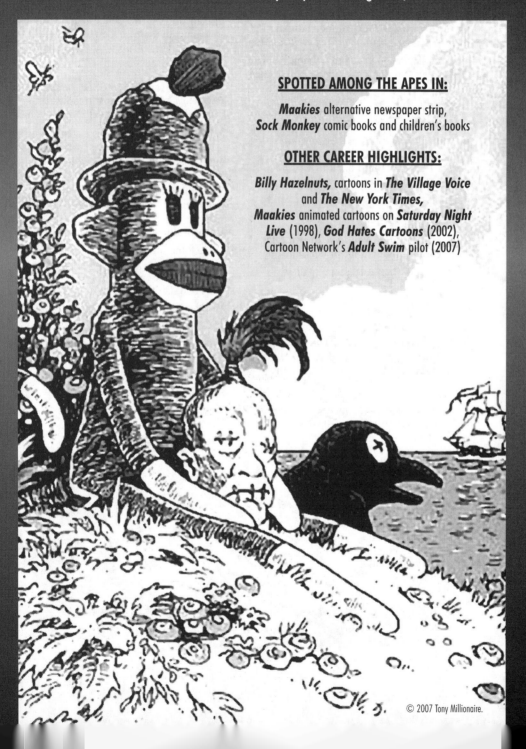

© 2007 Tony Millionaire.

**Why Sock *Monkey*? Why not
Sock *Puppet*? What attracted
you to monkeys?**

Well, when I was a little kid—I
think I was one year old—my
grandmother gave me a sock
monkey that she made. She
gave it to me and I took it and
she said, "It's name is Monkey,"
and I said, "Mummy," and my
mother said, "No, his name is
not Mummy, his name is Joe."
His name was Joe and I had
him for a long time.
   Years later I started
drawing the *Maakies* comic
strip, which has a monkey and
a crow in it. Then my sister
started making a new sock
monkey that looked like my
old one that I'd lost, so she
finished it one day and she
named it Uncle Gabby. I took it
and stuck it up in the corner of
my brownstone apartment in
Brooklyn and started doing
drawings of it going on adventures around the house.
Somebody at Dark Horse saw
the drawings and said, "What
about doing a comic strip
about this," and I said, "Okay,
let's do it."

**Was that the first time you
had drawn a monkey? Had
you ever sketched any type of
ape previous to that?**

The *Maakies* comic strip that
started 12 years ago featured a
monkey and crow. The monkey
doesn't look anything like the
sock monkey; he's a monkey
with a big head. I don't know
why I decided to do a monkey
and a crow; they are kind of
magical figures. They seemed
to be two who would be perfect
as alcoholic animals.
[*laughter*] I wanted to do
comic stories about my life,

more alcohol-riddled than even now. That's why I started drawing that monkey.

Are the Uncle Gabbys and Crows in *Sock Monkey* and *Maakies* parallel-universe versions of the same characters, or are they the same characters but at different stages of their lives?

They're completely different. I wanted to name the other one Uncle Gabby just for some weird cross reference. I don't even really know why—I didn't really put a lot of thought into it. But I wanted to do a monkey and a crow. When I started doing the *Sock Monkey* books, it was something more like from the softer side of my memories as a kid from my grandmother's house. It's much more realistically drawn. The original monkey and crow were more like straight cartoons, a tribute to old 1920s comics like *Mutt and Jeff*. Totally different styles: One is rough-and-tumble drunks shooting each other, and the other is toys playing in a grandmother's attic.

***Maakies* has been animated a few times on *Saturday Night Live* and such, but will there be a *Sock Monkey* cartoon?**

There have been a number of people who have tried to pitch a *Sock Monkey* movie—so far, no success. Not for lack of work… we did lots of stories, but we never came to the right story… lots of designs and situations he gets into, but no movie pitches based on a good story. That's the thing that I really have to work with the writer on. Writing a movie is a lot different from writing a comic.

Do you see this as a traditionally animated movie, a computer-animated movie, or a hybrid?

Yeah, the technology is advancing year after year… but I don't really know what it would look like. Whatever looks good! Look at the old *Bullwinkle* cartoons—

they're the simplest things imaginable, but funny and great. Then look at *Lord of the Rings*. You can go from one to the other, and now you can pick anything in between and say *this*'ll be the look of *Sock Monkey*.

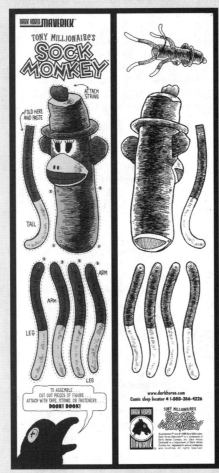

Tony Millionaire's Sock Monkey cut-out, front and back views, produced in 1999 by Dark Horse Comics. © 2007 Tony Millionaire.

I'd love to do it in a real Victorian house.

Was that house in *Sock Monkey* based on your grandmother's house?

It was, yeah. I remember the big, old staircase and the high ceilings and the sinks with two faucets, but I recently went back to see it and it wasn't quite as amazing as it was back then. [*laughter*]

Still, you do it justice in your renderings of it, and you have many readers who appreciate your artistry and level of detail.

How about Ann-Louise, the little girl in your *Sock Monkey* stories? Is she patterned after a real person in your family?

Ann-Louise is a real person. She was my cousin. When she was about 14, she would take us through grandmother's house and she'd take us up and down the back stairways from the kitchen to the back room. There was an attic and crazy stuff up there. She had us convinced that there was a little man living up there [*laughter*], a two-inch high guy she had in a little chair in there, and she'd leave a cookie on it, and we'd hear him poking around in there. We were completely convinced that this thing existed, so she brought that out for me and made it a really magical place.

Were you raised in Massachusetts? If so, is it connected with the name "Maakies"?

Yes, I was raised there, but no, it's not connected. It's very nonsensical—I was looking for a name that would look good on my comic strip. My friend, Spike Vrusho, and I would look into New York Harbor when I was living in New York, and whenever he'd see one of those tugboats, they'd have an "M" on the side.

© 2007 Tony Millionaire.

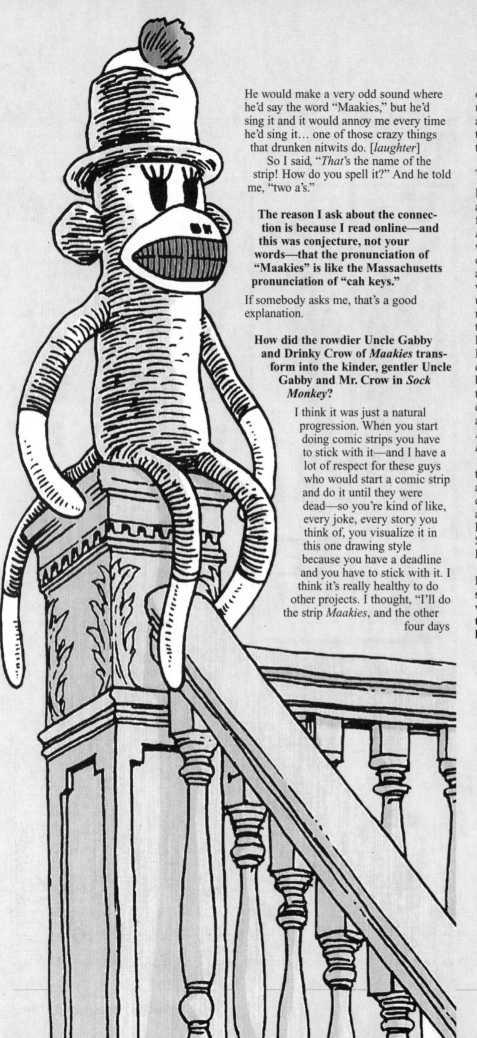

He would make a very odd sound where he'd say the word "Maakies," but he'd sing it and it would annoy me every time he'd sing it… one of those crazy things that drunken nitwits do. [*laughter*]

So I said, "*That*'s the name of the strip! How do you spell it?" And he told me, "two a's."

The reason I ask about the connection is because I read online—and this was conjecture, not your words—that the pronunciation of "Maakies" is like the Massachusetts pronunciation of "cah keys."

If somebody asks me, that's a good explanation.

How did the rowdier Uncle Gabby and Drinky Crow of *Maakies* transform into the kinder, gentler Uncle Gabby and Mr. Crow in *Sock Monkey*?

I think it was just a natural progression. When you start doing comic strips you have to stick with it—and I have a lot of respect for these guys who would start a comic strip and do it until they were dead—so you're kind of like, every joke, every story you think of, you visualize it in this one drawing style because you have a deadline and you have to stick with it. I think it's really healthy to do other projects. I thought, "I'll do the strip *Maakies*, and the other four days out of the week I'll do comic books and use a different style and use all the pen and ink techniques that my grandfather taught me. Very straightforward, representational pen-and-ink style.

Tell me about your grandfather.

He was a great illustrator. A lot of pen and ink, a lot of watercolor. He worked for magazines like the *Saturday Evening Post* and for boy's adventure books, where he would draw buffalo and cowboys and people shooting each other, and he noticed that I could draw while I was growing up. So he taught me how to use a nib, how to sharpen a pencil with a razor blade, and taught me all the techniques of pen-and-ink work. And he loved comics because he was friends with Roy Crane, who did the *Captain Easy* comic. He really wanted to do comics, but you didn't just start a fanzine back then, so it was harder to break into comics. He saw me drawing my comics and he'd say, "Keep 'em drawing, boy." And he'd show me his old collection, like *Prince Valiant*.

So I got an early taste of it. I saw it through the eyes of an illustrator and artist. Most kids would see these old comics and think about being Superman and flying around and punching things. I looked at it as the guy who could *draw* Superman and draw him flying around. Know what I mean?

I do. Most readers were looking at the strips for either their entertainment value or were living vicariously through the characters, but you got hands-on experience.

Did anyone else in your family draw?

My grandmother was even better than him. She was a watercolor portrait artist, seascapes and such… very straight, traditional, normal stuff. They lived in Rockport. Right out on the ocean, and they had a little gallery there… people would come in for portraits. Spectacular stuff—watercolor portraits are not easy. When you're painting, you can't erase it or go over it as with oils. She would get some amazing, beautiful faces!

My father works in advertising and designs trade shows. My mother was an art teacher… she taught junior-high kids. So, you know… she showed me how to hold a pen.

Did your grandfather introduce you to any cartoonists or famous illustrators? Like Roy Crane?

No, by the time I knew what he was talking about, he was living far from home. He grew up in Wichita Falls, Texas—that's where Roy Crane and friends of his were. He was the lonely guy living out in Massachusetts with his wife, happy to be drawing fishing boats rather than cowboys.

What's the storyline of your new *Sock Monkey* miniseries, *The Inches Incident* (2007)?

I wanted to do a longer story, so it's four books that tell one story. It's a story about Inches, a little ceramic doll in the house that's always getting into trouble. She gets her head cracked open and gets taken over by the ants in the house, and the ants are ferocious for reasons that you'll find out about into the book, and they turn her into their own personal robot, causing trouble. And hilarity ensues!

As hilarity always does! [*laughter*]
Sock Monkey is, at face value, a children's series, but it has a large adult readership. What makes it so appealing to older readers?

Well, the *Maakies* strip is obviously for adults… it's irreverent and wacky. The *Sock Monkey* books, they look like children's books and are drawn like old children's books, *Alice in Wonderland*-style, but they are mainly for people who *remember* old children's books, because the stories are a little more high-falutin'… they sort of play with the nostalgia of children's books.

I run into more and more people who don't remember the original *Winnie the Pooh* [children's books]. But they'll say, "I remember the original when it came out in the theaters." And I'll say, "No, no,

The Sock Monkey statue, produced in 2001 by Dark Horse Comics. © 2007 Tony Millionaire.

[there's something] more original than that!" So as I get older, people are more nostalgic for things I knew about in my twenties.

Other than your sock monkey, what

else was in your toy box as a kid?
I had a rabbit that I liked very much, and I used to sleep on it, not play with it. I grew up in the '60s and wanted a gun and plastic helmet to run around like an army guy… and model trains and models… but I remember seeing my sister with whole setups with tea parties and dolls, and I knew it was a world I couldn't go into because I'd be considered a sissy, but I loved the way she had everything all set up. It reminded me how I'd set up train sets with all these miniatures, building a little world. Now and then, I'd set up the sock monkey with the train sets.

What do you think about *The Secret Lives of Sock Monkeys*, the 2004 short film by "the Professor of Perverse Puppetry," Justin Bastard Sane?

I may have heard of it, but haven't seen it.

What did I not ask you?
I almost called *Maakies* "The Drinking Crow," but I didn't want to put the word "drinking" in the comic strip because I didn't know what would be happening ten years from now. But I found out the more I went along, the more situations needed somebody with hands and a face, so the monkey, Uncle Gabby, took more of a center stage. When you want to draw a guy brushing his teeth, you can't do that with a crow.

So hands and dexterity beat out feathers and wings!
That's why people really like monkeys. They can do things people can do.

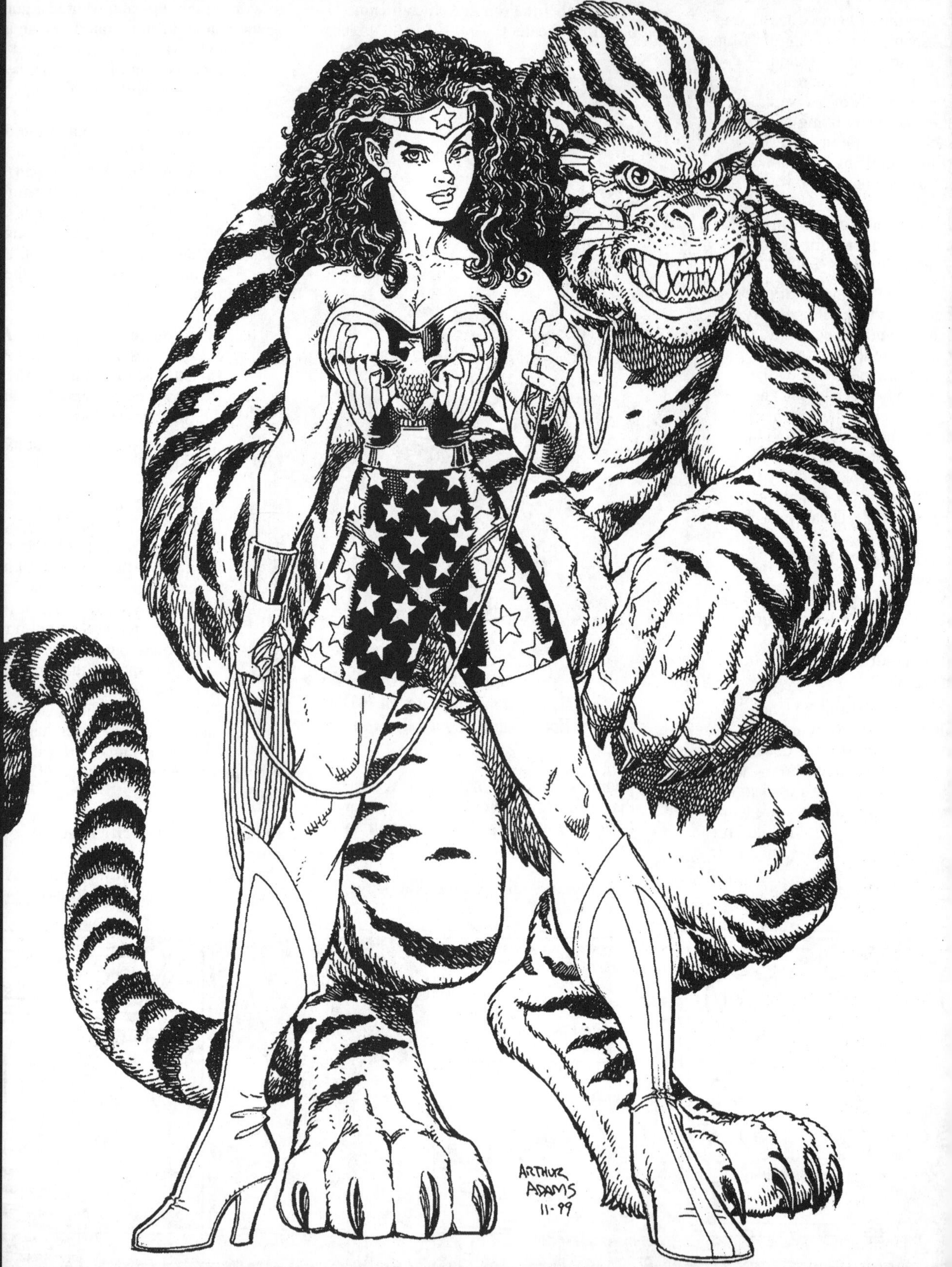
ARTHUR ADAMS
11-99

The Golden Age Amazon Princess and a Tigeape of Neptunia. Arthur Adams' homage to the cover of *Wonder Woman*

They walk among us... they talk among us... and you can never quite tell if they're friend or foe. You can run, but you can't hide from these...

GORILLAS IN OUR MIDST!

All hail Julius "Julie" Schwartz, patron saint of comic-book gorillas!

Schwartz (1915–2004), one of the founding fathers of science-fiction fandom, left a successful career as a sci-fi literary agent to become a DC Comics editor, a position he held for over four decades. Among his innumerable contributions to the field was the discovery (albeit by chance) that *intelligent gorillas sell comics.*

With the publication of the Schwartz-edited *Strange Adventures* #8 (May 1951), the comics business took a giant step forward in a story that took an evolutionary leap backward. "Evolution Plus!", scripted by longtime Schwartz collaborator Gardner Fox, penciled by former Terry Vance and future *Angel and the Ape* artist Bob Oksner, and inked by Bernard Sachs, told "the incredible story of an ape with a human brain!"

No doubt many vigilant mothers tsk-tsked such monkeyshines when noticing this funnybook peeking from under the beds of their pre-adolescent sons. Grown men also took notice of it, such as then-DC editorial director Irwin Donenfeld. Sales spiked upward with *Strange Adventures* #8, and Donenfeld wondered why.

Schwartz (with Brian M. Thomsen) wrote in his 2000 autobiography *Man of Two Worlds* that after deliberation, DC "decided that the magazine sold well because the gorilla was acting like a human being. So we decided to try it again… and every time we tried it, it sold fantastically well, with sales shooting sky high!"

For Schwartz, the success of *Strange Adventures* #8 opened the cage for more talking gorillas. The brainy beasts continued to

© 2007 DC Comics.

"act like human beings" in his *Strange Adventures*, but instead of evoking sympathy like Ralph of "Evolution Plus!" did, they became a simian Seven Deadly Sins. These gorillas were capable of robbing librarians at gunpoint, executing humans before a gorilla firing squad, and threatening a global takeover!

Schwartz's *Strange Adventures* was also home to societies of gorillas, in some cases quite amused by a human "missing link" who might blunder into their lives. A comics curiosity is the Otto Binder/Carmine Infantino story "The Gorilla World" from issue #45 (June 1954); its civilized gorillas dressed like humans and worked in offices (they even >gasp!< smoked!), almost a decade before the same concept was exposed to a wider audience by the 1963 publication of Pierre Boulle's *Monkey Planet* (a.k.a. *Planet of the Apes*).

"In due time every editor wanted to use a gorilla on the cover," wrote Schwartz in his memoirs. Contrary to Schwartz's recollection, comics historian and artist Jim Amash contends that not *every* DC editor went ape.

"George Kashdan was not fond of the idea," according to Amash, the last person to interview the editor of *Blackhawk*, *The Brave and the Bold*, and *Aquaman* before his death in 2006. Amash says that Kashdan used gorilla covers "because it was expected of editors."

Editor Jack Schiff seemed quite willing to do what was expected of him. Schiff had a lust for the incredible. His gawky infusion of fantasy into the urban landscape of *Batman* (alien invasions, bizarre Bat-transformations, and… well, Bat-Mite, a darn *pixie*!) nearly killed that book in the early 1960s, but his *Outer Limits*-like sensibility worked well with DC's *Strange Adventures*' companion titles *House of Mystery* and *My Greatest*

Adventure. Into those series Schiff introduced super-gorillas that fired ray blasts from their fingertips, pink-furred gorilla-creatures, and gorillas that got their jollies watching stupid human tricks in a "human zoo."

DC's gorillas weren't *all* bad, mind you… some were whizzes on TV game shows, or even unlucky enough to be tried for a crime they didn't commit. But overall, when a gorilla showed up on a DC Comics cover, he was up to something, and it wasn't good (for humans).

This Silver Age gorilla mania wasn't confined to DC Comics. Across the racks, gorillas were seen as super-villains (or as comic foils) in titles as wide-ranging as *Fantastic Four, Mighty Mouse, Popeye, Abbott and Costello, Magnus Robot Fighter,* and, believe it or not, *The Rawhide Kid.* Yet no one embraced gorilla covers (or stories) with DC's gusto. Schwartz wrote, "Eventually the law had to be laid down: No more than one DC cover that had a gorilla on it a month." It's even been said that DC had a "gorilla cover chart" to track ape appearances.

Although Julie "Be Original" Schwartz took immense pride in his inventiveness, sometimes his "original" ideas were simply novel spins on earlier concepts. Gorilla City, the hidden African civilization of super-intelligent apes first seen in 1959 in Schwartz's *The Flash,* expanded upon Otto Binder's "The Gorilla World" of five years earlier. Both Gorilla World and Gorilla City were throwbacks to the sci-fi pulps of the '30s—the stuff Schwartz read as a kid—where cunning, adversarial gorillas could sometimes be spied.

Nor did the enmity between the Flash and Gorilla City's most notorious native, megalomaniac Gorilla Grodd, make Grodd

Ralph goes ape for Ruth on the trailblazing Win Mortimer cover to *Strange Adventures* #8 (May 1951). © 2007 DC Comics.

the first super-villain gorilla (although he is, without a doubt, the most famous of the troop). As early as 1940, a superior-minded simian debuted in the form of Orang, the talking orangutan that met Will Eisner's masked man, the Spirit. And a generation before Grodd's first clash with the Flash in '59, gorillas had tangled with Golden Age super-heroes, with characters as diverse as the Green Hornet and Captain America occasionally taking a day off from pummeling Nazis and hoodlums to punch out an irritated ape.

Yet Julie Schwartz *can* be credited for making the intelligent gorilla a comic-book genre. Gorilla covers have since joined robot, "headlights" (buxom women), and bondage covers as desired collectibles. And talking gorillas (both good and evil) have become quite commonplace in comic-book continuities, coexisting with human characters in otherwise reality-based mythologies. Writer Alan Moore, for example, has used apes in a variety of his titles, from King Solomon and the Weeping Gorilla (you'll read about them momentarily) to Terrifo the Super-Ape (the companion of Tom Terrific, an alternate-universe version of Tom Strong) and the Titano tribute Stupendo (from *Supreme*). Kurt Busiek's character-rich *Astro City* includes the armored legionary Korrga, a movie monster given life by a "belief ray." DC itself continues to expand its Universe with simian characters like the Joker's underling Apeface (from the 2001 miniseries *Joker: Last Laugh*).

Certainly, gorillas are not an endangered species in comic books. If we didn't love 'em so much, you might call in Planned Primatehood to keep their population under control. With the dizzying array of comic-book gorillas that have made it into print over the decades, a reader needs a simian scorecard to keep up with them. So be it…!

A CHECKLIST OF CLASSIC STRANGE APE-VENTURES

[*Editor's note:* Not finding the issue you're looking for? See Chapter 5 for more.]

Strange Adventures #39 (Dec. 1953) "The Guilty Gorilla"

Strange Adventures #45 (June 1954) "The Gorilla World"

Strange Adventures #55 (Apr. 1955) "The Gorilla Who Challenged the World"

Tales of the Unexpected #2 (Apr.–May 1956) "The Gorilla Who Saved the World"

Strange Adventures #69 (June 1956) "The Gorilla Conquest of Space"

Strange Adventures #75 (Dec. 1956) "Secret of the Man-Ape"

My Greatest Adventure #14 (Mar.–Apr. 1957) "I Was a Prisoner in a Human Zoo"

Strange Adventures #88 (Jan. 1958) "The Gorilla War Against Earth"

Strange Adventures #100 (Jan. 1959) "The Amazing Trial of John (Gorilla) Doe"

House of Secrets #16 (Jan. 1959) "The Gorilla Genius"

Strange Adventures #108 (Sept. 1959) "The Human Pet of Gorilla Land"

Strange Adventures #117 (June 1960) "Challenge of the Gorilla Genius"

House of Mystery #105 (Dec. 1960) "The Creature of X-14"

Strange Adventures #125 (Feb. 1961) "The Flying Gorilla Menace"

House of Mystery #118 (Jan. 1962) "The Secret of the Super-Gorillas"

From Beyond the Unknown #5 (June–July 1970) reprints SA #55, "The Gorilla Who Challenged the World"

(See right for covers)

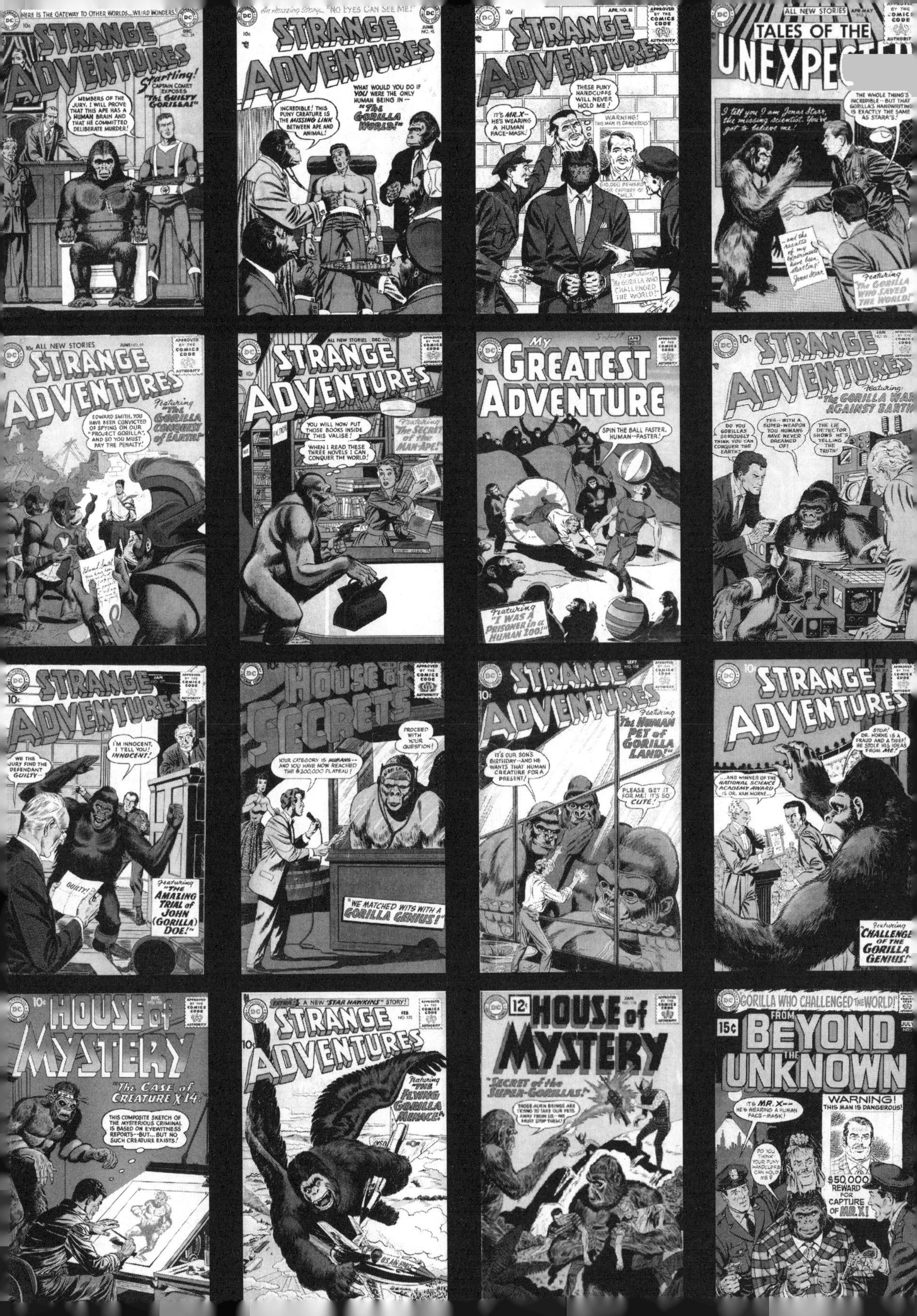
HERE IS THE GATEWAY TO OTHER WORLDS...WEIRD WONDERS!
STRANGE ADVENTURES
Starting! CAPTAIN COMET EXPOSES "THE GUILTY GORILLA!"
MEMBERS OF THE JURY, I WILL PROVE THAT THIS APE HAS A HUMAN BRAIN AND THAT HE COMMITTED DELIBERATE MURDER!
An Amazing Story..."NO EYES CAN SEE ME!"
STRANGE ADVENTURES
WHAT WOULD YOU DO IF YOU WERE THE ONLY HUMAN BEING IN -- "THE GORILLA WORLD!"
INCREDIBLE! THIS PUNY CREATURE IS THE MISSING LINK BETWEEN APE AND ANIMAL!
STRANGE ADVENTURES
THESE PUNY HANDCUFFS WILL NEVER HOLD ME!
IT'S MR. X-- HE'S WEARING A HUMAN FACE-MASK!
WARNING! THIS MAN IS DANGEROUS!
Featuring THE GORILLA WHO CHALLENGED THE WORLD!
ALL NEW STORIES
TALES OF THE UNEXPEC
THE WHOLE THING'S INCREDIBLE-- BUT THAT GORILLA'S HANDWRITING IS EXACTLY THE SAME AS STARR'S!
I tell you I am Jonas Starr, the missing scientist. You've got to believe me!
Featuring The GORILLA WHO SAVED THE WORLD!
ALL NEW STORIES
STRANGE ADVENTURES
Featuring "The GORILLA CONQUEST of EARTH!"
EDWARD SMITH, YOU HAVE BEEN CONVICTED OF SPYING ON OUR "PROJECT GORILLA"-- AND SO YOU MUST PAY THE PENALTY!
ALL NEW STORIES
STRANGE ADVENTURES
YOU WILL NOW PUT THOSE BOOKS INSIDE THIS VALISE!
WHEN I READ THESE THREE NOVELS I CAN CONQUER THE WORLD!
Featuring "The Secret of the Man-Ape!"
MY GREATEST ADVENTURE
SPIN THE BALL FASTER, HUMAN--FASTER!
Featuring "I WAS A PRISONER in a HUMAN ZOO!"
STRANGE ADVENTURES
Featuring: "The GORILLA WAR AGAINST EARTH"
DO YOU GORILLAS SERIOUSLY THINK YOU CAN CONQUER THE EARTH?
YES--WITH A SUPER-WEAPON YOU HUMANS HAVE NEVER DREAMED OF!
THE LIE DETECTOR SHOWS HE'S TELLING THE TRUTH!
STRANGE ADVENTURES
I'M INNOCENT, I TELL YOU! INNOCENT!
WE THE JURY FIND THE DEFENDANT GUILTY--
GUILTY!
Featuring "THE AMAZING TRIAL of JOHN (GORILLA) DOE!"
HOUSE of SECRETS
YOUR CATEGORY IS HUMANS-- AND YOU HAVE NOW REACHED THE $200,000 PLATEAU!
PROCEED WITH YOUR QUESTION!
"WE MATCHED WITS WITH A GORILLA GENIUS!"
STRANGE ADVENTURES
Featuring "The HUMAN PET of GORILLA LAND!"
IT'S OUR SON'S BIRTHDAY--AND HE WANTS THAT HUMAN CREATURE FOR A PRESENT!
PLEASE GET IT FOR ME! IT'S SO CUTE!
STRANGE ADVENTURES
STOP! DR. HORNE IS A FRAUD AND A THIEF! HE STOLE HIS IDEAS FROM ME!
...AND WINNER OF THE NATIONAL SCIENCE ACADEMY AWARD IS DR. VAN HORNE...
Featuring "CHALLENGE OF THE GORILLA GENIUS!"
HOUSE of MYSTERY
"The CASE of CREATURE X-14!"
THIS COMPOSITE SKETCH OF THE MYSTERIOUS CRIMINAL IS BASED ON EYEWITNESS REPORTS--BUT... BUT NO SUCH CREATURE EXISTS!
EXTRA! A NEW "STAR HAWKINS" STORY!
STRANGE ADVENTURES
Featuring "THE FLYING GORILLA MENACE!"
HOUSE of MYSTERY
"SECRET of the SUPER-GORILLAS!"
THOSE ALIEN BEINGS ARE TRYING TO TAKE OUR PETS AWAY FROM US--WE MUST STOP THEM!
GORILLA WHO CHALLENGED THE WORLD!
FROM BEYOND THE UNKNOWN
IT'S MR. X-- HE'S WEARING A HUMAN FACE-MASK!
WARNING! THIS MAN IS DANGEROUS!
DO YOU THINK YOUR PUNY HANDCUFFS CAN HOLD ME?
$50,000 REWARD FOR CAPTURE OF MR. X!

Pesty and Jesty "GORILLA GRIPES"

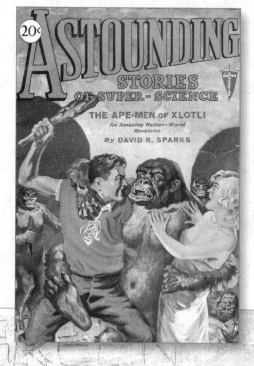

Quarrelsome gorilla societies such as the Ape-Men of Xlotli (pictured on this 1930 Hans Wessolowski cover for the pulp magazine *Astounding Stories of Super-Science* vol. 4 #3) guided pulp reader and eventual DC Comics editor Julius Schwartz toward Gorilla City. © 1930 Street & Smith.

While gorillas were taking over sci-fi comics in the '50s, humor titles occasionally used them for comedy. This 1954 "Pesty and Jesty" page by artist Marty Taras is attributed to *Rags Rabbit #19*, but this page's previous publication remains uncertain since Harvey Comics cancelled that title with issue #18. © 2007 Harvey. Courtesy of Heritage Auctions.

Will Eisner's "Orang, the Ape Man," from the Sept. 1, 1940 episode of *The Spirit*.
© 2007 Will Eisner estate.

"The Monster Roars in German," an early super-hero vs. gorilla story, from Harvey's *Green Hornet Comics #19 (July 1944)*. Art by Arturo (Arthur) Cazeneuve.
© 2007 Green Hornet, Inc.

Stuntman takes on a gorilla in this unpublished, unfinished Jack Kirby page from Kirby and Joe Simon's late-1940s *Stuntman* series from Harvey Comics. © 2007 Jack Kirby estate and Joe Simon. Courtesy of Heritage Auctions.

Comics Gone Ape!'s
Go-To
GORILLA GUIDE

[Editor's note: Human-to-ape transformations and humans disguised as apes appear in Chapter 5.]

ANGEL AND THE APE

Felix and Oscar weren't the only odd couple making news in 1968. On the heels of a summer DC Comics house ad teasing readers with silhouettes of two of comics' conventional cover archetypes—a shapely girl and a gorilla—the tryout title *Showcase* premiered "Angel and the Ape" in issue #77 (Sept. 1968). Angel O'Day, a clever, comely platinum blonde (no dumb bunny, she!) with martial-arts skills that would make Emma Peel green with envy, and Sam Simeon, a gorilla that dressed in men's clothing and illustrated comic books, teamed together as O'Day and Simeon, private eyes. Were this pairing not bizarre enough, people rarely seemed to notice that Sam was an ape, even though his speech was mostly grunts understood only by Angel.

If you think the crazy concept of a pretty girl and a gorilla running a detective agency sounds like a gag out of *MAD* magazine, you're not too far off base. Angel and the Ape was conceived by *MAD* cartoonist-turned-DC Comics editor Joe Orlando, in cahoots with (according to conflicting reports) humorists E. Nelson Bridwell, Al Jaffee, Sergio Aragonés, and

DC Comics' 1968 teaser ad for *Angel and the Ape.*
© 2007 DC Comics.

Howie Post. Post was slated to draw the feature but opted out while Angel and the Ape was still in the development stage, with Orlando wisely anointing Bob Oksner—renowned for rendering coquettish girls and, upon occasion, comical primates—as the series' penciler (see this chapter's Oksner Q & Ape).

Like their *Showcase* contemporaries of '68 (the Creeper, Anthro, the Hawk and the Dove, and Bat Lash), O'Day and Simeon immediately jumped from the tyro title into their own book, *Angel and the Ape* #1, cover-dated Nov.–Dec. 1968. At last—after decades of cover walk-ons, guest-appearances, and one-shot stories, a gorilla had finally become a *headliner!*

But not for long—despite witty scripts by John Albano, Aragonés, and Oksner, as well as Oksner's delightful art—*Angel and the Ape* didn't connect with late-'60s readers. "It was a rather sophisticated comic book," Oksner observes, "and it went 'backstage' of comic-book publishing." That in-jokey element, with Sam drawing comics first for the Stan Lee parody Stan Bragg of Brainpix Comics, then for Morton I. Stoops, a takeoff of DC's Mort Weisinger, is appreciated by today's comics junkies but was lost upon the kid audience of the day. With issue #4

© 2007 DC Comics.

(May–June 1969) the book's logo was altered to *Meet Angel*, with "*and the Ape*" appearing as a subtitle… and the series' seventh and final issue dropped Sam Simeon from the logo, becoming solely *Meet Angel*. Sorry, ya big gorilla, better luck next time.

A 15-page tale commissioned for the unpublished *Angel and the Ape* #8 was remaindered into the "Christmas with the Super-Heroes" tabloid *Limited Collectors' Edition* #C-34 (Feb.–Mar. 1975), and the duo appeared in the DC character free-for-all *Showcase* #100 (May 1978). Aside from a cameo in *Crisis on Infinite Earths* #11 (Feb. 1986) and a return to action (with other DC gorillas) in *Swamp Thing Annual* #3 (1987), O'Day and Simeon remained a footnote in DC history until 1991, when cartoonist Phil Foglio wrote and penciled a four-issue *Angel and the Ape* miniseries, revealing that Sam's grandpa

© 2007 DC Comics.

was none other than Flash foe Gorilla Grodd! Ten years later, writers Howard Chaykin and David Tischman and artist Philip Bond produced a harder-edged ("The Naked City Just Got Hairier") four-issue *Angel and the Ape* miniseries for DC's Vertigo imprint, with covers by Arthur Adams.

THE APE

Quick: Make a mental list of the perils of the American Wild West. Done? Chances are, "a raging gorilla" didn't come to

© 2007 Marvel Characters, Inc.

mind—unless you've read Marvel's *Rawhide Kid* #39 (Apr. 1964)… or its reprint in issue #107 (Jan. 1973).

Did writer/editor Stan Lee have lunch with Julie Schwartz the day he conceived "The Ape Strikes"? (If so, it must've been a three-cocktail meal!) This goofy tale, drawn by Dick Ayers (with a Jack Kirby cover), had the range-rovin' Rawhide Kid riding into a town where he was grabbed by a gorilla! He was taken to the secret lab of mad scientist Dr. Karlbad, who had in mind transplanting the Kid's brain into his anthropoid's head. Old plot, new twist, odd comic!

APE MAN AND MONKEY BOY

A gorilla named Clarence (and *you* thought he was a cross-eyed lion) and a chimpanzee named Bobo (not to be confused with Detective Chimp) were minding their own business in the jungle when they were captured by a creepy cabal of scientists who perform experiments on hapless animals. Little did the researchers know that their tests would give the simians augmented prowess and super-strength. The gifted apes liberated their fellow beasts and then did what any justice-minded monkeys would do: become super-heroes! Thus was born the team of Ape Man and Monkey Boy, a.k.a. the Zoo Crusaders, Batman and Robin-like talking-animal heroes living and fighting crime in a world of humans.

Operating from their gadget-ridden secret HQ at the San Diablo Zoo, Ape Man and Monkey Boy, created by writers (and siblings) Larry and Tim Williams and artist Matthew Smith, were first seen in *Bubba the Redneck Werewolf's Super Sci-fi Special* #1 (Feb. 2006), where they fought John Cockroach, a bugged-out insect insurrectionist from the year 3005. As of this writing, Ape Man and Monkey Boy are scheduled for another *Bubba* backup in 2007, to be followed by their own comic.

Matthew Smith's cover art to the forthcoming (as of this writing) *Ape Man and Monkey Boy* #1.
© 2007 Larry Williams, Tim Williams, and Matthew Smith.

APE-X

The "wheelchair"-bound Ape-X might look like the gorilla equivalent of Professor X, but she was actually Marvel Comics' counterpart to Gorilla Grodd. As seen in the 12-issue maxiseries *Squadron Supreme* (Sept. 1985–Aug. 1986), Ape-X was originally a gorilla named Xina that was afforded artificial intelligence in experiments that also amputated her lower body. Dependent upon her tank-like, weapons-loaded mobile base for movement, Ape-X was a member of the Institute of Evil (based upon DC's Secret Society of Super-Villains) until the Justice League analogues the Squadron Supreme reformed her (and other members of the Institute) with their Behavior Modification Machine. The holier-than-thou Squadron should not have monkeyed around with poor Ape-X—resulting psychological turmoil from her alteration induced a coma.

BAT-APE

Ah, the days when *Batman* editor Jack Schiff could slap a Bat-mask on whatever critter was popular in the media (love Lassie? Meet Ace the Bat-Hound!) and put it into a story. And "a" story was all that Mogo the Bat-Ape garnered, even during DC's gorilla craze.

© 2007 DC Comics.

In *Batman* #114 (Mar. 1958), an uncredited writer and artists Sheldon Moldoff and Charles Paris introduced Mogo, a trained circus gorilla befriended by Batman and Robin at a big-top charity event. The thankful ape trailed the Dynamic Duo to the Batcave (sheesh, if a beast was smart enough to do that, why couldn't the Penguin or the Joker?) and put on a Bat-cowl and cape, helping the heroes track down a thief who had robbed the circus' box office receipts.

THE BEASTS OF BERLIN

It takes a big man to stand up against six intellectually enhanced Communist gorillas—and fortunately, Henry (Giant-Man) Pym rose to the occasion! Writer Stan Lee and penciler Dick Ayers introduced this simian sextet in *Tales to Astonish* vol. 1 #60 (Oct. 1964) as a new breed of Red Super-Soldiers, augmented by an evolutionary ray. Giant-Man, using the shrinking powers of his original identity Ant-Man, turned the Commies' ray against them, devolving them to a primitive state.

Steve Englehart and Al Milgrom brought back the Beasts of Berlin for another Red-romp beginning in *West Coast Avengers* #33 (June 1988).

BIG JULIE, THE GANGSTER GORILLA

Tom DeFalco and Ron Lim pitted "the son of the original Juggernaut" against a talking mobster monkey named Big Julie (if you don't know after whom this ape was named, go back and read the beginning of this chapter, book skimmer!) in *J2* #9 (June 1999), part of Marvel's M2 alternate universe of next-generation characters. Its cover parodied a classic (and oft-imitated) 1970s *National Lampoon* cover.

© 2007 Marvel Characters, Inc.

BIG MAX

"Why, in *my* day, you couldn't swing a cat in a comic-book world without hitting an ape!" reminisced writer Dan Slott on the Mr. Comics website (*www.mrcomics.ca*). "And then you'd look down and realize, 'Hey! That WASN'T a cat—but some kinda alien-midget-ape crammed into a cat suit!' And THAT'S when comics were GREAT!"

Page 3 of *Big Max Comics* #1 pits the Mammal of Might against a malevolent mime. By Dan Slott, James Fry, and Andrew Pepoy.
© 2007 Dan Slott. Courtesy of Ty Templeton and Mr. Comics.

And so in 2006 Slott, with penciler James Fry and inker Andrew Pepoy, introduced the gorilla super-hero Big Max, a.k.a. the Ape Wonder of the World, the Super Simian, the Mammal of Might, the Top Banana, and the Primate Who Lowers the Crime Rate! Actually, Slott came up with Big Max years earlier but found no home for it, but after his star rose from his Marvel Comics serio-comedy hits *She-Hulk* and *The Thing*, he earned the clout to bring his crime-crushing anthropoid into print (abetted by Mr. Comics' Ty Templeton, who drew the cover of the one-shot *Big Max Comics* #1).

Despite his Captain America-like garb, the super-strong Big Max is the gorilla-hero equivalent of the Silver Age Weisinger

Superman. Secretly Homer Sapien, who runs a business called Gorilla-Grams, Big Max has his own "Lois Lane" (reporter Anne Fries) and a "Lex Luthor" (Dr. Galapagos). Unlike other contemporary ape-starring series that broadly or sophomorically parody the super-hero genre, *Big Max Comics* is a relatively straightforward book whose humor is situational (although those situations are often absolutely nutty).

THE BLUE GORILLA

No, that wasn't the X-Men's Beast pretending to be Conan in the biweekly anthology *Marvel Comics Presents* #137–142 (late Sept.–late Nov. 1993). It was instead a Cerulean-furred gorilla warrior created by plotter Erik Larsen and scripter/penciler Chris Marrinan. In the "Rumble in the Jungle" Wolverine storyline, this ape escapee from a zoo freighter was armed with a battleaxe and a shield (as well as an eyemask!) and dispatched as the strong arm of a race of mechanical-organic insects.

BRAINIAPE

They saved Hitler's brain! And they put it in a gorilla's body!

"They" were Erik Larsen and Mike Mignola, but before the Hitler revelation, BrainiApe might've been mistaken as a Grodd knockoff (or as Monsieur Mallah *wearing* his jarred companion, the Brain). First seen issue #23 (Oct. 1995) of writer/artist Larsen's long-running Image Comics title *The Savage Dragon*, BrainiApe—one of many extraordinary enemies of the titular fin-headed, green-skinned super-cop—was a power-mad primate jockeying for the leadership of the villainous Vicious Circle. But BrainiApe was much more than a Grodd wannabe: He was dimmer and much less "civilized" than Grodd, and prone to ranting and chest-pounding (energetically drawn by Larsen with monstrously proportioned arms)… plus there was BrainiApe's

© 2007 Erik Larsen.

exposed brain, floating in what looks like a fishbowl atop his noggin!

When Larsen partnered with co-writer Mike Mignola for a Dragon/Hellboy team-up in *Savage Dragon* #34 (Dec. 1996), the secret of BrainiApe's brain was revealed—to the previously clueless gorilla as well as the reader. After an earlier Hellboy/Hitler confrontation destroyed der Fuhrer's body, Hitler's head was preserved, and ultimately his brain was relocated into its hairy new home. In subsequent stories, Hitler's brain was separated from the gorilla's body and BrainiApe deservedly bit the dust—but does any super-villain in comics stay dead for long?

CHANDU, THE GORILLA WITH SUPER-EYES

Monkey see—through boxes, walls, and young Clark Kent's shirt (and look: there's a big, red "S" underneath)! In the Superboy tale in *Adventure Comics* #219 (Dec. 1955), the Boy of Steel rescued Professor Lang, on an African safari, from the berserk Chandu, a "giant gorilla" (he's not *that* big, by *Comics Gone Ape!* standards: eight feet, tops… although the beast-to-human size ratio fluctuated in this otherwise perfectly penciled Curt Swan tale). Placed on exhibit in Smallville, gruff Chandu acquired X-ray and heat vision during lightning storms, a trait observed by ex-con

© 2007 DC Comics.

"Doc" Baird, who stole the gorilla to pull heists. As Superboy soon discovered, Chandu's eye beams were kryptonite-irradiated due to the ape's ingestion of green K-tainted water, giving the Boy of Steel 12 pages of headaches—and providing story editor Mort Weisinger with a gimmick he'd revisit in 1959 by introducing Titano, the giant ape with kryptonite vision.

CY-GOR

If you're drawing from outside sources when creating a new character, then borrow from the best. That's what Spawn creator Todd McFarlane (with co-writer Julia Simmons) and penciler Tony Daniel did when rolling the thundering cybernetic silverback Cy-Gor off the assembly line in Image Comics' *Spawn* #38 (Dec. 1995).

Cy-Gor is part Mighty Joe Young, part Robocop (or Deathlok), part Frankenstein, and even part Captain America. A top-secret agency (known in Image's continuity as, quite conveniently, "the Agency") that manufactures brutal super-soldiers cherry-picked the brain of commando Michael Konieczny, a former protégé of Al (Spawn) Simmons (continuity was later altered to make the brain's host Sgt. Stephen Smith), for "Project: Simian," an insidious program intended to create a

© 2007 Todd McFarlane.

bestial killing machine with a man's intelligence. Borrowing yet another story element—the scientific plan gone awry—McFarlane's Cy-Gor emerged as an uncontrollable killing machine with only a hint of human thoughts, mainly residual memories that ignite a feral vengeance. Topping off Cy-Gor's rampaging might is his ability to interface with computers and communications networks. This recurring Spawn foe has been popular enough to score his own 1999 miniseries (written by Rick Veitch and drawn by Joel Thomas), plus action figures and appearances on the *Spawn* animated cartoon.

DON UGGIE APELINO AND THE APE GANG

Among the criminal element plaguing Judge Dredd's Mega-City One was the Ape Gang, a syndicate of intelligent ape mobsters, introduced by writer John Wagner and artist Mike McMahon in the British comic *2000AD* prog. [issue #] 39 (Nov. 19, 1977). Fronted by Don Uggie Apelino, a dapper-dressed anthropoid (think: *The Godfather*'s Don Corleone by way of Gorilla Grodd), the Ape Gang networked with human mobs and proved that Britain's monkey-mania did not die with the 1977 cancellation of *Planet of the Apes*. In the 1980s a 25mm role-playing game miniature of Apelino, in a pinstriped suit, was produced.

DJUBA

Since editor George Kashdan reportedly didn't care for DC's gorilla comics trend, you've got to wonder what was going on in his head when B'Wana Beast was plopped onto his desk. Penciled by Mike Sekowsky and possibly (in those days of uncredited stories) written by Bob Haney, B'Wana Beast, introduced during the campy super-hero fad of the mid-'60s, was Batman-meets-Tarzan, a masked jungle super-hero that premiered in *Showcase* #66 (Jan.–Feb. 1967)… and disappeared after the very next issue (except for a few random appearances including, oddly enough, a mid-2000s revival on TV's *Justice League Unlimited* cartoon).

But since the title of this book isn't *Jungle Super-Heroes*, you've probably guessed that B'Wana Beast's partner-in-crime-fighting was a gorilla named Djuba. The "Alfred" to B'Wana Beast's "Batman," Djuba was fundamental in the hero's origin, feeding a strange brew to Mike Maxwell, a white game warden in the African wild. After taking the serum and donning a pelt-masked helmet, Maxwell gained increased stamina and the ability to command the beasts of the wild.

FLYING GORILLAS

Bartenders know that a "flying gorilla" is a cocktail made with dark crème de cacao, liqueur, and cream. Comics readers might wonder if flying gorillas were responsible for the creation of the Flying Gorillas seen in two Silver Age issues of *Hawkman* (#6, Feb.–Mar. 1965, and #16, Oct.–Nov. 1966), but instead, their genesis lies in the more sobering Julie Schwartz editorial directive of, "Let's have Hawkman fight a gorilla with wings." These Gardner Fox-scripted/Murphy Anderson-drawn issues involved the Dimension World, an illogical place

© 2007 DC Comics.

described in the first issue's title as "The World Where Evolution Ran Wild." After Schwartz's passing in 2004, *DC Comics Presents Hawkman* #1, one of several tributes to the late editor, reimagined the Flying Gorillas in stories drawn by John Byrne and Walter Simonson.

GARGANTUA, THE PHI BETA GORILLA

In the surreal world of Jack Cole's Plastic Man, no concept seemed out of place—including a cigar-smoking gorilla! In Quality Comics' *Police Comics* #81 (Aug. 1948), Plas and his roly-poly partner Woozy Winks met the sharp-witted, sharply dressed Gargantua, a displaced zoo gorilla given smarts from a mishap with a scientist's (Professor Brewster) cosmic-ray experiment. You'd think that with his increased intelligence this "Phi Beta Gorilla" would know that smoking was bad for his health, but Gargantua's attempt to transplant his brain into Woozy's dumpy body demonstrated that the big ape still had a thing or two to learn.

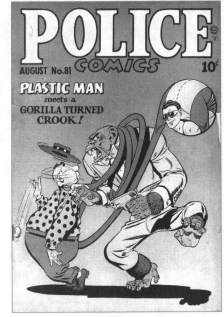

© 2007 DC Comics.

GO-GO GORILLA

In the tradition of DC's early-'80s funny-animal super-team comic *Captain Carrot and His Amazing Zoo Crew* is Ape Entertainment's mid-2000s' series of *Go-Go Gorilla and the Jungle Crew* one-shots. Joining the costumed anthropoid as defenders of Jungle City in this super-hero satire are Anubia, Lady Waterdragon, Mega Mouse, Shellhead, and Quick Cat, uniting in battles against bestial baddies like Polar Paw and Sasquatch.

© 2007 Ape Entertainment.

The super-hero Go-Go Gorilla is not to be confused with the cover copy of *Hawkman* vol. 1 #16 (see "Flying Gorillas"), where a winged ape walloping the Winged Wonder is blurbed as a "Go-Go Gorilla" (a reference to DC's "Go-Go Checks" adorning the top borders of their swingin' mid-'60s comics).

GORILLA GALAXY'S PRIMATE LEGION

In the 1998 crossover *DC One Million*, which glimpsed into the far-future of the company's colorful Universe, readers were introduced to the Gorilla Galaxy's Primate Legion, led by the super-mentalist Titano and consisting of simian variations of classic DC characters: the cyborg Groddchild, the Bat-ape Detective Chimp, the ocean king Sea Ape, the size-diminishing Atomarsupial, and Negative Gorilla Woman (this Negative Man/Negative Woman doppelganger had a human head on a bandaged girl-gorilla body).

GORILLA GRODD

Grodd is not only the comics world's most famous talking gorilla, but he is also quite possibly its ultimate super-villain.

Grodd's megalomania puts him on par with Dr. Doom while his scientific genius rivals Lex Luthor's. He is as blackhearted as Ming the Merciless and his "Force of Mind" makes Darth Vader's control of *Star Wars*' "Force" seem like a cheesy parlor trick. Yet despite his vast intellect and insidious cunning, Gorilla Grodd is a *beast*, providing him a savagery denied human villains. Mind, muscle, and primordial fury, all in one horrific package.

The solo series you didn't see: Page 1 of 1977's unreleased *Grodd of Gorilla City* #1. Art by Joe Barney and Terry Austin.
© 2007 DC Comics. Courtesy of Terry Austin.

KNEEL BEFORE GRODD!

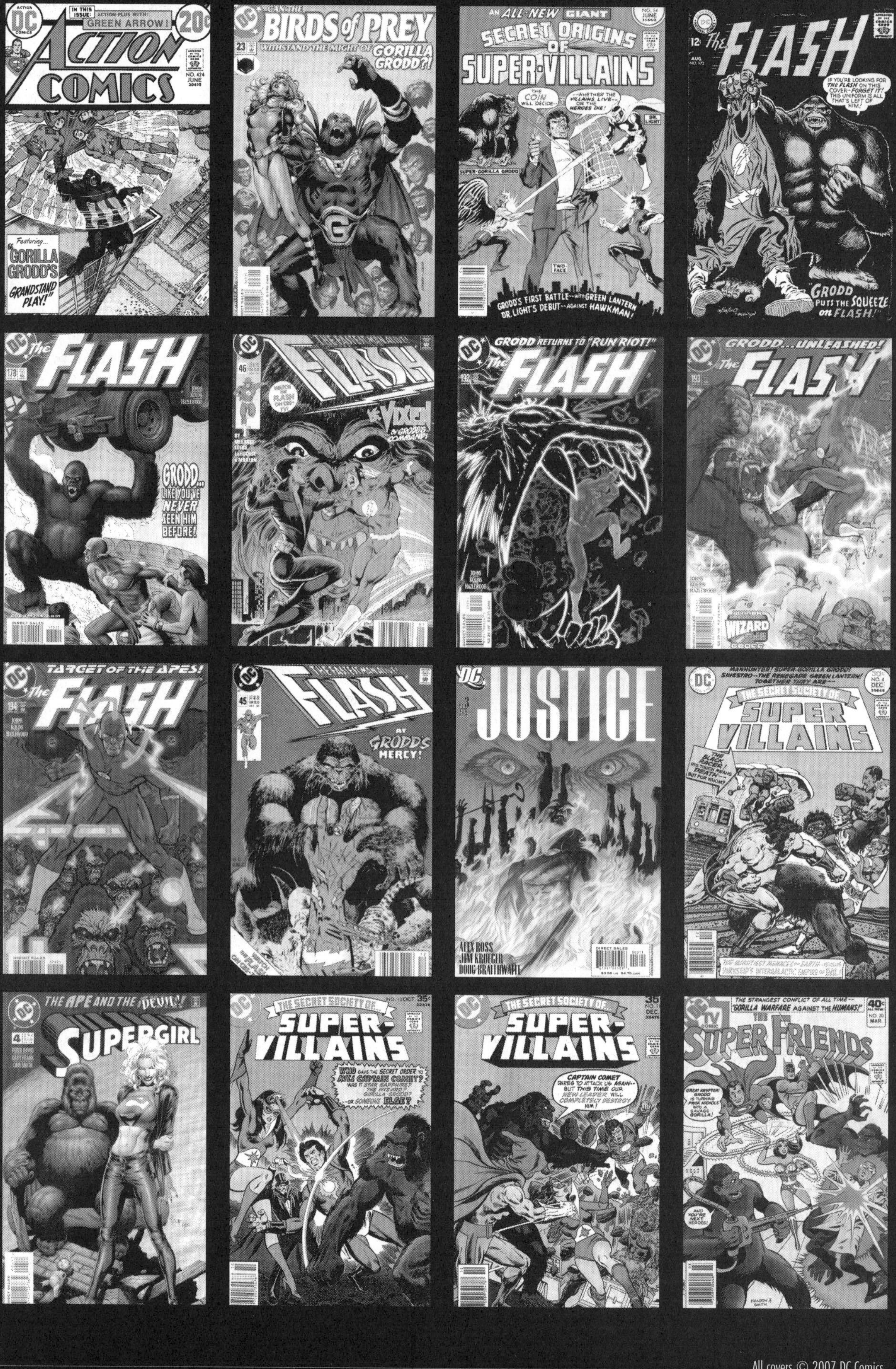

ACTION COMICS
IN THIS ISSUE: ACTION-PLUS WITH: GREEN ARROW!
20¢
Featuring... "GORILLA GRODD'S GRANDSTAND PLAY!"
CAN THE BIRDS of PREY WITHSTAND THE MIGHT OF GORILLA GRODD?!
AN ALL-NEW GIANT SECRET ORIGINS OF SUPER-VILLAINS
THE COIN WILL DECIDE--
--WHETHER THE VILLAINS LIVE-- OR THE HEROES DIE!
SUPER-GORILLA GRODD
DR. LIGHT
TWO-FACE
GRODD'S FIRST BATTLE--with GREEN LANTERN
DR. LIGHT'S DEBUT--AGAINST HAWKMAN!
The FLASH
IF YOU'RE LOOKING FOR THE FLASH ON THIS COVER--FORGET IT! THIS UNIFORM IS ALL THAT'S LEFT OF HIM!
GRODD PUTS THE SQUEEZE on FLASH!
The FLASH
GRODD... LIKE YOU'VE NEVER SEEN HIM BEFORE!
FLASH
VIXEN IN GRODD'S COMMAND!
GRODD RETURNS TO "RUN RIOT!"
The FLASH
GRODD...UNLEASHED!
The FLASH
TARGET OF THE APES!
The FLASH
FLASH
AT GRODD'S MERCY!
JUSTICE
ALEX ROSS
JIM KRUEGER
DOUG BRAITHWAITE
THE SECRET SOCIETY OF... SUPER VILLAINS
THE APE AND THE DEVIL!
SUPERGIRL
THE SECRET SOCIETY OF... SUPER-VILLAINS
THE SECRET SOCIETY OF... SUPER-VILLAINS
CAPTAIN COMET DARES TO ATTACK US AGAIN-- BUT THIS TIME OUR NEW LEADER WILL COMPLETELY DESTROY HIM!
THE STRANGEST CONFLICT OF ALL TIME-- "GORILLA WARFARE AGAINST THE HUMANS!"
TV COMICS
THE SUPER FRIENDS
40¢
AND YOU'RE NEXT, HEROES!

REVEALED AT LAST! **SECRET ORIGINS OF SUPER-VILLAINS** **3 NEW ACTION EPICS!**

SUPER GORILLA GRODD IS THE FLASH'S MORTAL FOE, RIGHT? THEN WHY IS HE BATTLING GREEN LANTERN?

JOURNEY TO A FAR-OFF WORLD AND LEARN THE SECRET STORY OF THE SUPER GORILLA—HOW HE CAME TO EARTH—AND HOW HE FOUGHT GL BEFORE HIS FIRST BATTLE WITH THE FLASH!

Artist Jim Aparo infrequently drew super-gorillas. This Grodd vs. Green Lantern panel might be Aparo's rarest ape illo; it's from the title page of *DC Super Stars* #14 (May–June 1977).

© 2007 DC Comics. Courtesy of Chris Khalaf.

It wasn't always that way with Grodd, however. "Super-Gorilla" Grodd was first seen in *The Flash* vol. 1 #106 (Apr.–May 1959)—although you wouldn't have known it from its cover, which featured the Scarlet Speedster running up against the blowhard Pied Piper. The brainchild of writer John Broome (visually abetted by artist Carmine Infantino; see Chapter 3's Infantino Q & Ape), Grodd was clearly the synthesis of many of the elements that peppered the gorilla sci-fi tales that *Flash* editor Julius Schwartz had previously employed in *Strange Adventures*.

Hailing from Gorilla City, a hidden African society of genius gorillas, Grodd in his earliest stories boasted psionic blasts and mind-over-matter manipulation, could project his intellect into other bodies, and wielded a high-tech arsenal that often kept him one step ahead of his enemies, Solovar, the sagacious simian leader of Gorilla City, and the Flash. No prison, be it man– or gorilla–made, could hold Grodd for long.

And what a braggart, that Grodd! The Super-Gorilla was so full of himself that in his fifth appearance (*Flash* #127, Mar. 1962) he made himself irresistible to others, even the Flash, chortling that the Scarlet Speedster was the newest member of the

"G.A.S.—Grodd Appreciation Society!"

Grodd puppeted the first gathering of the Flash's Rogues' Gallery in *Flash* #155 (Sept. 1965)—although he chose to keep himself at a shaggy arm's length from these costumed humans. This began Grodd's occasional role as team "player," although the calculating criminal usually played those with whom he sided for his own diabolical means. When DC's gorilla fad had become a distant memory in the '70s (outside of Schwartz's *Super-Heroes Battle Super-Gorillas* Giant collections in 1975 and 1976), Grodd stomped forth as his species' badwill ambassador and hogged the limelight—he took on Superman, was one of the stars of DC's *Secret Society of Super-Villains* (1976–1978), and was on the tube as a member of the Legion of Doom in Saturday morning's *Challenge of the Super Friends* (1978–1979). The Super-Gorilla was just a hair away from getting his own comic book in the late 1970s, as *Flash* scribe Cary Bates teamed with Elliot S! Maggin to co-write *Grodd of Gorilla City* #1, illustrated by Joe Barney, Carl Potts, and Terry Austin, the first issue of a planned series that never made it into print.

Grodd appeared infrequently in the 1980s as DC's titles darkened their tone. The Silver Age Flash himself was running out of steam, tripping into oblivion in *Crisis on Infinite Earths* #8 (Nov. 1985). Flash was succeeded by his former sidekick, who by late 1990 resumed his predecessor's rivalry with Grodd. Gorilla Grodd was mentioned by name as a former Central City crime boss on TV's live-action series *The Flash* (1990–1991); budget restrictions and the show's cancellation after only one season prohibited an actual Grodd appearance. Phil Foglio's 1991 *Angel and the Ape* miniseries linked that duo's Sam Simeon to the Grodd family in a fun and flippant romp that unintentionally illustrated just how out of step Gorilla Grodd had become with the rest of the DC Universe. Tradition dictated that Grodd continue to be a part of DC lore, but *a talking gorilla super-villain, in the world of "grownup" super-hero comics? Please…!*

And so taking a cue from *The Flash* #172 (Aug. 1967), one of the few

Tom Raney and Scott Hanna's terrifying rendition of Grodd, from *Outsiders* vol. 3 #1 (Aug. 2003).

© 2007 DC Comics. Courtesy of Scott Trego.

times in the Silver Age that Grodd got off his hirsute heinie to actually mix it up with his fleet-footed foe (by "squeezing the life" out of the Flash), writers made Grodd more frightening. Most noteworthy is the 1999 "JLApe: Gorilla Warfare" crossover serialized throughout DC's Annuals, where Grodd ordered a hit on Solovar and led Gorilla City into a war with humanity (okay, he was also connected to the ridiculous—for the '90s—transformation of DC's super-heroes into gorillas with his "Gorillabomb," but with all those wonderful Arthur Adams-drawn JLApe covers, who's gonna complain?). Grodd's son, Gorbul Mammit (first seen in *Legends of the DC Universe* #19, Aug. 1999), was part of this conspiracy.

Today's Grodd is quite capable of murder, and has become an all-purpose DC villain, seen in battles against the Flash and almost every other DC hero with his or her own title. Folks outside of DC's comics also have a case of "G.A.S."— Grodd has appeared on the Cartoon Network's *Justice League Unlimited* and has been manufactured by DC Direct as an action figure and a mini-statue.

GORRO

Joe Simon and Jack Kirby's Star-Spangled Avenger and his sidekick Bucky checked into the "Horror Hospital" in Timely's (Marvel) *Captain America Comics* #4 (June 1941), where the fiendish Dr. Grimm was the physician on duty, creating monstrosities such as the long-maned gorilla-beast Gorro. Although Gorro perished in that tale, his significance as one of the earliest super-villain gorillas made up for his short lifespan.

GREASE MONKEY

Grease Monkey, writer/artist Tim Eldred's black-and-white graphic novel from Tor Books, is "a tale of growing up in orbit" from the perspective of junior mechanic Robin Plotnik. In the near future, after an unprovoked alien attacks wipes out much of Earth's population, Robin is assigned to the mega-starship *Fist of Earth*, from which fighter pilots train for their inevitable retaliation against their attackers.

And how does this involve gorillas, you ask? Robin is human. His boss, chief "grease monkey" Mac Gimbensky, is a talking gorilla who's outwardly gruff but in actuality is a nice… guy.

In *Grease Monkey*, benevolent extraterrestrials replenish some of Earth's fractured populace by accelerating the evolution of gorillas, and Eldred deftly explores their assimilation into society in a charismatic blend of *Star Wars* and a mellower *Planet of the Apes*. Originally serialized in comics 1990s miniseries from publishers Kitchen Sink and Image, *Grease Monkey* was collected, expanded, and completed in graphic-novel form in 2006, earning the award for "Best Book for Young Adults 2007" by the American Library Association. (See this chapter's Eldred Q & Ape.)

© 2007 DC Comics.

THE GROONK

You're a mean one, Mister… *Groonk*. The Groonk was a green-furred, gorilla-like creature in a Santa Claus suit that safeguarded a group of sewer-dwelling nomads in *Thor* #444 (Feb. 1992). In a compassionate *How the Grinch Stole Christmas* tribute by writer Tom DeFalco and penciler Ron Frenz, the Groonk crawled out of his subterranean tunnels, snatching Christmas packages from New Yorkers, until the intervening Thunder God stopped his shopping spree. After mixing it up with the Groonk, Thor discovered a heartwarming motive behind the Santa-rilla's actions. (And yes, the story also featured an adorable moppet and a dog with clip-on reindeer antlers.)

GRUNT

The reunion of one-time *X-Men* team supreme Chris Claremont and John Byrne in the 2004 *JLA* story arc "The Tenth Circle" generated industry buzz, as did its "introduction" of the Doom Patrol (which ignored the DP's previous continuity and earned some fans' ire). For gorilla lovers, though, the introduction of Grunt was the big story.

"Mega-hominid" Grunt was a four-armed gorilla—visually, sort of the love child of BrainiApe and Jack Kirby's Four-Armed Terror from *Jimmy Olsen*—who premiered in *JLA* #94 (early May 2004) as one of Niles "Chief" Caulder's Doom Patrol recruits. His fury could only be quelled by his companion, the telepath Nudge, another DP member. Once Byrne, as writer/penciler, spun off the reworked Doom Patrol into its own title with an Aug. 2004 cover-dated first issue, Grunt was part of the world's strangest super-team throughout the series until the title expired with issue #18 (Jan. 2006). In the wake of *Infinite Crisis*' 2005–2006 continuity restructuring, Byrne's DP is no more, but c'mon, a snarling four-armed gorilla can't stay in limbo for long!

KING SOLOMON

King Solomon was the articulate, Cockney-accented gorilla right-arm to "Science Hero" Tom Strong, the Doc Savage-by-way-of-Tarzan (with a nod to the Silver Age Superman, too) pulpish hero co-created by writer Alan Moore and artist Chris Sprouse. First seen in *Tom Strong* #1 (June 1999),

© 2007 America's Best Comics.

published under the DC imprint America's Best Comics, Solomon got his smarts from Strong's brain amplifications. Undeniably an homage to the gaggle of gorillas in DC lore, Solomon sometimes slipped into cliché, especially when bickering with the steam-punk-C3P0 robot sidekick Pneuman. But exceptional artwork—including covers and special tales by Arthur Adams and Sergio Aragonés—and Moore's respect for comics and pulp archetypes made King Solomon a welcome addition to the primate pantheon.

KRIEGAFFE

Kriegaffe Number Ten was the latest in a line of talking bionic killer-gorillas engineered by Nazi scientist Dr. Herman Von Klempt, as writer/artist Mike Mignola disclosed in his 2001 *Hellboy* miniseries *Conqueror Worm*. His grotesque, hulkish form dotted with rivets, Kriegaffe (German for "war ape") Number Ten was sicced on the "World's Greatest Paranormal Investigator" by the vengeful Von Klempt in retribution for Hellboy's killing of the previous model of the monster-monkey. Hellboy completists recall that the murdered Kriegaffe Number Nine was called Brutus in his appearance in a mid-'90s Hellboy tale appearing in *The Comic Buyer's Guide* (and reprinted in the Dark Horse Comics trade paperback *Hellboy: Seed of Destruction*). Mezco produced a hard-to-find "Kriegaffe #10" deluxe action figure in 2005.

MAGILLA GORILLA

Hanna-Barbera's animated *The Magilla Gorilla Show* (sponsored by Ideal Toys, as Magilla the corporate mouth-piece reminded viewers in a tag to the show's theme song) premiered on syndicated television in 1964. A play on the kiddie tune "How Much is That Doggie in the Window?", Magilla was an overzealous gorilla for sale in Mr. Peebles' Pet Shop. He desperately wanted a home, but Peebles couldn't shake the beast for more than a seven-minute episode (and let's face it—you'd have to be a mad scientist to want a pet gorilla!).

That narrow premise didn't dissuade Gold Key Comics from licensing the character, and *Magilla Gorilla* ran ten issues, from May 1964 through Dec. 1968. The series' most famous issue was #3, published prior to the presidential election of 1964, where Magilla and Yogi Bear faced off in a bid for the Oval Office! Charlton Comics published five issues of *Magilla Gorilla* from Nov. 1970 through July 1971. Magilla was seen a few times in Marvel's late-'70s H-B comics line, where he headlined *Spotlight* #4 (Mar. 1979), and at DC in the 1990s, even lending his name to the Hanna-Barberape "Magilla's Guerillas" team in *Cartoon Network Presents* #4 (Nov. 1997).

MONKEYMAN AND O'BRIEN

Axwell Tiberius, a.k.a. Monkeyman, is a whopper of a mega-intelligent gorilla, standing ten feet tall. He met his she-hulk of a human partner, pretty Ann Darrow O'Brien, when she accidentally triggered her missing-in-action scientist father's interdimensional machine, sucking Monkeyman into our realm—San Francisco, to be exact. Trapped in a world he

never made! Which was lucky for the Bay City's rollers, because writer/artist Arthur Adams quaked the city with grotesqueries like the Shrewmanoid and the Frogolodytes, freakish fiends that only a super-smart gorilla and a super-strong gal could stop.

Adams, along with other top-flight comics creators including Mike Mignola (*Hellboy*) and Frank Miller (*Sin City*), united to form the Legend imprint for Dark Horse Comics in 1994, with Monkeyman and O'Brien premiering as a *Hellboy* backup before spinning off into its own miniseries. Since then, this dynamic duo's infrequent appearances included a two-issue 1998 *Gen13/Monkeyman and O'Brien* miniseries, but Adams' hyper-detailed artwork and hilarious scripts have kept Monkeyman and O'Brien fresh in readers' minds. (See Chapter 2 for an Adams Q & Ape.)

MONSIEUR MALLAH

Would you allow a gorilla to perform your brain surgery? A French scientist did… but this was no mundane monkey.

The unnamed scientist's strict regimen of educational and electroshock conditioning elevated the beast's I.Q. to 178, and the gorilla, now brilliant and quite verbose (and pretty good with firearms, too), was named Monsieur Mallah. When the scientist's body was destroyed in an explosion, Mallah encased his mentor's brain under glass in life-supporting liquid, and hooked it up to wiring (straight out of a grade-B sci-fi movie) which allowed him to speak. And thus was born the Brain, who, with his loyal ape aide Mallah, became the linchpins of the Brotherhood of Evil, created by writer Arnold Drake and artist Bruno Premiani in DC Comics' *Doom Patrol* vol. 1 #86 (Mar. 1964).

After several tangles with "the World's Strangest Heroes," Mallah, the Brain, and the rest of the Brother-hood appeared to

© 2007 Hanna-Barbera.

die when *Doom Patrol* was cancelled with issue #121 (Sept.–Oct. 1968). Marv Wolfman and George Pérez gave Monsieur Mallah a new lease on life—and a French accent—when they revived the Brotherhood in *The New Teen Titans* #14–15 (Dec. 1981–Jan. 1982). In *Doom Patrol* vol. 2 #34 (July 1990), during writer Grant Morrison's avant garde *DP* stint, Morrison and penciler Richard Case revealed Mallah's and Brain's love for one another. Comics' first gay gorilla! Despite the Doom Patrol's fluctuating continuity in the 2000s, the Mallah/Brain partnership has endured in non-DP appearances, including a 2006 encounter with the Outsiders. (Don't expect to see Mallah canoodling with the Brain in any of the gorilla's six 2005–2006 appearances on the Cartoon Network's kid-friendly *Teen Titans*, though…)

ORANG, THE APE THAT IS HUMAN

Leave it to pathfinder Will Eisner to introduce yet another comics staple…

While not a super-gorilla, Orang (who debuted in "Orang, the Ape Man" in *The Spirit*, Sept. 1, 1940), a slack-jawed orangutan endowed with human brainpower (and a wardrobe) by the training and surgical brain implants of Dr. Egel, paved the way for the super-villainous gorillas that would follow. Considering his evolutionary boost a nightmare, the societal outcast Orang turned against Egel—who also *de*volved a contemporary's gorgeous daughter into a savage—and killed him, putting him in the Spirit's sights. Orang seemingly perished at the end of the *Spirit* weekly newspaper comic supplement, but resurfaced the following week, attempting to lead an uprising of "normal" apes against the Spirit and humankind.

Orang was inspired by Edgar Allan Poe's "Murders in the Rue Morgue," with King Kong and Beauty and the Beast overtones, but creator Eisner was stymied by the objections to the character by his editors, who feared controversy and charges of miscegenation from creationists. (Imagine what they'd say about the Monsieur Mallah/ Brain relationship!)

PRIME8

Finally, an equal ape-ortunity comic book! After decades of being cast as super-villains or supporting-cast members, simian *super-heroes* finally got their moment in the sun in TwoMorrows' *Prime8: Creation* #1 (July 2001).

Co-written by brothers Jon B. and Andrew D. Cooke and penciled by Chris Knowles (with a rockin' wraparound cover by Neal Adams), this black-and-white one-shot took a familiar concept—apes augmented into powerful pawns by a covert organization's top-secret program (in this case, Project: Bruteforce)—and tilted it into new territory. A father-daughter scientist duo rescued six primates from execution when Project: Bruteforce was disbanded and granted them enhanced abilities via a serum. Of course, Silverbak, a gorilla, headed the group (Julie Schwartz would be proud!), and was joined by a chimp (Gltch), baboon (Ryot), orangutan (Churchill), aye-aye (Imp), and spider monkey (Re:jkt), plus two human hangers-on. *Prime8: Creation* was a fun, fast-paced comic that unfortunately did not find a large enough audience to sustain its continued publication.

Criminal gorilla Monsieur Mallah and the Brotherhood of Evil, illustrated by George Pérez and Romeo Tanghal. From *New Teen Titans* #31 (May 1983), page 8. © 2007 DC Comics.

PRIMATE

One might regard Image Comics' *Primate* as Angel and the Ape reimagined as a gory revenge flick. Its gorilla star, an intelligent silverback with the ever-popular comics ape name of Bobo, survived the slaughter of his troop and set out on a bloody path of retribution against the poachers responsible. Bobo was not alone: This ape's "angel" was Dr. Catherine Lim, an anthropologist who had worked with the massacred gorilla family.

Released in 2001 with variant covers by Alex Garner and David Michael Beck, the one-shot *Image Introduces... Primate: The Sword of Darwin* #1 was one of several projects published under the company's short-lived *Showcase*-like *Image Introduces...* title. It was co-written by Beau Smith and Kevin Bernhardt and illustrated by Mitch Byrd.

RADIOACTIVE APE

When Radioactive Man shielded Grrk-Grrk, the gorilla prince of the secret monkey metropolis known as Simian City, from a Xeno Ray Mini-Bomb, residual fallout imbued the anthropoid with super-strength, the power of flight, and invulnerability. This

© 2007 Bongo Entertainment, Inc.

Radioactive Ape joined the universe of Bongo Comics' *Simpsons* spin-off *Radioactive Man* in *Radioactive Man 80-Page Colossal* #1 ("Summer 1968," actually 1995; Bongo's irregularly published *Radioactive Man* comics contain faux cover dates symbolizing the era they are parodying).

A member of the Secret Society of Super Simians, Radioactive Ape, who, like Radioactive Man, has a lightning bolt protruding from his noggin, is the super-powered protector of the African wild. His biggest challenge, however, is concealing his Grrk-Grrk identity from prying primate reporter G'rrla G'rll. Somewhere, in the Great Beyond, Silver Age Superman editor Mort Weisinger is looking down upon cartoonist Bill Morrison's creation with a content smile… or a copyright-infringement lawsuit.

RED GHOST AND HIS SUPER-APES

Ivan Kragoff, one of the Fantastic Four's earliest foes (first seen in *FF* #13, Apr. 1963, by Stan Lee and Jack Kirby), is a dumpy Russian space pioneer who can become wraithlike. Big whoop—so can Space Ghost and Phantom Girl, and they've got better hairstyles. What's interesting about Kragoff, a.k.a. the Red Ghost,

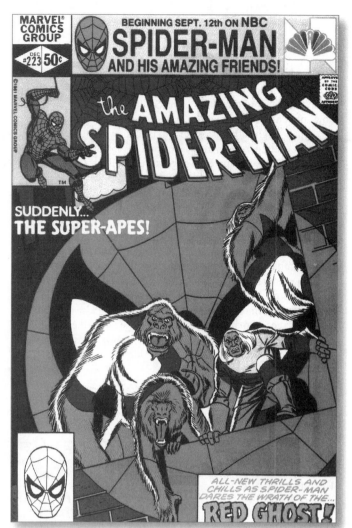

© 2007 Marvel Characters, Inc.

is the company he keeps.

Back in '63, during the famed Space Race between the US and the USSR, Kragoff gathered three apes—a gorilla named Mikhlo, a baboon named Igor, and an orangutan named Peotr—and with them duplicated the famous space flight of Reed Richards and his fantastic friends. Like the FF, Kragoff and the beasts were exposed to cosmic rays, and emerged as the Red Ghost and the Super-Apes—the gorilla gained super-strength, the baboon became a shapeshifter, and the orangutan developed control over gravity and magnetic fields.

These Super-Apes followed their no-goodnik Commie leader into conflicts with the FF, and later with Iron Man, Spider-Man, and even Marvel's "Teen Titans" of the '90s, the New Warriors. In more recent years, the Super-Apes have developed human-level intelligence have attempted to remake Earth into a monkey planet by purging it of people and repopulating it with primates (apparently, their intellectual boost was accompanied by a library of *Planet of the Apes* movies).

Karl Kesel and Tom Grummett offered a variation on the Super-Apes theme in *Challengers of the Fantastic* #1 (June 1997), one of a series of "Amalgam" DC/Marvel hybrids spinning out of the popular *DC vs. Marvel* crossover. In this merger of the Challengers of the Unknown and the Fantastic Four, the Red Ghost, an official from the nation of Gorillagrad (a Communist Gorilla City), controlled Super-Apes Congo-Red, Comrade Grodd, and Moon Boy (an alternate version of Moon-Boy from Kirby's *Devil Dinosaur* series).

REX MANTOOTH, KUNG-FU GORILLA

Rex Mantooth is, more or less, James Bond as a gorilla. No, make that Austin Powers. Or John Shaft. Or Blackbelt Jones. Or how 'bout all of the above?

This delightfully insane spoof, created by writer Matt Fraction (with penciler Andy Kuhn and inker/washtone artist Tim Fisher), appeared in three 13-page stories in Funk-O-Tron's two-in-one tyro title *Double Take* #6–8 (Nov. 2001–Jan. 2002). Like 007 and other super-spies, Mantooth has a "Bond girl," Honey Hamptonwick. But being a gorilla secret agent in a comic gives Rex license to kill every cliché in the book, and then some. If you've been disappointed that Bond has never fought a giant robot, lesbian revolutionaries, or a Stephen Hawking zombie, then Mantooth is your spy!

The three *Double Take* stories were compiled in a 96-page trade paperback published by AiT/Planet Lar, titled *The Annotated Mantooth!* If you're doing the math and wondering how 39 pages of material can fill a 96-page book, the trade edition is loaded with extras like pin-ups, essays, script pages, and Fraction's whacked-out annotations, reading like a Pop-Up Video or DVD special edition.

SGT. GORILLA

Long before Jeff Parker's "Congo-Happy Joes" of Ape Company (see Chapter 5's Parker Q & Ape), DC's battle team supreme, writer Robert Kanigher and artist Joe Kubert, joined forces for what might very well be the strangest "straight" war story ever published: "You Can't Pin a Medal on a Gorilla!" in *Star Spangled War Stories* #126 (Apr.–May 1966). "Sgt. Gorilla" was actually a Charlie, a trained ape on hand to entertain the troops in the South Pacific during WWII. Charlie mimicked his trainer, Cpl. Pinky Donovan, by dressing as a Marine—a regular Jungle G. I.! The Commanding Officer scoffed at such monkeyshines… until valiant Charlie saved the boys' bacon.

Says cartoonist Fred Hembeck, responsible for this 2001 recreation of Joe Kubert's 1966 Sgt. Gorilla cover: "Most people seem to think the tactic originated with the Vietnam War, but Kanigher and Kubert—inside the pages of DC's *Star Spangled War Stories* #126—give us plenty of reason to believe otherwise. Yup, thanks to Bob and Joe, we discover that gorilla warfare goes all the way back to WWII (...and gags this creaky go back even further, I'm afraid...)!" Star Spangled War Stories TM & © 2007 DC Comics. Recreation art © 2007 Fred Hembeck.

SKY APE

You'll believe a gorilla can fly! Especially when he has a jetpack strapped onto his back.

Sky Ape is actually Kirk Madge, a talking millionaire gorilla, who responds to crises by flying into action as a simian crime-crusher. It's a tough job—Kirk is rich enough just to sit back and enjoy smoking cigars, and once he even tried to walk away from the burden of duty by becoming a C.P.A.—but with

nutcases like Mister Doctor Powerful and Poeticus, the Liberal Arts Robot milling about, *somebody*'s gotta take to the skies to protect America ("England's ballsy ex-wife").

Sky Ape reads like an episode of *Animaniacs* on acid—free-form, ludicrous but hysterical plots buttressed by non sequiturs and pop-culture references. Its world is also inhabited by a legion of lame super-heroes that make Bob Burden's Mystery Men seem Justice League-worthy—the Swimsuit Bastards, Monja: the Last Shogun, Frances Bird, Doctor Asteroid, Mrs. Burglar (she's reformed, but kept her name), and Hall and Oates (yes, Hall and Oates) are among the weirdos zipping in and out of stories.

It takes a whole team of creators to keep this big ape airborne: Writers Phil Amara, Tim McCarney, and Mike Russo and artist Richard Jenkins are responsible for Sky Ape's adventures. *Sky Ape* started as a 1997 miniseries from Slave Labor Graphics and has appeared in a total of four volumes, attracting a cult audience of fans… including comics-industry pros, some of whom have contributed pin-ups to the book. The character's last outing (as of this writing), the one-shot *Sky Ape: King of Girls* (Mar. 2006, from AiT/Planet Lar), might very well be Sky Ape's last flight, as other assignments have separated the creative team.

SOLOVAR

He would have preferred to have been remembered as the brilliant sovereign of Gorilla City, DC Comics' secret society of super-smart simians. But poor Solovar is probably best known as the world's worst warden, as he could never keep his city's vilest villain, Gorilla Grodd, behind bars for long.

When first seen in *The Flash* vol. 1 #106 (Apr.–May 1959)—also the first appearance of Grodd and Gorilla City—Solovar was caged, keeping mum in a zoo rather than disclose the existence of his enlightened race. A close confidant to Barry Allen, a.k.a. the Silver Age Flash, Solovar's extraordinary Force of Mind was stolen by Grodd in their very first story. For decades Solovar held off Grodd's attempts to seize Gorilla City, but was assassinated in the 1999 JLApe crossover and succeeded by Ulgo, his nephew.

THE SUPER-APE FROM KRYPTON

The first of a succession of Kryptonian apes making their way to Earth in 1950s stories, Super-Ape was a talking gorilla that dressed like Fred Flintstone (in an orange pelt with black spots). In the Superman story in *Action Comics* #218 (July 1956), readers learned that before Krypton's explosion a scientist named Shir Kan (author Edmond Hamilton's nod to *The Jungle Book*'s Shere Khan) launched a young gorilla to Earth in an experimental rocket. Like Burroughs' Tarzan, this Super-Ape was raised by African gorillas, and joined forces with the Man of Steel to battle African animal poachers. At story's end, Superman reunited Super-Ape with other Kryptonian apes displaced throughout the galaxy by Shir Kan's test flights and relocated them to a new planet all their own.

© 2007 DC Comics.

UPROAR

Before the debuts of the better-known bionic apes Cy-Gor and Kreigaffe, Marvel Comics introduced the cybernetic gorilla Uproar in the 1990 four-issue miniseries *Brute Force*. Created with high hopes by Marvel as a potential licensed property (that went nowhere), Brute Force was a *Captain Planet*-inspired team of genetically enhanced animals, augmented to serve as ecological peacekeepers. Uproar was a member of Heavy Metal (insert your own joke here), a super-villain team of scientifically altered creatures that stood in opposition to the heroic Brute Force. Uproar's teammates were Armory the octopus, Bloodbath the shark, Ramrod the rhino, and Tailgunner the vulture.

VOZ

Since the Guardians of the Universe assigned power rings to all sorts of alien creatures—magenta-skinned cuties, turnip-headed and bird-beaked humanoids, even talking chipmunks and dogs—it was only a matter of time before a *gorilla* became a Green Lantern (GL). And that time was *Guy Gardner* #11 (Aug. 1993), when writer Chuck Dixon and penciler Joe Staton introduced Voz, a hunchbacked, gorilla-like GL from an undetermined world. When first seen, Voz was enslaved by a race called the Draal that was, in an *Invasion of the Body Snatchers*-inspired move, attempting to supplant GLs with duplicates. The big guy has been known to use violent force at times.

WEEPING GORILLA

No other gorilla in comic books better resonates with cynical contemporary audiences than the Weeping Gorilla, from creator Alan Moore's *Promethea* series (1999–2005, from the DC imprint America's Best Comics). Like an ape version of cartoon everyman (or every-*whiner*) Ziggy, the disheartened Weeping Gorilla is depicted more as an impressionistic icon than a legitimate story character, seen sobbing through philosophical queries and laments. (Read "You Can't Pin a Medal on a Gorilla!", you crybaby— *that*'ll put a smile on your face!)

© 2007 America's Best Comics.

YANGO THE SUPER-APE

When *Superboy* #172 (Mar. 1971) hit the stands, longtime Superman readers began to wonder if *any* of Krypton's simians actually perished in the planet's explosion, as yet another Kryptonian critter was revealed to be living on Earth. According to writer Frank Robbins and the art team of Bob Brown and Murphy Anderson, Kryptonian anthropologist An-Kal rocketed a young ape named Yango to Earth in a prototype spacecraft that departed the doomed planet moments before its demise… on a simultaneous intergalactic journey with the soon-to-be-super baby Kal-El. Years later, when Superboy was summoned to Kenya to deal with ivory poachers (a far-fetched concept in itself—why not give Congo Bill a buzz?), the Boy of Steel discovered an underground simian city, lorded over by Yango the Super-Ape. After an obligatory Superboy vs. Super-Ape bout, the Kryptonian evolutionary cousins patched up their relationship, the Boy of Steel leaving Yango behind to be the jungle's super-guardian.

SUPER-HEROES BATTLE SUPER- (AND NOT-SO-SUPER) GORILLAS!

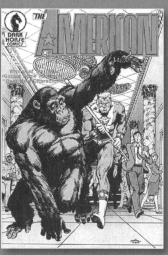

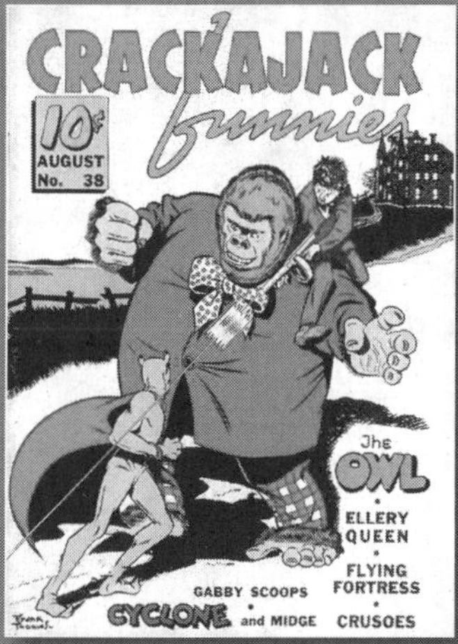
CRACKAJACK funnies
10¢
AUGUST No. 38
The OWL
ELLERY QUEEN
FLYING FORTRESS
GABBY SCOOPS
CYCLONE and MIDGE
CRUSOES

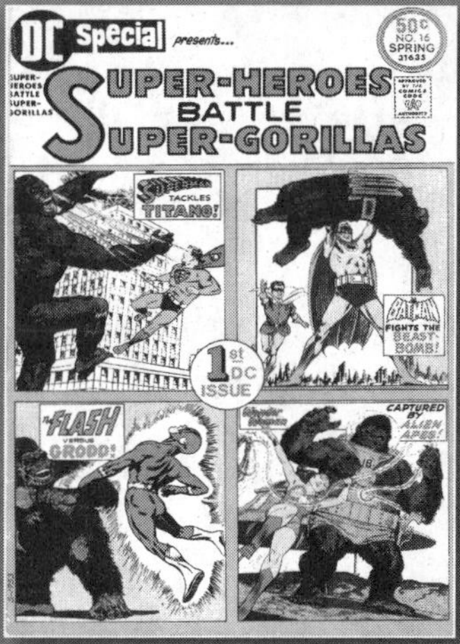
DC Special presents...
50¢ NO. 16 SPRING
SUPER-HEROES BATTLE SUPER-GORILLAS
TACKLES TITANO!
FIGHTS THE BEAST BOMB!
1st DC ISSUE
FLASH VERSUS GRODD!
CAPTURED BY ALIEN APE!

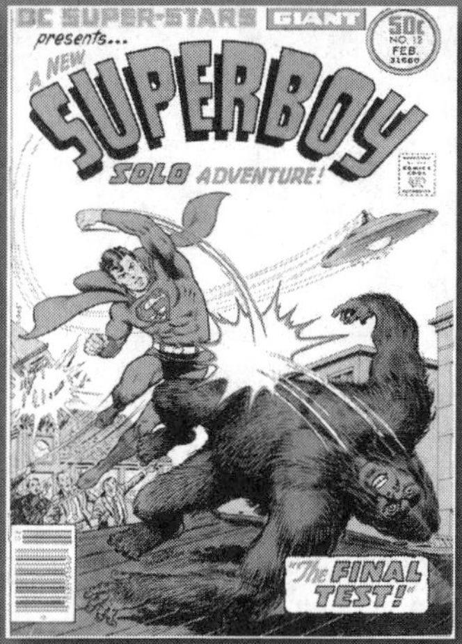
DC SUPER-STARS GIANT
50¢ NO. 12 FEB
presents...
A NEW SUPERBOY SOLO ADVENTURE!
"The FINAL TEST!"

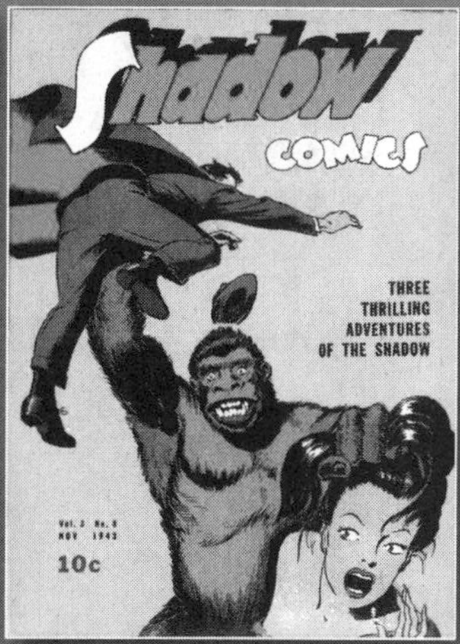
Shadow COMICS
THREE THRILLING ADVENTURES OF THE SHADOW
10c

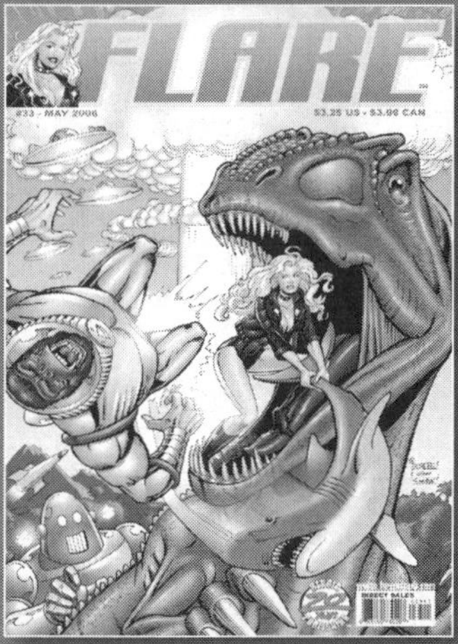
FLARE
#33 - MAY 2006

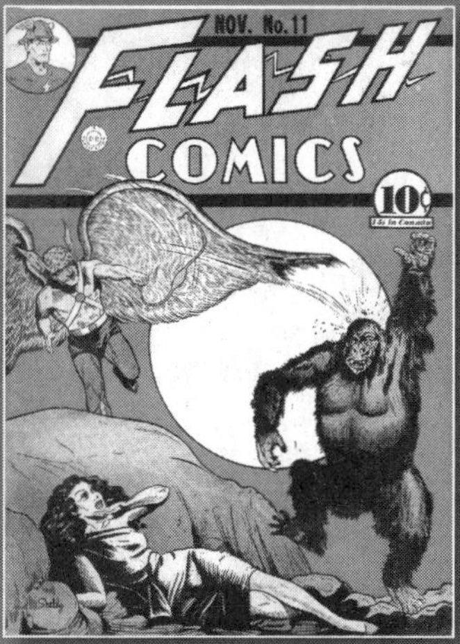
NOV. No. 11
FLASH COMICS
10¢

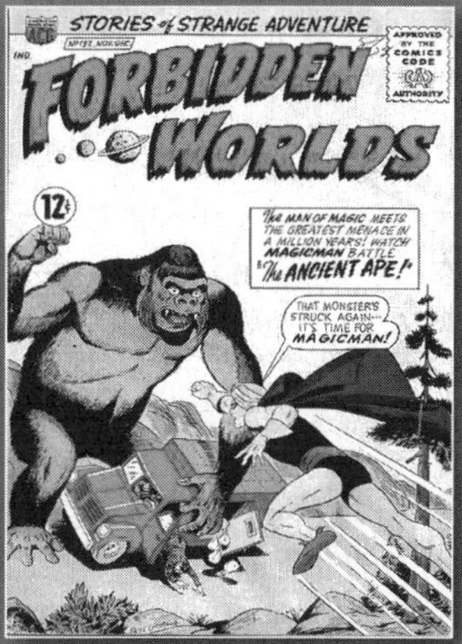
STORIES of STRANGE ADVENTURE
APPROVED BY THE COMICS CODE AUTHORITY
FORBIDDEN WORLDS
12¢
THE MAN OF MAGIC MEETS THE GREATEST MENACE IN A MILLION YEARS! WATCH MAGICMAN BATTLE "The ANCIENT APE!"
THAT MONSTER'S STRUCK AGAIN-- IT'S TIME FOR MAGICMAN!

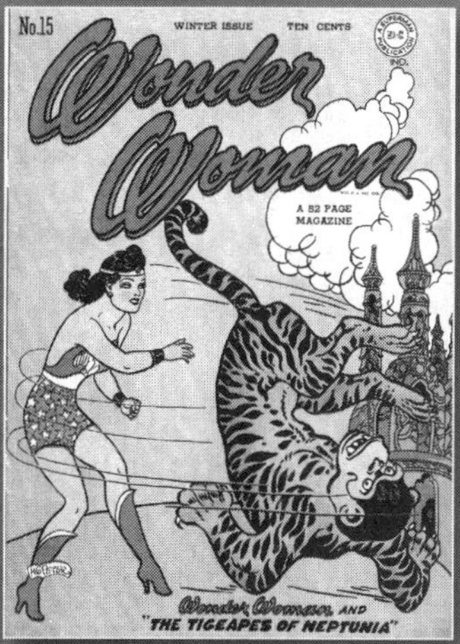
No.15
WINTER ISSUE
TEN CENTS
Wonder Woman
A 52 PAGE MAGAZINE
Wonder Woman AND "THE TIGEAPES OF NEPTUNIA"

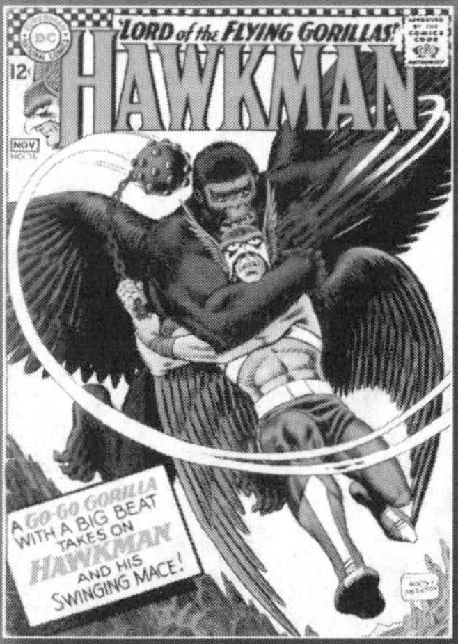
LORD of the FLYING GORILLAS!
HAWKMAN
12¢
NOV
A GO-GO GORILLA WITH A BIG BEAT TAKES ON HAWKMAN AND HIS SWINGING MACE!

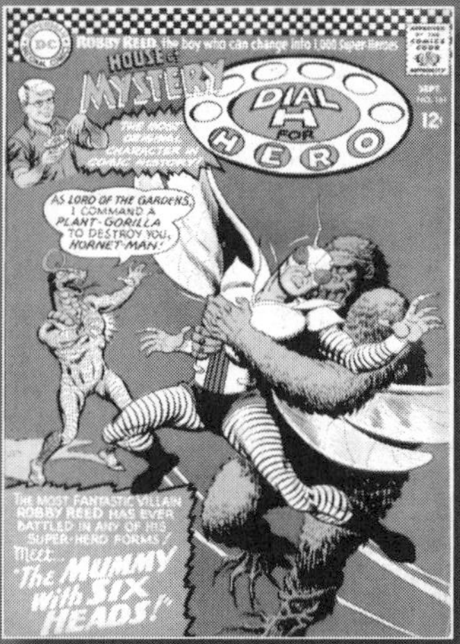
ROBBY REED, the boy who can change into 1,000 Super-Heroes
HOUSE of MYSTERY
DIAL H FOR HERO
12¢
AS LORD OF THE GARDENS, I COMMAND A PLANT-GORILLA TO DESTROY YOU, HORNET-MAN!
THE MOST FANTASTIC VILLAIN ROBBY REED HAS EVER BATTLED IN ANY OF HIS SUPER-HERO FORMS!
Meet... "The MUMMY with SIX HEADS!"

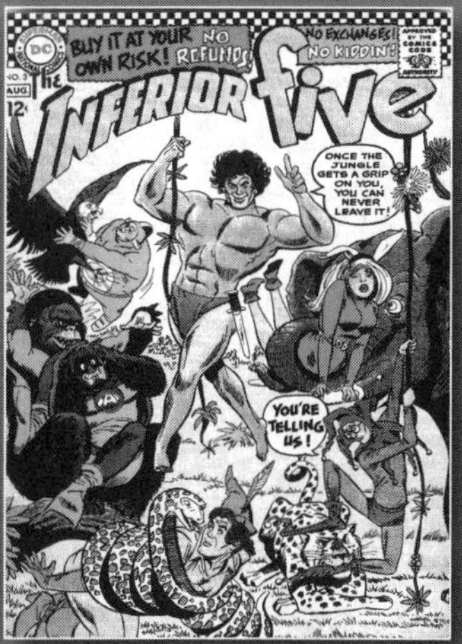
BUY IT AT YOUR OWN RISK! NO REFUNDS!
NO EXCHANGES! NO KIDDIN'!
The INFERIOR five
12¢
ONCE THE JUNGLE GETS A GRIP ON YOU, YOU CAN NEVER LEAVE IT!
YOU'RE TELLING US!

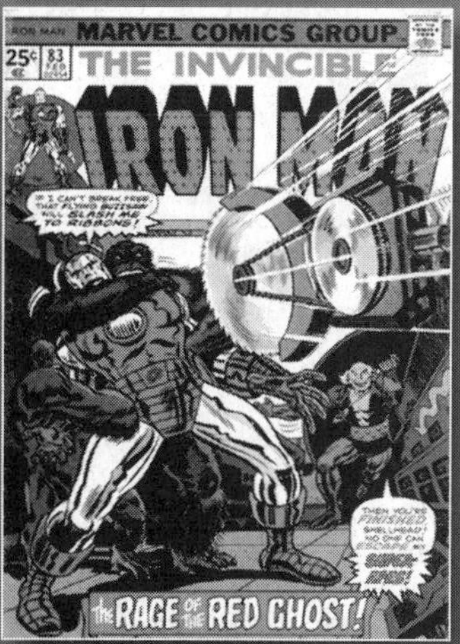
MARVEL COMICS GROUP
25¢ 83 FEB
THE INVINCIBLE IRON MAN
THE RAGE of the RED GHOST!

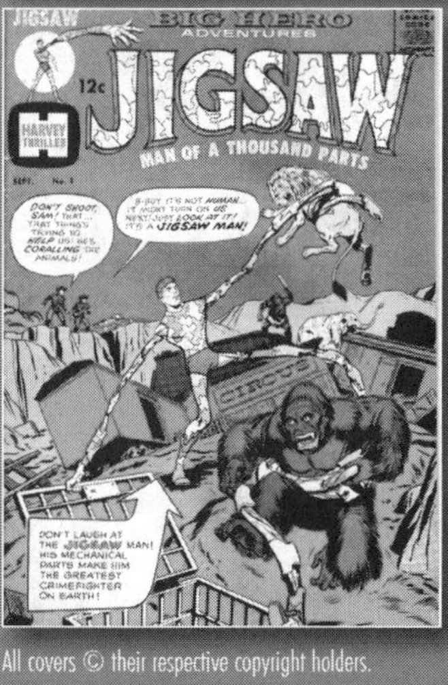
JIGSAW
BIG HERO ADVENTURES
12c
HARVEY THRILLER
JIGSAW
MAN OF A THOUSAND PARTS
DON'T LAUGH AT THE JIGSAW MAN! HIS MECHANICAL PARTS MAKE HIM THE GREATEST CRIMEFIGHTER ON EARTH!

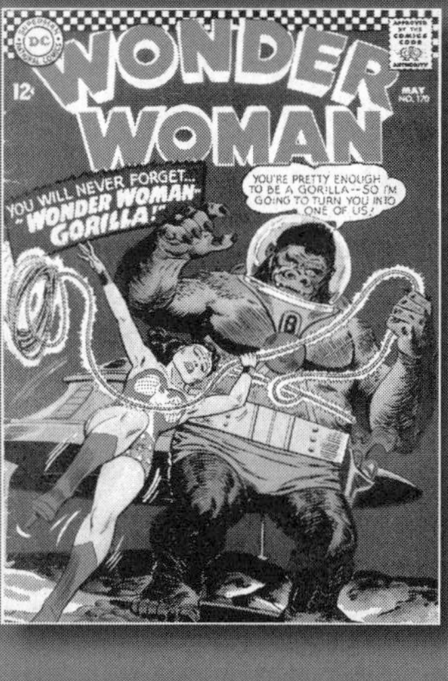
WONDER WOMAN
12¢
YOU WILL NEVER FORGET... "WONDER WOMAN-GORILLA!"
YOU'RE PRETTY ENOUGH TO BE A GORILLA--SO I'M GOING TO TURN YOU INTO ONE OF US!

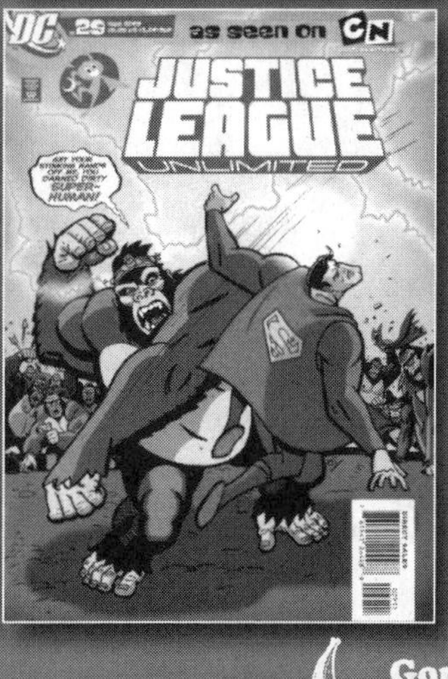
DC
as seen on CN
JUSTICE LEAGUE UNLIMITED

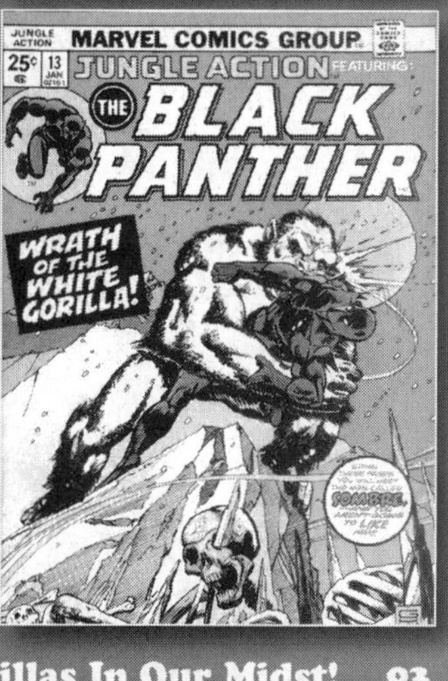
JUNGLE ACTION
MARVEL COMICS GROUP
25¢ 13 JAN
JUNGLE ACTION FEATURING: THE BLACK PANTHER
WRATH OF THE WHITE GORILLA!

APE Q with BOB OKSNER

Conducted by telephone on August 22, 2006

SPOTTED AMONG THE APES IN:

Terry Vance feature in ***Marvel Mystery Comics* (1940s),** ***Angel and the Ape*** (1960s DC Comics series), miscellaneous humor covers with gorillas

OTHER CAREER HIGHLIGHTS:

Miss Cairo Jones comic strip, ***Leave it to Binky,*** various teen and romance series, ***The Adventures of Bob Hope, The Adventures of Jerry Lewis, I Love Lucy*** comic strip, ***Stanley and His Monster, Supergirl,*** Black Orchid in ***Adventure Comics, Superman, Shazam!, Welcome Back Kotter, Ambush Bug***

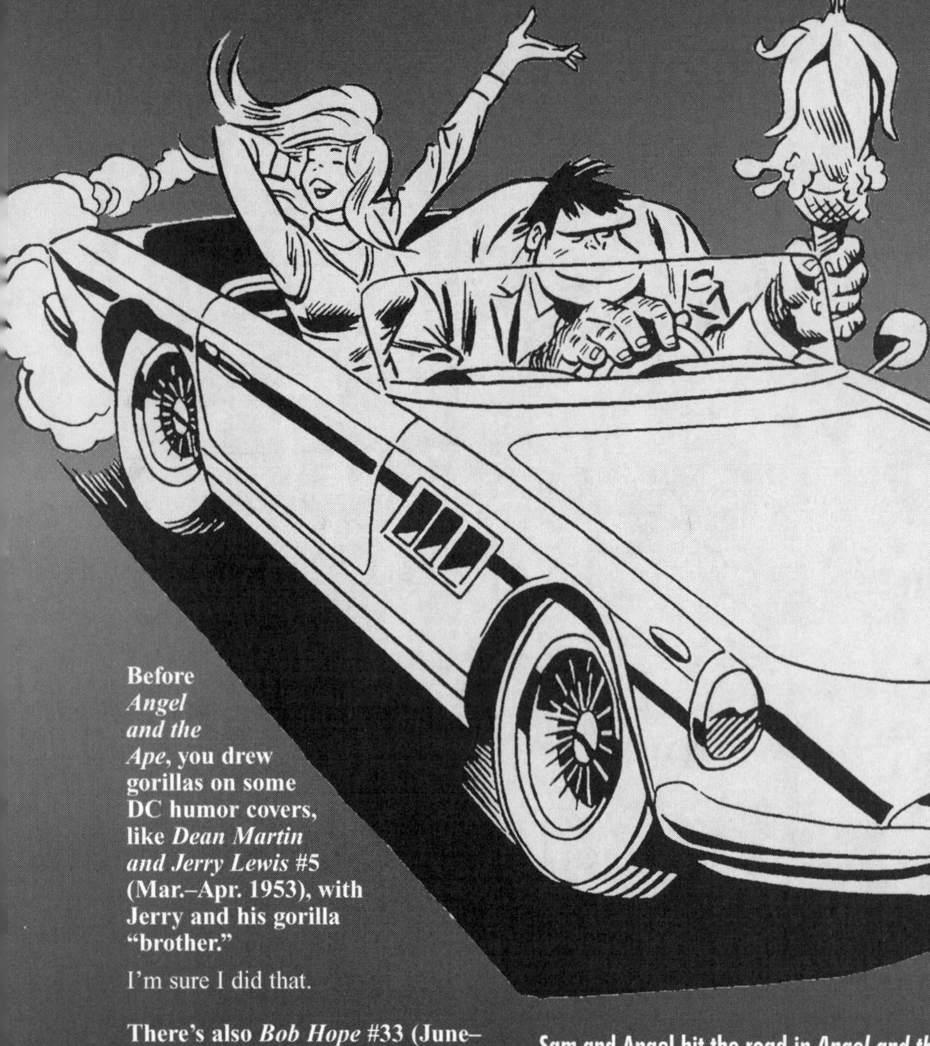

Sam and Angel hit the road in *Angel and the Ape* #2. TM & © 2007 DC Comics.

Before *Angel and the Ape*, you drew gorillas on some DC humor covers, like *Dean Martin and Jerry Lewis* #5 (Mar.–Apr. 1953), with Jerry and his gorilla "brother."

I'm sure I did that.

There's also *Bob Hope* #33 (June–July 1955), with a gorilla beating Bob at poker, and #41 (Oct.–Nov. 1956), with a gorilla golf caddy.

With *Jerry Lewis* and *Bob Hope*, if it's with a gorilla, it's very likely I did them.

***Jerry Lewis* #41, from Nov. 1957, is an interesting one: I found a source that credited you as the *writer* of "Watching Nuts Talk to Apes," a story with Jerry being invited on an African safari because he could talk to apes.**

Sounds reasonable [*laughs*]. In those days I wrote *Jerry Lewis* before Arnold Drake did.

That source also credited Owen Fitzgerald and Graham Place as your story's artists; they also did the cover.

I don't know that I ever worked with Owen Fitzgerald. He was a great cartoonist. I don't remember if we worked together, though.

Jerry's cowering from a gorilla with boxing gloves on the cover of *Jerry Lewis* #69 (Mar.–Apr. 1962)—the pretty girl on that cover tells me it's probably your work.

Oh, I did that.

Do you remember "King Klonk," the giant ape climbing the "Tower of Pizza" on the cover of *Jerry Lewis* #86 (Jan.–Feb. 1965)? And that's "pizza" as in "pepperoni."

I vaguely remember that [*laughs*]. By the way, the first monkey I did was when I was working for Lloyd Jacquet; this was way back. Does that name ring a bell with you?

No… who was he?

He ran an agency, where he bought work from cartoonists and sold it to publishers, and at that time Mickey Spillane was also working for him. We did a strip about a boy who had a pet monkey. Let me try to think of the name… "Terry Vance," that's it. A play on Philo Vance, who was a very popular detective in hardcover books back in those days.

Oh, that strip was the adventures of Terry Vance, "Boy Detective," or "the Schoolboy Sleuth," from *Marvel Mystery Comics* in the early '40s, some of your earliest work. Terry's sidekick was his pet monkey, Dr. Watson.

That was the first monkey I ever drew [*laughs*]. I was going to college at that time. I was going to Columbia and I picked up that work from Lloyd Jacquet.

Angel and the Ape premiered in *Showcase* #77 (Sept. 1968), then went to its own book. What do you recall about how the series started?

For a couple years before that, I was doing a syndicated strip called *Soozie* for a North American syndicate, in Chicago, I think. The strip went out of business, then I immediately went up to DC and [editor] Joe Orlando told me he was working on the concept for Angel and the Ape, and that it was waiting for me!

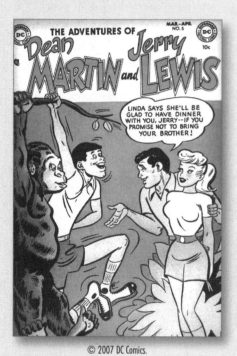

© 2007 DC Comics.

Did Joe Orlando involve you in the development of the series?

At that time, if I recollect, he was going through the process of a divorce, or in the process of remarrying. In any event, he had a lot of free nights [*laughter*]. We went out to dinner quite a lot and discussed the concept of the book.

The "Ape" in the title, Sam Simeon, wasn't your average gorilla.

From the beginning, I was not going to draw a real ape; it was going to be my concept of a sophisticated ape. He was a cartoonist and rather sophisticated; he wore men's clothes—ties, a shirt—and he was very sensitive. He did not like to be called "ape"—if anyone called him "ape," he'd go into a rage.

  After meeting with Joe for about five or six dinners, I drew the character— there was no worry about the girl [*laughter*]… I *knew* how to draw a girl. So I sat

and drew the ape more like a Cro-Magnon man.

Sam Simeon was always impeccably dressed, although he didn't wear shoes.

[*laughs*] Right.

So you helped shape the characters— you weren't just brought on board to draw.

Both Joe and I did… and Sergio Aragonés contributed to the story.

Did Sergio draw storyboards for the script?

Not for me. We were both credited with doing the script.

As you recall, back then DC stories rarely had credits in print, so sometimes it's a guessing game to figure out who wrote what. Some sources have reported that E. Nelson Bridwell or John Albano scripted *Angel and the Ape*.

John Albano wrote one issue of *Angel and the Ape*, and I may have done some writing on the book. At that time, I was also writing *Dondi*, the comic strip.

© 2007 DC Comics.

Angel and the Ape was created during Carmine Infantino's tenure as editorial director. Was he involved with the *Angel and the Ape* startup?

No… just Joe Orlando, the editor.

Orlando had a reputation as a practical joker. Were you the target of any of his

gags, or do you remember any particularly funny jokes of his?

Not as far as I was concerned.

Carmine Infantino designed most of DC's covers then. Did he lay out the *Angel and the Ape* covers?

I would do those covers, with Joe. When Carmine got me into doing Superman stuff in '70, '71, *then* he would lay out a cover on typewriter paper. I would take it home and put it in an artograph and draw into it. A lot of fun. He was a great layout

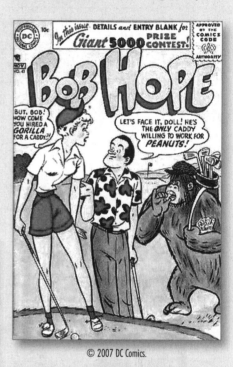

© 2007 DC Comics.

man. I was very busy with many things going on [during my Superman years], so having an anchor cover was a big help.

Wasn't Howie Post also involved with *Angel and the Ape*?

He was involved earlier, much earlier, before I signed on to it.

I've read that Post was involved with developmental work on *Angel and the Ape*.

No, not at all. For a brief period, Howie was going to be the *Angel and the Ape* artist. He was a wonderful cartoonist and he worked on *Jerry Lewis*, and then left [DC Comics] and I don't know why. He was in Glen Rock, New Jersey, and I lived in Teaneck, New Jersey, so we weren't far from each other. But I took over [*Angel and the Ape*] from him, and that's the only connection I have with him as far as comic books go.

Sam Simeon shows his smarts on page 12 of "The Most Fantastic Robbery in History!" From *Angel and the Ape* #2 (Jan.–Feb. 1969). Pencils by Bob Oksner and inks by Wally Wood.

TM & © 2007 DC Comics. Courtesy of Heritage Auctions.

that *Angel and the Ape* was sophisticated, despite its campiness. It came out at a time when DC was experimenting with new types of comics [the offbeat Western *Bat Lash*, Steve Ditko's *Creeper* and *Hawk and the Dove*, horror anthologies like *House of Mystery*, etc.]. I read it as a child and liked the art, but I didn't quite "get it." Now I go back and read it and realize that it was a little ahead of its time.

Much ahead!

You mentioned your children… I know your daughters modeled for you. Which one was Angel?

My middle daughter, Peggy… Margaret.

Is she the one who had the acting career?

Yes, didn't last too long, thank God [*laughs*]. She was in the acting company of *1776*, playing the wife of Thomas Jefferson. She was in several movies— one was John Travolta's *Saturday Night Fever*. She was in a bar and he comes over and kisses her; big moment.

She was in *Superman*, the first one. She was a stand-in, the same facial bone structure as Margot Kidder [Lois Lane]. At that time, there was a blackout in New York City, when the movie was being shot there. My daughter lived in Greenwich Village, and the star—oh, what's his name…?

Christopher Reeve.

Yes. Christopher Reeve walked her home.

She was walked home by Chris Reeve? With Superman is a good place to be in a blackout.

She was very thankful, and so was I!

Didn't another of your daughters pose for you?

My oldest daughter posed for the *Mary Hartman* strip.

There was a comic strip based upon the sitcom soap opera *Mary Hartman, Mary Hartman* (1976–1978)?

I did six weeks and was highly paid for doing them… can't complain. Unfortunately, Mary Hartman [actress Louise Lasser] was picked up on drugs [and that killed the show]. The producer, Norman Lear, he has all the strips.

You had three different inkers on *Angel and the Ape*: Tex Blaisdell, Wally Wood, and Henry Scarpelli.

I inked all the covers, of course.

That you did. If you had to choose

From your view, what was the primary appeal of *Angel and the Ape*?

It was a rather sophisticated comic book, and it went "backstage" of comic-book publishing. I did it with no interest of it as a fiction opus or in the kids who were supposed to buy it.

I do know that in '68, '69, in the East Village in New York, which was a place of lesbians and off-center, rather wild life, they took to *Angel and the Ape*

and published a paper called *The East Village Other*, which covered things that were not conventional. They would have features on *Angel and the Ape*, and they would send them to me. My children at that time were about nine to 18, and they saw these newspapers. The oldest didn't ask any questions, but the youngest asked, "Daddy, what's a fairy?" [*laughter*]

You make a very important observation,

between those inkers, which one best handled your pencils?

Well, Tex worked with me on many things, but Wally Wood I would choose over everybody.

Wood's style was very strong; do you think he overpowered you?

No, no. What I liked about Wood was he followed the pencils and added some blacks.

Whose idea was it to make Sam Simeon, the Ape, a cartoonist?

Joe Orlando's and mine. That's what we talked about. On the first cover [*Showcase* #77], the Ape's drawing.

Was the "monkey" cartoonist an in-joke about the comic-book sweatshops of the '40s?

There were too many in-jokes to count [*laughs*]! Especially with someone like Stan Lee drawn like [DC editor/cartoonist] Shelly Mayer. "Stan Bragg" [a Stan Lee parody] was the character's name but he looked like Shelly Mayer. And the slave fellow in the office who worshiped Stan was Tex Blaisdell.

In the stories, only Angel could understand Sam Simeon. Whose idea was that?

I don't know. May have been both Joe's and mine.

That was a funny bit, and the Ape's speech was translated for the reader in word balloons. The reader was in on the joke.

Unfortunately that at the time, the audience wasn't quite ready for something like that.

Do you remember the cover to *Angel and the Ape* #4 (May–June 1969)?

The one with them surrounded by Chinese with weapons of destructions?

That's the cover *art*. But with issue #4, the *logo* changed to *Meet Angel*, with "*and the Ape*" in small type, and by the last issue, #7, the title was simply *Meet Angel*, looking like a typical teen book. Presumably Joe Orlando was getting pressure to make changes to improve sales.

Another thing with Joe was his use of monsters: Frankenstein and Dracula started to appear [on the covers to issues #5 and 6]. When you do that once or twice it's not too bad, but they did it nearly every

issue. And *Bob Hope* had that, too. Enough. Of course, it sold, and they weren't going to fool around with was sold, but it crimped the style and progress of *Angel and the Ape*, I think.

Have you ever been interviewed about *Angel and the Ape* before this?

I think this might be the first and probably the last time!

Did you know that *Angel and the Ape* inspired other creators? The characters returned in two miniseries, in 1991 and 2001.

No, I didn't see them. I did get a letter from Kevin Nowlan, the artist. According to Kevin, he's a great admirer of *Angel and the Ape*.

Anything else you'd like to add about *Angel and the Ape*?

Angel and the Ape was one of my favorite books to work on; most of my other books were based on TV personalities and sitcoms. So I was less constricted with *Angel and the Ape*, and I was free to create my own characters. I enjoyed that very much.

Superman editor Mort Weisinger was lampooned as Morton I. Stoops in *Angel and the Ape* #2. TM & © 2007 DC Comics.

APE Q with TIM ELDRED

Conducted via email on August 26, 2006

SPOTTED AMONG THE APES IN:

Grease Monkey (1990s miniseries and 2006 graphic novel)

OTHER CAREER HIGHLIGHTS:

Star Blazers Perfect Album, Armored Trooper Votoms: Supreme Survivor, The Man Who Grew Young, animation storyboard artist for *Legion of Super-Heroes, Ultimate Avengers II,* and other series

I understand that *Grease Monkey* was inspired in part by the use of the term "monkeywrenching" in the Stan Ridgway song "The Overlords."

Yeah, that was the catalyst that moved the idea out of my head and onto paper. I should drop back and punt to explain. When I first read *Lord of the Rings* I decided that Sam was my favorite character because he embodied the common man better than anyone else, and he was best suited to carry on with an "ordinary" life after the adventure was over. That got me thinking about the value of the proletariat; those people who don't get to make the high-stakes decisions, but usually end up carrying the load. I like stories about larger-than-life heroes, too, but the tradition of mythology says they can't return to real life after their battle is over. They've tasted transcendence and they are obliged to move on to a higher plane. And I say, fine, who needs ya? The rest of us have dishes and laundry to do!

So for most of the '80s I'm thinking, there's got to be a way to write an interesting story about the guys who have to stay behind and do the dishes. It should be easy for anyone to relate to, because that's really all of us. The Stan Ridgway song used the term "monkeywrenching" in the context of someone in a resistance movement against alien overlords, which gave me the image of a hidden rebel camp somewhere, a good setting for a story. Then I got to thinking about a mechanic working in that camp who had to fix all the machinery that the soldiers were ruining on a daily basis and I thought, that's the guy I want to write about.

Then I thought, what if he's not a guy at all, but is instead a monkey? Everything else spun outward from there. The rebel camp turned into a spaceship and the overlords turned into middle management. *Monkey Wrench* was the working title for all of this until it occurred to me later that *Grease Monkey* would be a better one.

Did you have an interest in apes before *Grease Monkey*?

How could I not? Monkeys and apes are the most humanoid creatures on the planet next to us, and they're completely fascinating to watch. I can stare at them forever in a zoo, moving between the ideas that this is what we were once like, and maybe these are "alternate" human beings who share our planet. And I wonder what observations they would make of us if they could speak. That's what made Mac so much fun to write; it would give me a chance to see the human world from an outside perspective. It's amazing what gets revealed when you step outside your own bubble from time to time.

I read several primatology books as I worked on *Grease Monkey,* and I was sensitive from the beginning about the scientific ineptitude of using the M-word to describe a gorilla. I was determined from the start to make a story point out of it; that on one hand it would simply be his job description and on the other hand it would symbolize the ignorance most humans have toward apes and provide an immediate talking point. In fact, there's an entire chapter devoted to it.

Do you remember the first time you drew an ape?

It was probably after seeing one in a zoo, or watching *King Kong.* As a child of the '70s, it was still easy to see gorillas in this mode of perpetual savagery, like all you had to do was make eye contact with one and you'd be in for a throw-down. So, of course, one of the standard villains (along with robots, aliens, and dinosaurs) for an adolescent hero to fight would always be a gorilla. Even an intelligent one would somehow end up beating the snot out of you to make his point.

I don't know if the kids of today have inherited this same provincial viewpoint. Maybe since most of our cultural education about apes has happened since the '70s, it has removed the gorilla from the lineup of standard villains. I'd like to think so. It would speak well of us as a species if we could stop saddling them with our own faults.

What reference did you use when designing Mac and the other gorillas in the *Grease Monkey* cast? Your original designs for Mac depicted him as more gorilla-like than the "humanized" interpretation we know from print. What prompted the change?

I began with photo-reference and no

matter how much I worked it, I couldn't get away from the image of a gorilla as a dumpy, pot-bellied slob. I had a feeling that if I forced myself to stick with that, my tendency would be to recreate Homer Simpson, which would be the wrong way to go. So while developing the backstory in which gorillas go through this evolutionary acceleration, I figured their bodies could be modified along with their brains. Maybe the aliens who do this to them are advanced enough to see several different evolutionary paths, and choose the one that would best suit everyone's purposes.

Therefore, since the accelerated gorillas would have to fit into a world already designed by and for humans, they'd benefit from having humanoid bodies. So the hip joints would be modified to let them stand upright and free the hands for work, and their dexterity would improve. They wouldn't live in jungles anymore, so their diets would change and they wouldn't

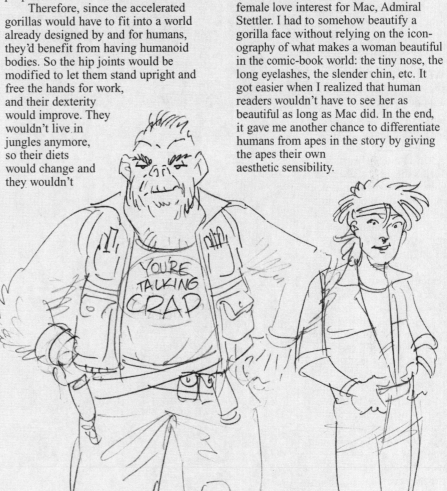

need those huge jaw muscles, so they wouldn't need the sagittal crest on the head, and on and on. The trick was giving them more humanoid bodies without losing their non-human perspective. And, as a natural consequence of this, gorillas all end up bigger and more imposing than humans, which immediately gives us all an inferiority complex around them.

As the central character, Mac provided me with a basic body model and all the other gorillas became variations of him. Some with bigger shoulders, some with longer arms, some with a little more crouch, etc. And then there was the female love interest for Mac, Admiral Stettler. I had to somehow beautify a gorilla face without relying on the iconography of what makes a woman beautiful in the comic-book world: the tiny nose, the long eyelashes, the slender chin, etc. It got easier when I realized that human readers wouldn't have to see her as beautiful as long as Mac did. In the end, it gave me another chance to differentiate humans from apes in the story by giving the apes their own aesthetic sensibility.

(above and next page) Tim Eldred's earliest sketches of Mac and Robin. TM & © 2007 Tim Eldred.

Is it true that the character of junior mechanic Robin Plotnik is based upon a younger version of you?

Absolutely. I think it's inevitable that as an artist you tend to copy the face you see in the mirror and as a writer you tend to relive your own experiences through your craft, so I didn't make any pretense about Robin not representing me in this story. Whenever I decided to explore some aspect of the world, I'd have to send him off to do it in my place. He would be the one to make the discoveries for the benefit of the reader, so he had to be a very "real" character to pull it off. Since I'm pretty much the most "real" person I know, naturally he'd be based on me.

What about Mac? Is his personality patterned after anyone you know?

He's the guy I wish I knew back when I was Robin's age. Whenever some aspect of human behavior defied logic, it would have been great to have him as a mentor with an uncluttered perspective who could just say, "Well, humans think this way." That's the kind of father I've always tried to be with my own daughter. She just turned 17, and she recently read *Grease Monkey* for the first time. She told me afterward that she appreciated it for not being preachy or giving easy answers, that it made her think a little bit and provided a positive example.

The hardest part of mentoring anyone, I think, is knowing how much to say and when to shut up so they can figure out the rest of it for themselves, otherwise they don't get the actual experience of solving a problem and they'll probably repeat it over and over until they do. So when writing for Mac, just like when advising my daughter on various life issues, I tried to skate on that thin line. And by necessity, other people will have to judge whether or not I've been successful.

What's the story behind Mac's "no crap" (originally "you're talking crap") T-shirt, which became, more or less, an icon for *Grease Monkey*?

One of my favorite TV shows from the '80s was a Brit comedy called *The Young Ones,* which I rewatch every couple of years. When I was first conceiving Mac's personality, I patterned him a little bit after one of the characters in the show, Mike (the cool one). Mike was always a step ahead of everyone else and he was impossible to trick. In one episode another character is winding him up for a minute or so and Mike completely trumps him with the line: "It's simple. You're talking crap." That went onto

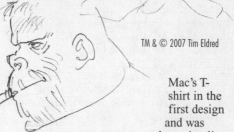

TM & © 2007 Tim Eldred

Mac's T-shirt in the first design and was later simplified to the "no crap" symbol. I'd like it to one day become the battle cry of an entire generation.

You started *Grease Monkey* in 1992, but due to bumps in the publishing road you didn't finish your original storyline until 2002. What challenges did you face resuming a dormant storyline?

It wasn't ever really dormant. It's true that I didn't draw any actual comic pages for a long period in the middle there, but I did a lot of the writing then and I also developed the series for animation, which included spending an entire year making animated shorts all on my own. Out of that whole ten-year period, there was maybe a year or year-and-a-half at most when I wasn't doing something with it. And even during this downtime it was always in my head at some level. I pretty much figured this would be the best idea I ever came up with, so I couldn't let it wither.

Some of the last installments were written and drawn immediately on the heels of September 11, 2001. Did the terrorist attacks affect the way you approached your material?

It only affected one chapter, which I had written in '96 and drew in '01 shortly after 9/11. It just so happened to be the only chapter in the book that reviewed events in the 20th century, and the three moments that I chose for their overall impact on us were the two atomic bomb blasts in 1945 and the first moon landing in 1969. It was with great regret that I had to remove the moon landing and substitute 9/11 in its place, but I think anyone who reads that chapter would understand why the context made this change necessary.

I'll be very happy when we finish with the stupid stuff here on Earth and start doing cool things again, like getting the hell off the Earth.

One of *Grease Monkey*'s most impressive qualities is how each of its episodes are accessible and succeed as stand-alone stories, but when read in succession they interconnect into a broader, well-oiled tapestry. You make that look easy, but I suspect it's *far* from easy…

I think any writer has the option at the beginning of a project of making it easy or hard on themselves. It all comes down to knowing how to create opportunities.

Developing characters with depth and personality is the first step, because once you become comfortable with them they can take over. The second step is to create a world with multiple layers to explore, then peel back just one layer at a time. For this you need patience, foresight, and a good sense of pacing. Telling a complex story is like letting the air out of a balloon a little at a time so you don't lose control of it and have it fly out of your hands with a big wet farty sound.

In my case, I kept the first few chapters small and intimate so I'd have the opportunity to get comfortable with the characters, drop a few hints about the larger world, and then expand outward later. And since the story was originally formatted for monthly consumption, I put a premium on keeping the chapters self-contained for a satisfying read. I also like stories that have a shelf life, meaning you can go back and find something new the second time around. That gets easier when you write an entire book before you start drawing it, which gives you the

A still from the *Grease Monkey* animated pilot.
TM & © 2007 Tim Eldred.

chance to go back through and add details, build subplots, and help the thing to unfold sensibly. A second read can be just as interesting as a first read because you know what's coming and you can see how an author puts events into motion.

Despite its backstory of genocide and its backdrop of war, *Grease Monkey* is remarkably optimistic. What would you consider to be the underlying message of your series?

I'd prefer for readers to decide that for themselves, since the story is sort of an exercise for learning how to find your way through life. But if I were to pick out one aspect of it for special attention, it would have to be the importance of seeing people in all their shades of grey rather than simple black and white. I

think it's important to recognize that nobody, including our so-called authority figures, is entirely right or entirely wrong about any given thing, and the truth is usually somewhere in the middle. We spend a lot of time fighting to stay on one side of an issue or another only to end up somewhere back in the middleground again. Although it makes for good drama, this wastes an awful lot of energy.

Would you welcome sentient gorillas into your neighborhood?

One of the "secret" agendas I had going into this project was to break down some of the prejudice we humans seem to have against animals. You're confronted by a character like Mac or any of the other gorillas in the story, and it doesn't even occur to you to classify them as animals because they're capable of communicating with us on our own terms. Remove that ability, though, and suddenly they don't measure up to our standard and they're reduced to being animals again and we feel like we have the right to decide their fate. If their method of communication is the only thing that's keeping them from getting a fair shake and peaceful coexistence, it doesn't say much for us as a species.

Adjacent to that issue is the way we treat each other, making divisions based on gender, age, sexual orientation, and ethnicity. All that looks ridiculous when you throw an entirely different species into the mix and put an umbrella of alien invasion over the whole thing. There was a story idea I had early on where Robin would have to interact with a gay character on the ship and get all weirded out by it, then Mac would say, "You work with a gorilla and you're all knotted up over a homosexual?" I dropped this idea when I realized that Robin's culture would have already worked through those issues, but I still like that line of dialogue. Maybe if we had sentient gorillas in our neighborhood it would finally force the whole human race to grow the hell up.

What type of changes, if any, did you make to the *Grease Monkey* concept when adapting it to animation for the unsold pilots?

None whatsoever. In fact, the graphic novel and the animated version grew up together. I started developing it for animation after drawing the first six chapters. I came up with a story that would work in an animated format, then went back to writing comics with this story in mind as a sequel. So everything in the graphic novel leads up to the animated version. And it doesn't matter if

TM & © 2007 Tim Eldred

it actually gets animated, because I've already started turning that story into Book 2.

So what's the storyline of your sequel, *Grease Monkey Book 2: A Tale of Two Species*?

In Book 1 you learn the history of what brought humans and apes together, a massive alien attack and subsequent assistance from a godlike race called the Benefactors. The purpose of Book 1 is to explore the implications on a personal, cultural, and societal level. We never actually meet the attacking aliens, but the underlying mission is to prepare for the day when we do. In Book 2, that day finally comes.

Mac, Robin, and the Barbarians [female fighter pilots] are there on the front lines and all have to face the threat together. There's also a new character, a girl who joins the squadron and becomes pretty much the focal point of the book. She's a fantastic pilot, but she's got a secret that might end up sinking the whole ship if it gets out, so the story swings back and forth between personal politics and white-knuckle space battles.

As I said, this story started out as an animated project. I actually wrote it as a screenplay and later adapted it into a graphic novel. It's going to feel a lot like a big-screen movie but also retain the humor and personality of Book 1. After that, there's more ground I want to cover in which we'll find out that having intelligent gorillas on our side may just be the best thing that will ever happen to anyone anywhere in all of galactic history. So we better hope they don't go extinct in the meantime!

Would-be Spidey sidekick the Gibbon suits up in this pin-up by Keith Pollard. From *Amazing Spider-Man Annual* #13 (1979).

*Are we not men? In these cases, <u>no</u>. At least not anymore,
due to brain transferences, evolutionary experiments, and furry costumes designed to...*

MAKE A MONKEY OUT OF ME!

Humans and chimpanzees share nearly 99% of their DNA, reported *Time* magazine in an Oct. 9, 2006 cover feature. Despite this biological similarity, there are many who refuse to believe in the kinship between Man and Ape. A century and a half after Charles Darwin published his controversial [On] *The Origin of Species* in 1859, the creation vs. evolution debate still rocks us, joining conservative vs. liberal, PC vs. Mac, straight vs. gay, and Paris vs. Nicole as some of society's most divisive disputes.

Even those who steadfastly discredit Darwin's evolution theory as "dangerous" or dismiss it as just plain nutty might find an inexplicable attraction to those "cute, little monkeys" discussed in Chapter 3. It's easy to become entranced by the antics of apes at the zoo, dwarfing the time we might spend observing a tiger or a rhino. It's like looking in a mirror.

And so it should come as no surprise that fiction is filled with stories merging humans and apes. In some, a man—usually by the whim of a mad scientist, but sometimes by his own choice—exchanges his brain with an ape. To many this notion might be considered horrific, or even humorous—after all, "as" a gorilla you'd be turned away from most four-star restaurants—but this simian swap is also the ultimate power fantasy,

Arthur J. Burks' Manape the Mighty, the gorilla with the human mind, on artist Hans Wessolowski's painted cover to the June 1931 edition (vol. 6 #3) of Street & Smith's *Astounding Stories*. © 1931 Street & Smith.

guaranteeing its "victim" amplified strength without civilization's restraints.

This familiar motif might be traced back to Robert Louis Stevenson's *Strange Case of Dr. Jekyll and Mr. Hyde*, the 1886 novella about a scientist who reverts to a misanthropic state. Arthur J. Burks' brief series of pulp tales starring Manape the Mighty, a gorilla with a human brain, helped the concept evolve in 1931 in Street & Smith's *Astounding Stories*. Three of the earliest instances of a man becoming an ape in comic books took place in Fox's *Blue Beetle* #9 and 10 (Oct. and Dec. 1941), in a backup featuring starring Jack Castle, a.k.a. the Gorilla, a simian with a human brain; *Captain America Comics* #17 (Aug. 1942), in a story by Stan Lee and Al Avison, where the brain of bad guy Killer Kole was transplanted into a gorilla's body; and in issue #1 (Jan.–Feb. 1946) of the little-known, short-lived O. W. (Ogden Whitney) Comics Corp. title *Mad Hatter,* where a criminal cheated death by returning to life as a gorilla. But thanks to the horror and mystery comic-book craze of the 1950s, including the landmark *Strange Adventures* #8, comics snatched up this concept (like they did so many others) and ran with it.

Editor Julie Schwartz's *Strange Adventures* was home to many such

Early man-to-gorilla transformations occurred in *Captain America Comics #17 (Aug. 1942)* and *Mad Hatter #1 (Jan.–Feb. 1946)*. © 2007 Marvel Characters, Inc. and © 1946 O. W. Comics Corp.

© 1953 Comic Media.

tales. In addition to the stories mentioned in Chapter 4 that featured gorillas with human brains, *Strange Adventures #32* (May 1953) took the mutant spaceman Captain Comet—the DC Comics character whose 1951 debut predated the premieres of Silver Age super-heroes Martian Manhunter and the Flash—and deposited his smarts into a gorilla in the John Broome/Murphy Anderson tale "The Challenge of Man-Ape the Mighty" (a title which suggests that Broome was an admirer of Burks' *Astounding Stories*). And in 1959 DC took its ailing jungle voyager Congo Bill, star of an *Action Comics* backup, and blended a super-hero sensibility into the strip by allowing Bill to become the Golden Gorilla Congorilla (see biography).

Marvel and other publishers beat this same drum with similar tales. An early non-DC example was Man-Ape (yet another of the many characters employing that name, with or without the hyphen) from Comic Media's *Weird Terror* #10 (Mar. 1954). This Man-Ape, the star of a story illustrated by stalwart Don Heck, was a poor schmuck named Peter Gargan who was roped by his pal Dr. Marik into a gorilla brain trade.

Other characters yearning for ape-dom made the jump cosmetically, or sartorially, including the longtime foe of the Avengers (and other Marvel heroes) known as Man-Ape (there's that name again). And with some, nature, usually in the form of a genetic mutation (as with Marvel's Mandrill), caused them to "become" a simian.

Today, the world of comic books contains a troop of titans that have experienced such monkey makeovers. This outbreak of characters might have surprised even the trailblazing Julie Schwartz, but Don Martin saw it coming. Martin (1931–2000), often hyped as "*MAD*'s Maddest Artist," created a holiday (of sorts) in *Don Martin Bounces Back*, a 1962 Signet paperback containing original material. In a riotously funny comic story (and sly commentary on the over-commercialization of Christmas), Martin's characters Fester Bestertester and Karbunkle groused that the strip's "National Gorilla Suit Day" was a ruse to sell gorilla suits. In its wake, January 31 has been "officially" deemed National Gorilla Suit Day, with observers encouraged to wear gorilla suits.

And now, *Comics Gone Ape!* chronicles the histories of the fearsome and freaky folks who turned their soon-to-be hairy backs on humanity, thereby creating…

Captain Comet suffers Dr. Sarcon's brain-drain on Murphy Anderson's cover to *Strange Adventures #32 (May 1953)*. © 2007 DC Comics.

The Invasion of the
MONKEY MEN (AND WOMEN)

(with apologies to Arthur Adams)

ANIMAL MAN

DC Comics' Animal Man (originally Animal-Man) did not, like the other characters in this chapter, become an ape—but he did, in his very first appearance, become "as strong as a gorilla." Created by writers Dave Wood and France Herron and artists Carmine Infantino and George Roussos in *Strange Adventures (SA)* #180 (Sept. 1965), Buddy Baker was a stuntman bombarded by radiation while witnessing a UFO crash. As a result, Baker learned he could temporarily duplicate the abilities of any animal he encountered, claiming, per the title of his initial outing, "I Was the Man with Animal Powers."

At first, Animal Man was similar to Marvel's Henry Pym, a.k.a. Ant-Man—more a sci-fi movie knockoff than a costumed super-hero (the super-shrinking Pym premiered, without costume, in *Tales to Astonish* #27, Jan. 1962, in a story called "The Man in the Anthill," and later became a uniformed crimefighter). Baker wasn't intended to be a regular character, but a positive response to *Strange Adventures* #180 led to "The Return of the Man with Animal Powers" in *SA* #184 (Jan.

© 2007 DC Comics.

1966). He disappeared again until #190 (July 1966), when he came back in orange spandex with a big, blue "A" (for Animal Man or, as he was nicknamed, A-Man). He was now as an honest-to-gosh super-hero…

…but an irregularly seen one, since Animal Man stepped in and out of *Strange Adventures* a few more times before fading away until 1980s guest-shots in other titles (including *Action Comics* #552, Feb. 1984, where he returned with fellow Monkey Man Congorilla as one of the "Forgotten Heroes").

It wasn't until writer Grant Morrison got his hands on Buddy Baker that the character came into his own. With penciler Chas Truog and cover artist Brian Bolland, Morrison launched a monthly *Animal Man* series with a Sept. 1988 first issue (A-Man joined Justice League Europe the very next year). Morrison often portrayed A-Man as an animal-rights crusader, and apes were common in the series (and were spectacularly drawn on covers by Bolland). Ape aficionados affectionately recall *Animal Man* #25's (July 1990) "Monkey Puzzle," which began a story arc where Morrison took Buddy Baker into comic-book limbo, where he met an array of retired characters like Merryman of the Inferior Five. Issue #25's cover and interior story depicted a monkey at a typewriter, a nod to the "infinite monkey theorem," the notion that a monkey hitting

random typewriter keys will eventually type the works of Shakespeare. Morrison and company eventually vacated *Animal Man*, but the series ran until issue #89 (Sept. 1995).

THE APE

One-time *Planet of the Apes* scribe Doug Moench (see the Moench Q & Ape in Chapter 6) told the woeful tale of "The Ogre and the Ape" in *Batman* #535 (Oct. 1996). An under-the-table evolutionary-research project in Gotham City agonizingly evolved a lab monkey into the intelligent Ape while devolving a human victim into the brutish Ogre. The vengeful duo executed the scientists responsible, one by one, until the Dark Knight intervened. Moench's tension-building script and Kelley Jones' moody artwork elevated what could have been a routine revenge tale into a riveting study of isolation and animal/human rights.

THE APE MAN

Once you were sentenced to Lost Island Prison, you were there for good—if the surrounding shark-infested waters weren't intimidating enough, the dreadful Ape Man rumored to lumber throughout the nearby jungle would keep you in your cell. Chisel-faced convict Salty Gruner didn't believe in legendary monster-men, however, as artist Steve Ditko and an uncredited writer (more than likely either Stan Lee or Larry Lieber) disclosed in "The Ape Man" in Marvel Comics' *Strange Tales* vol. 1 #85 (June 1961). At nightfall Gruner snuck out of the penitentiary and into the isle's forest, before long stumbling across the golden-furred, Mighty Joe Young-sized Ape Man. The Ape Man, formerly a human being, was the victim of a witch doctor's curse—a curse which was transferable, as Gruner regrettably discovered when his meeting with the creature freed the man of his ape-affliction and turned Salty into a simian. "The Ape Man," a five-page tale, has been twice reprinted, in *Where Monsters Dwell* #24 (Oct. 1973) and *Giant-Size Werewolf by Night* #2 (Oct. 1974).

APE-MAN (of the ANI-MEN)

In the early days of Marvel's Daredevil, the Man without Fear was, more or less, the company's answer to Batman, even down to his copycat villains (DD's Jester and Owl to Batman's Joker and Penguin, as examples). In the vein of lower-tier Bat-baddies the Terrible Trio, the '50s fiends that plundered Gotham City wearing Mardi Gras-like

© 2007 Marvel Characters, Inc.

animal heads (becoming the Fox, the Shark, and the Vulture), the Ani-Men fought Ol' Hornhead in *Daredevil* vol. 1 #10 and 11 (Oct. and Dec. 1965), by Wally Wood, Stan Lee, and Bob Powell. Gordon "Monk" Keefer was one of this felonious foursome given animal-themed super-suits by the criminal strategist called the Organizer.

As Ape-Man, Keefer had slightly boosted strength and athleticism, and with his partners Cat-Man, Bird-Man, and Frog-Man became costumed muscle for hire, occasionally venturing outside of *Daredevil* into other Marvel titles. (Frog-Man was ousted from the team, which then was sometimes called the Unholy Three.) Ape-Man was killed by Spymaster in *Iron Man* vol. 1 #116 (Nov. 1978), and Roy McVey replaced Monk Keefer in the simian suit. This second Ape-Man, along with Cat-Man, was murdered by Death-Stalker in *Daredevil* #158 (May 1979). The Ani-Men have since experienced roster changes, but as of this writing no new Ape-Man has suited up.

BEAST BOY (a.k.a. CHANGELING)

Garfield "Gar" Logan—you probably know him as either Beast Boy or the Changeling (maybe both), depending upon when you discovered *The Teen Titans*—owes his life to a green monkey.

He was kid with a rare blood disease who was cured by a monkey-based serum in DC's *Doom Patrol* #99 (Nov. 1965). This was before the days of pharmaceutical commercials' 20-second precautionary voiceovers, so how could young Logan know that *potential side effects include green skin, green hair, and the ability to transform into animals*?

© 2007 DC Comics.

So Gar Logan mutated into Beast Boy, the hyperactive teen who could become any animal. And many of those animals were monkeys, recurring favorites in his shape-shifting repertoire. He was dubbed Changeling when he joined the New Teen Titans in 1980, and weathered a decade of bad-hair days in the '90s during a mullet phase. By 2000 he had returned to his Beast Boy name and even received his own miniseries—and scored much wider acclaim (including merchandising galore) once the Cartoon Network's *Teen Titans* premiered in 2003.

© 2007 Scott McCloud.

BUTCH

Ever date someone with an obnoxious sibling? You know, the kind of jerk who acts like a monkey? In Scott McCloud's *Zot!*, the sanguine sci-fi series published by Eclipse Comics from 1984 through 1991, Butch—a.k.a. Horton Everett Weaver—was the exasperating older brother of the titular character's girlfriend Jenny. First seen in *Zot!* #1 (Apr. 1984), Butch was turned into a chimp by terrorists called the De-Evolutionaries (or Devoes, for you '80s music fans) and provided laughs throughout the critically acclaimed series. Butch wasn't permanently a chimp—while on his bleaker (more reality-based) Earth he was human, but he went ape each time he visited Zot's optimistic parallel world.

THE CHANGELING

The 400th issue of *Action Comics* (May 1971) presented the jaw-dropping concept of Superman's *son* (not an Imaginary Story or an "Earth-B" Super Son, mind you) who could transform into a *gorilla*—all this, and a Neal Adams cover, too! A triple-whammy anniversary treat!

Writer Leo Dorfman and the "Swanderson" art team of Curt Swan and Murphy Anderson gave the

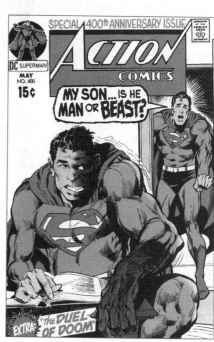

© 2007 DC Comics.

Man of Steel a teenage ward in "My Son… Is He Man or Beast?" Gregor Nagy, the offspring of Superman's scientist friend Dr. Jan Nagy, ended up in the Man of Steel's care upon his father's passing. Gregor was pretty darn bitter about it, since the Man of Steel's earlier disruption of one of Dr. Nagy's malfunctioning experiments gave the teen the ability to transform into other living creatures (including a gorilla). Eventually, Gregor changed his tune and averted a crisis by appropriating both his guardian's powers and one of his Super-suits, climaxing in a tearjerker of a scene where Super-son Gregor died in Superman's arms.

CONGORILLA

Congo Bill was one of those second-tier comic-book characters (like Aquaman and Green Arrow) that luckily managed to survive when most other Golden Age characters were being shown the door in the 1950s.

DC Comics' imitation of Jungle Jim, the explorer-hero first seen in 1934 in a King Features syndicated comic strip and later in Hollywood (in 1937 and 1948 movie serials and in a 1955–1956 TV series, with former film Tarzan Johnny Weissmuller slipping into a pith helmet and jodhpurs as Jungle Jim in the second serial and on television), Congo Bill premiered in *More Fun Comics* #56 (June 1940) and remained a B- (as in backup series) player for years. Not long after his debut, Congo Bill jumped to *Action Comics*, loyally serving as one of big Kahuna Superman's support features until the end of the 1950s. Along the way, Congo Bill, like Jungle Jim, earned a movie serial (in 1948, starring Don McGuire), a sidekick (Janu the Jungle Boy, "Boy" to Bill's

© 2007 DC Comics.

civilized "Tarzan," in *Action* #191, Apr. 1954), his own "Cheeta" (Janu's pet chimp, Chota), and his own short-lived title. *Congo Bill* ran seven issues (cover-dated Sept. 1954 through Sept. 1955) and was expertly drawn by Nick Cardy (see the Cardy Q & Ape in this chapter).

The emergence of a flashy new breed of super-heroes during the Silver Age made Congo Bill quite boring by comparison, and as Mort Weisinger firmly took control of the Superman franchise in the late '50s, *Action* backup Bill, like the Man of Steel, got a facelift—and a hairier face.

In *Action* #248 (Jan. 1959), writer Robert Bernstein and artist Howard Sherman turned the Anglo adventurer into "The Amazing Congorilla" by having Bill inherit from a tribal chief a magic ring bearing a gorilla silhouette; whenever Bill rubbed the ring, for one hour he would switch bodies with the Golden Gorilla after which the feature was renamed (incidentally, Congorilla, without Bill's brain, had made one earlier appearance). Once the co-stars swapped forms, Bill would storm into action as an "intelligent" ape while readers got a chuckle from his human form grunting and pounding his chest like a gorilla. And so Congo Bill became a supporting-cast member in his own series, but, hey, how could a well-groomed guy with a Ricky Ricardo moustache hope to complete with an orange (comics' version of "golden") anthropoid? Congorilla was moved from *Action* to *Adventure Comics* in 1960, but by *Adventure* #283 (Apr. 1961) Congorilla was canned.

Of course, no DC gorilla stays in limbo forever, and Congorilla made infrequent reprint or token appearances for years. Congo Bill/Congorilla's most unorthodox outing was as one of a prototype JLA (along with DC's 1950s lineup, including the Blackhawks and Rex the Wonder Dog) in writer Steve Englehart's and penciler Dick Dillin's *Justice League of America* #144 (July 1977), and the Golden Gorilla was seen again as one of the Forgotten Heroes in *Action Comics* #552 (Feb. 1984). Englehart, with penciler Neil Vokes, resurrected the Golden Gorilla in 1992 in a four-issue *Congorilla* series that featured Janu in Congorilla's body, with Congo Bill in Janu's (!).

Writer Robert Bernstein and artist Howard Sherman turned Congo Bill into Congorilla in *Action Comics* **#248 (Jan. 1959).** © 2007 DC Comics.

THE 800-LB. GORILLA

Writer/artist Batton Lash's Alanna Wolff and Jeff Byrd, stars of the comic *Supernatural Law* (published by Exhibit A Press) and "counselors of the macabre," have developed a cult audience from their courtroom defense of paranormal clients. Lash paid homage to the DC gorilla stories of yesteryear in the 2003 Harvey Award-nominated issue #35. In the "The Trial of the 800-lb. Gorilla," Wolff and Byrd represented a New York mobster named Nicky Gorillo, whose brain was transplanted into the body of an 800-lb. gorilla. Lash skewered the apes-in-comics phenomenon with non-stop one-liners, and as an added treat, his cover art was inked by Murphy Anderson, certainly no stranger to gorilla covers.

THE GIBBON

The Gibbon was a Spider-Man wannabe who premiered in Stan Lee and John Romita, Sr.'s *Amazing Spider-Man* vol. 1 #110 (July 1972). Born Martin Blank, an apish mutant with astounding agility, he thought he'd overcome a lifetime of ridicule by becoming the Wall-Crawler's crimefighting partner. Costuming himself in a monkey suit he'd once worn as a circus performer, Blank, calling himself the Gibbon, took to the rooftops until he found Spidey, who (unwisely) laughed at this nimble nebbish's request to work with him. "Nobody's ever gonna laugh at me—ever again!" snapped the Gibbon as he tore into Spider-Man… and he was back the next issue, with enhanced powers thanks to one of Kraven the Hunter's mystical potions. Spidey whipped the Gibbon, who took his place in the annals of idiotic super-villains…

…a role cemented by his return in *Spectacular Spider-Man* #246 (May 1997) alongside a ragtag team of bargain-basement Spider-foes (including the Grizzly, the Kangaroo, and the Spot) called… the Legion of Losers. (Before being officially branded as a loser, the Gibbon made a guest appearance in the two-part *Spectacular Spider-Man* #59–60, Oct.–Nov. 1981.)

GIGANTA

You might not know it from her *Attack of the 50 Ft. Woman*-ish mid-2000s appearances in DC's post–Infinite Crisis *Wonder Woman* relaunch, but statuesque Giganta first went ape way back during World War II.

In *Wonder Woman* vol. 1 #9 (Summer 1944), writer/artist team William Moulton Marston and H. G. Peter's "Evolution Goes Haywire" introduced Professor Zool, a bearded, shaggy-

Original John Romita, Sr. cover art to the Gibbon's second appearance. From *Amazing Spider-Man* #111 (Aug. 1972).
© 2007 Marvel Characters, Inc. Courtesy of Heritage Auctions.

haired male instructor at the Holliday College for Women. Zool's "electronic evolutionizer" turned a female gorilla into Giganta, a busty, redheaded wild woman in a leopard-pelt swimsuit (and beaded wrist- and ankle-bracelets). What heresy, some readers must've thought, with Zool's boasted goal of making out men of monkeys! Most readers didn't mind, though, as Wonder Woman going head-to-head with the rampant Giganta was tons of fun.

Giganta palled around with other Wonder Woman rogues (including Cheetah, who shared Giganta's spotted fashion sense) as Villainy Inc. in *Wonder Woman* #28 (Mar.–Apr. 1948), then disappeared until July 1966, when she was dusted off by *WW* writer/editor Robert Kanigher for "Giganta—the Gorilla Girl," drawn by Ross Andru and Mike Esposito, in *Wonder Woman* #163. Over a decade later, television offered

"Giganta and Grodd, sittin' in a tree…" Monkey love from *Super Friends* #30 (Mar. 1980).
© 2007 DC Comics.

Giganta her greatest stature: She was one of the Legion of Doom on Saturday morning's *Challenge of the Super Friends* (1978–1979, where she was voiced by Ruth Forman) and was played by A'lesha (also A'leshia and Alesha) Brevard on the live-action TV farce *Legends of the Superheroes* (1979). On *Super Friends*, Giganta received the super-power of growth, and towered over the Amazon Princess and her uber-allies in a season's worth of adventures.

Giganta's Saturday-morning fame inspired an utterly weird story in a DC title, in its "TV Comic" spin-off *Super Friends* #30 (Mar. 1980). In writer E. Nelson Bridwell's "Gorilla Warfare Against Humans!", illustrated by Ramona Fradon and Bob Smith, super-gorilla Grodd and former-gorilla Giganta had the hots for one another, although they were mutually repulsed by each other's appearances. Improving upon Zool's original device, Grodd intended to alter Giganta into an intelligent gorilla until the Super Friends upended his plans. Miscegenation? Bestiality? Since Giganta was originally a gorilla, one can argue that neither charge applied, but nonetheless the mere implication of a relationship between ape and "woman" was downright kinky, especially since it was packaged as a kid-friendly fable.

Zool was gender-retrofitted into Dr. Doris Zeul courtesy of writer/artist John Byrne in *Wonder Woman* vol. 2 #125 (Sept. 1997). In a somewhat convoluted storyline Zeul died, had her soul transferred into the body of a gorilla named Giganta, then transplanted her mind into the form of a carnival strongwoman named Olga. Somehow amidst these transformations Zeul, calling herself Giganta, obtained the ability to grow into a giantess. Since then she's used this lofty trait to become a regular baddie in DC's titles and on the Cartoon Networks' 2000s *Justice League* toons, where she was voiced by Jennifer Hale.

GORILLA BOSS OF GOTHAM CITY
According to the Batcomputer, George "Boss" Dyke's specialty was "crimes of violence," and his trademark was the theft of "big denomination bills only." No wonder Boss Dyke got the gas chamber on page two of "The Gorilla Boss of Gotham City!" in *Batman* #75 (Feb.–Mar. 1953), written by David Vern, penciled by Lew Sayre Schwartz (with Batman figures drawn by Bob Kane), and inked by Charles Paris. Ever the strategist, prior to his execution Dyke had arranged with the unscrupulous Doc Willard to transplant his brain into the body of a giant gorilla. As the mute but intelligent Gorilla Boss, Dyke pulled heists in Gotham City to lure its cowled protector, Batman, into the crush

of his mammoth arms for phase two of his insidious plan: to transfer his brain into the body of Batman! "And for laughs, Dyke insists I put Batman's brain in the gorilla!" chuckled Willard, about to make the cranial swap, but the wily Caped Crusader outsmarted the Gorilla Boss, and after a climb to the top of a Gotham skyscraper, Dyke took a Kong-sized fatal fall…

…but his brain was back in action—or in *World's Finest Comics*, rather—courtesy of Bob Haney, a writer who never let continuity get in the way of a story, in the Superman/Batman tale "Invasion of the Deathless Brain" in issue #251 (June–July 1978; Boss Dyke also appeared in a flashback in issue #254). The Gorilla Boss of Gotham City made one more appearance as one of several legendary DC apes mind-controlled by Gorilla Grodd in "Distant Cousins" in *Swamp Thing Annual* #3 (1987). In this story by writer Rick Veitch, Dyke was reduced in size (to that of a "normal" gorilla) and stature (to performing celebrity impressions from his zoo cage). While these changes disregarded the original tale's continuity, by giving Gorilla Boss voice Veitch also awarded the villain one of the best lines in the Annual: "I'm on a mission from Grodd." "The Gorilla Boss of Gotham City" was reprinted in 1963's *Batman Annual* #3 and 1976's *Super-Heroes Battle Super-Gorillas* #1.

Lew Sayre Schwartz's original pencil art to the cover of *Batman* #75 (Feb.–March 1953), featuring the Gorilla Boss of Gotham City. Win Mortimer redrew the Batman and Robin figures on the final version of the cover. (For a full progression of this cover art, see *Alter Ego* vol. 3 #51, Aug. 2005.)

GORILLA COMICS

In 1999 a "Banana Trust" collective was formed between comic-book writers and artists Kurt Busiek, Tom Grummett, Karl Kesel, Barry Kitson, George Pérez, Mark Waid, and Mike Wieringo (with Todd DeZago and Stuart Immonen signing on shortly thereafter), with the highly publicized goal of releasing creator-owned properties under an imprint called Gorilla Comics. Distributed by Image Comics, Gorilla had high hopes—but, to the creators' surprise, no money. Gorilla Comics was financially backed by an Internet startup company, and the dot-com bust of the early 21st century squashed the Banana Trust's plans when they discovered the investors and capital they were promised simply did not exist. Only a few Gorilla titles trickled out, and the most visible of the batch, Waid and Kitson's *Empire* and DeZago and Wieringo's *Tellos*, continued at other publishers. *Comics Gone Ape!* extends a furry-pawed salute to these talented monkey men for their valiant effort.

GORILLA GANG

Most run-of-the-mill cat burglars would cloak themselves in black, but a trio of thieves seen in the landmark Silver Age tale "Robin Dies at Dawn" in *Batman* #156 (June 1963) instead chose much more conspicuous garb. The Gorilla Gang, three crooks in gorilla suits, enjoyed a brief crime spree in Gotham City during a time when Batman was incapacitated by a recurring hallucination foretelling the death of his sidekick. Fortunately writer Bill Finger and penciler Sheldon Moldoff spared Robin, and treated

Batman goes undercover to infiltrate the Gorilla Gang in *Batman* #156 (June 1963).
© 2007 DC Comics.

readers with an appreciation for the absurd with a sequence of Batman wearing a gorilla suit when infiltrating the monkey mob.

These lawbreaking one-hit wonders are not to the confused with the Don F. Glut-produced fan-film *Superman vs. the Gorilla Gang* (1965). Glut's mini-movie included in its cast Glenn Strange, reprising his earlier role of the Frankenstein Monster, and fantasy-film authority Bob Burns, in his "Kogar, the Gorilla" suit. Over the years Burns zipped himself into his gorilla suit for a host of TV appearances on series such as *The Lucy Show* and *The Mickey Mouse Club*; he also played Tracy the Gorilla in the 1975 live-action Saturday-morning show *The Ghost Busters* (bearing no relation to the "Who Ya Gonna Call?" Ghostbusters made popular during the '80s).

GORILLA GIRL (a.k.a. GORILLA WOMAN)

You'd have to dig deep into the back-issue bins to find a more obscure ape character than this one. Gorilla Woman was originally shown only on a circus billboard in a Spider-Man/Ghost Rider story in *Marvel Team-Up* vol. 1 #91 (Mar. 1980). She was "revived," along with the six-armed carnival attraction dubbed

Six and the Man-Thing-like Muck Monster (both of whom actually appeared in that *MTU* tale), as "the Freaks" in a backup story in *Marvel Tales* #256 (Dec. 1991). Called Gorilla Girl in the *Marvel Tales* story, she was an attractive young woman who could turn herself into a talking gorilla. After a chance skirmish with the super-villains Hammer and Anvil, the Freaks dedicated themselves to super-heroics in what was intended as a tryout for further adventures.

GORILLA MAN I (KEN HALE)

Marvel Comics' *Men's Adventures* was in the midst of morphing from a "rugged tales of real adventure!" omnibus to a horror anthology when writer Stan Lee and artist Robert Q. Sale's "The Gorilla Man" saw print in issue #26 (Mar. 1954). This unpretentious six-pager introduced Kenneth Hale, an adventurer led to Kenya after a series of perplexing dreams introduced him to the fabled ape-human hybrids called Gorilla Men. Hale's quest to discover this race led him deep in the jungle, where he came upon a testy Gorilla Man. A fierce hand-to-hand battle followed, and Hale bested

© 2007 Marvel Characters, Inc.

the creature—and was magically transformed into a Gorilla Man himself. See what happens when you follow your dreams, Ken?

Gorilla Man was originally a throwaway character, just another story in just another series. Then co-writers Don Glut and Roy Thomas got a hold of Ken Hale—and other stray characters that had populated Marvel's titles during the 1950s, such as Marvel Boy, Venus, and the Human Robot. With artists Alan Kupperberg and Bill Black they asked readers "What If the Avengers Had Fought Evil in the 1950s?" in *What If?* vol. 1 #9 (June 1978). This tale, not unlike the similar concept introduced a year earlier by competitor DC Comics in *Justice League of America* #144, gathered together a prototype Avengers before the "true" formation of the team. Here, Gorilla Man (called Gorilla-Man, with the hyphen) and his mismatched teammates battled the international despot the Yellow Claw, as well as other '50s-vintage villains. It was revealed that Hale had been hiding out in Africa since his transformation into Gorilla Man, disassociating himself from his past. Marvel Boy pledged to use his extraterrestrial (he's from Uranus—please don't snicker) technology to return Hale to his original state (Gorilla Man's still waiting, M-Boy).

Gorilla Man returned to active duty in the 2005–2006 miniseries *Nick Fury's Howling Commandos*, a monster super-team, and in 2006–2007 reunited with his proto-Avengers in the six-issue miniseries *Agents of Atlas*, written by Jeff Parker (see the Parker Q & Ape in this chapter) and illustrated by Leonard Kirk and Kris Justice. Regrouping these retro heroes in the modern day, *Agents of Atlas*—borrowing its name from Marvel's 1950s imprint, Atlas—pitted the offbeat heroes against their old enemy the Yellow (now Golden) Claw. In *Atlas*, Hale, deliciously drawn by Kirk, provided both firearm expertise and, through his irascible demeanor, comic relief.

GORILLA-MAN II (DR. ARTHUR NAGAN)

A pop-music-savvy comics reader might think that Marvel Comics' second Gorilla-Man, Dr. Arthur Nagan, the super-villain with a man's head on a gorilla's body, was a swipe at crooner Paul Anka's "Put Your Head on My Shoulder." But Anka's hit platter made *Billboard*'s Top 100 in 1959, while Nagan premiered five years earlier in *Mystery Tales* #21 (Sept. 1954, and reprinted in *Weird Wonder Tales* #7, Dec. 1974) in a story illustrated by Bob Powell and possibly written by Stan Lee. Nagan was an

unscrupulous surgeon, operating from an African base, who felt no compunctions about using animals' internal organs in human transplants. After performing surgery upon a gorilla, substituting some of its organs with faulty human ones, the ape's troop exacted their revenge by relocating Nagan's head onto the body of a gorilla (*that*'ll teach ya!). Now, gorillas might be bright, but unless they're of the sentient, *Strange Adventures* variety, they're not smart enough to perform a head transplant, so it's anyone's guess just how they pulled off this surgery.

This grotesque Gorilla-Man was, like his namesake, pulled out of mothballs many years later, in Nagan's case by writer Steve Gerber. Gerber's *The Defenders* #21 (Mar. 1975), penciled by Sal Buscema, placed Nagan as the head honcho of the Headmen, bizarre bad guys with unusually shaped craniums (the Headmen included the turban-topped Chondu the Mystic; Jerry Morgan, a putty-faced biologist; and Ruby Tuesday, a shapely woman with a malleable crimson sphere as a noggin). The Headmen returned to fight the Defenders upon several occasions, with Gerber extrapolating from Nagan's *Mystery Tales* shtick for a series of oddball brain transfer-ences in a 1976 storyline. In addition to the Defenders, Nagan, along with the Headmen, has made enemies of Power Man, Spider-Man, and She-Hulk.

GORILLA-MAN III
(FRANZ RADZIK)

In *Tales to Astonish* #28 (Feb. 1962), Stan Lee resuscitated his Gorilla Man idea from *Men's Adventures* #26 (this was, of course, well before Gorilla Man's 1978 reintroduction) and partnered with artists Jack Kirby and Dick Ayers to produce "I Am the Gorilla-Man." This version of the character was Transylvanian scientist Franz Radzik, inventor of a device that exchanged minds between beings. Radzik ripped off a zoo gorilla and transferred his intellect into its fearsome form, intending to use it for crime. In a *Twilight Zone*-worthy twist, Gorilla Man, who was unable to speak, was arrested when the real gorilla, inside Radzik's body, alerted zoo authorities to reclaim their escaped ape.

Two months later, *Tales to Astonish* #30 presented "The Return of the Gorilla-Man." Gorilla-Man Radzik busted loose from the zoo and attempted to exploit this "gorilla's" intellect for scientific gain. Once again he got something he didn't bargain for: a one-way ticket into space in an experimental rocket. Gorilla-Man and the gorilla inhabiting Radzik's body haven't been seen since 1962, discounting the reprinting of both Gorilla-Man tales in *Fear* #5 (Nov. 1971).

THE GORILLA WITCH

Anyone who's ever watched a television soap opera knows that in fiction, only bad guys wear eye patches. Or, in the case of DC's *Strange Adventures* #186

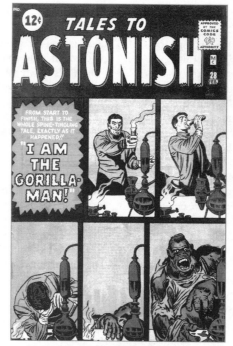

© 2007 Marvel Characters, Inc.

© 2007 DC Comics.

DON'T BREATHE IN THESE FUMES FROM MY WITCH'S BREW, HUMANS-- OR *YOU* WILL LIVE TO REGRET IT AS OTHERS HAVE!

(Mar. 1966), bad *gorillas*. And since the gorilla on that comic's Bernard Baily-drawn cover warned against breathing in the fumes of his cauldron's brew, only the most naïve of comic-book readers approached this issue thinking that the Gorilla Witch was anything short of a sinister simian.

In writer Dave Wood and artist Baily's "Beware the Gorilla Witch," a man named Reed ventured to Africa to uncover the secret of communicating with wild creatures. After obtaining a magic formula from a witch doctor named Karuu, Reed whipped up a batch of the supernatural soup. Tangling with a gorilla named Taro while stirring the stew, Reed mutated into a mindless ape, while Taro gained Reed's intelligence. Taro the Gorilla Witch planned to stir up more of his brew to create obedient gorilla armies… "And then, I will establish myself as king—ruler of the world!" Luckily, Reed's friend Bruce tracked down his buddy in the jungle and, by slipping a "Mickey Finn" into the witch's potion, helped Reed return to normal and put Taro behind bars.

GRAYSON'S GORILLA

Among Silver Age collectors, *Tales to Astonish* #48 (Oct. 1963) is noteworthy for its debut of Ant-Man's prickliest foe, the Porcupine. Following that tale was a rather pedestrian five-pager by Stan Lee and Larry Lieber titled "Grayson's Gorilla," the sole appearance of inventor Harvey Grayson. Grayson constructed a device that would transfer a gorilla's might into his own body, but to his surprise swapped minds with the anthropoid instead.

JAYNA

Wonder Twins Zan and Jayna and their pet monkey Gleek first appeared in comic books in 1977 in issue #7 of DC's TV spin-off *Super Friends*. "Wonder Twins powers, activate!" chimed the super-siblings when touching their fists and triggering their shapeshifting abilities. Brother Zan's transmutations were pretty darn lame—water-based alterations, such as cloudbursts and snow, a super-power ridiculed on the Cartoon Network in an animated spot where the boy Wonder Twin, as a puddle of water, was mopped up by a janitor. Sister Jayna, however, like Beast Boy/Changeling, could become a virtual zoo, one creature at a time. Zayna occasionally turned into an ape, such as a Giganto-Pithecus ("A type of prehistoric ape of Asia, the largest ape known," according to editor Julius Schwartz in *Super Friends* #30, the Giganta/Grodd issue).

KARMAK, THE LIVING BEAST-BOMB

Some days, you just can't get rid of a Beast-Bomb! That was Caped Crusader's lament in "Batman Battles the Living Beast-Bomb!" in *Detective Comics* #339 (May 1965), written by Gardner Fox, penciled by Carmine Infantino, and inked by Joe Giella.

"Worthless Wally" Hewitt was a downtrodden nebbish who used bionics—"The study of living creatures and the attempt to duplicate their special properties," per Julius Schwartz's editor's note, a surprise to those of you who grew up with *The Six Million Dollar Man* and *The Bionic Woman*—to absorb the amazing properties of a variety of animals (Schwartz's *Strange Adventures* #180 would use a similar gimmick a mere four months later with its introduction of Animal Man). Buying a gorilla named Karmak from a circus passing through town, Hewitt used his "bioni-former" to successfully duplicate the anthropoid's strength… but unexpectedly the ape also acquired the ability to think just like a man! And as readers discovered through his thought balloons, Karmak was, like so many men, quite undeniably evil.

Karmak schemed to mimic Batman's "experience and knowledge" to make him a more formidable threat, and after an exciting two-page fight sequence he clobbered Batman and copied his Bat-"mojo," using those gifts on a rampant crime spree. To keep Batman at bay, Karmak strapped bombs onto his hirsute torso, threatening to blow up Gotham City. Batman overcame the gorilla, but in an Atlas-esque gesture had to hoist Karmak over his head for what must have seemed like an eternity to keep the bombs from detonating.

KING KRYPTON, THE SUPER-GORILLA

Encouraged by the healthy sales of the appearances of Chandu the Gorilla with Super-Eyes and the Super-Ape from Krypton, Superman editor Mort Weisinger inched closer his launching of Titano and Beppo by introducing a king-sized super-gorilla in a Superman costume on the Curt Swan/Stan Kaye cover of *Action Comics* #238 (Mar. 1958).

© 2007 DC Comics.

The gorilla-fitted Super-suit was nowhere to be found in the actual story, written by Otto Binder and penciled by Wayne Boring, but the ape's super-powers were clearly on display—and noticed by the *Daily Planet*'s cub reporter Jimmy Olsen, on photographic assignment in Africa. Jimmy used his Superman signal watch to call the Man of Steel, who surmised that this "Gorilla of Steel" was a refugee from Krypton, sent to Earth in an experimental rocket. Dubbed King Krypton by young Olsen, the untamed Super-Gorilla wreaked havoc with its powers, ripping wings off of airplanes and leading to an inevitable battle with Superman (where King Krypton wore Superman's cape during their climactic clash). Exposure to a kryptonite meteor revealed the truth about King Krypton: He was actually a human, a Kryptonian scientist turned into a gorilla by a malfunctioning "evolution accelerator"

and blasted into space in hopes that cosmic radiation would reverse his transformation. "Strangely, the kryptonite rays had the power to restore your human form!" noted Superman as the unnamed scientist perished before his eyes.

MANDRILL

Mandrill is the ladies' man among comic-book apes. Women fawn over him, following him anywhere, obeying his every command. This attribute, however, comes not from Mandrill's looks (he's no Heath Ledger—heck, Steve Buscemi's handsomer than this Marvel Comics villain), but from his mutant ability to emit tremendously potent pheromones.

First seen in *Shanna the She-Devil* vol. 1 #4 (June 1973), in a tale co-written by Carol Seuling and Steve Gerber and penciled by Ross Andru, Mandrill is

© 2007 Marvel Characters, Inc.

actually Jerome Beechman, the son of a Los Alamos atomic researcher. The senior Beechman was, years earlier, accidentally exposed to radiation while on the job, which caused a genetic mutation with his son. Jerome was a black child born to white parents; as he aged his appearance grew apelike, with his face elongating into a snout and tufts of hair sprouting across his body. Abused and outcast because of his unusual appearance, Jerome allied with a young woman similarly mutated by radiation, the vampiric Nekra Sinclair. Calling himself Mandrill (how could he not, with a puss like his?), Jerome and Nekra tried to form an African nation all their own, until Shanna closed them down.

The next year Gerber brought back Mandrill, with Nekra, in *Daredevil* #108–112 (Mar.–Aug. 1974), where Mandrill led an all-female band of followers called Black Spectre in an attempt to take over the White House. Daredevil, Black Widow, and Shanna thwarted that plan. In later appearances Mandrill also controlled an army of radical feminists called Fem-Force and a mutant team called Mutant Force. Mandrill, who also boasts enhanced strength and, when needed, a primal fury, has become one of those second-banana Marvel villains who rears his ugly head from time to time, fighting the Avengers, the Defenders, and the Thunderbolts, among others. In a comical turn, he was seen giving Valentine's Day gift tips to Spider-Man in *I ♥ Marvel: Web of Romance* #1 (Feb. 2006).

Man-Ape returns to plague the Black Panther. Original art to page 17 of *Avengers* #78 (July 1970), penciled by Sal Buscema and inked by Tom Palmer. © 2007 Marvel Characters, Inc. Courtesy of Heritage Auctions.

MAN-APE

Not to be confused with the previously mentioned Man-Apes—or Marvel's own Maa-gor the Man-Ape, a caveman from its Ka-Zar and X-Men continuities—Man-Ape, the strapping African warrior-turned-gorilla-suited troublemaker, was originally the second-in-command to Prince T'Challa, better known as the Black Panther. In "The Monarch and the Man-Ape!" in *Avengers* vol. 1 #62 (Mar. 1969), writer Roy Thomas and artists John Buscema and George Klein introduced T'Challa's aide M'Baku, who was determined to take over the prince's throne in Wakanda. Wearing "the forbidden guise of the white gorilla—in our legends, the most savage… most merciless of beasts," M'Baku literally became one with this notorious creature by consuming white gorilla blood and flesh, magically becoming a superman. Man-Ape nearly killed the Black Panther before being crushed to death under the collapse of a giant, stone panther idol.

Death didn't last long for Man-Ape, as he

was revived supernaturally and was back in *Avengers* #78 (July 1970), this time part of the super-villain team the Lethal Legion; in later appearances, Man-Ape also joined up with the Masters of Evil. M'Baku's grudge match against T'Challa has continued for decades, but the Wakandan prince has made a reconciliatory gesture: Man-Ape showed up at the wedding of T'Challa and Storm in *Black Panther* vol. 4 #18 (Sept. 2006), ready to "wreak revenge for not being invited." M'Baku was surprised, however, to find that T'Challa had included him on the guest list! Instead of busting up the ceremony, Man-Ape got soused and scrapped with Spider-Man.

MOD GORILLA BOSS

Let's count the transgressions of the Mod Gorilla Boss, whose sole appearance was in the Animal Man tale in *Strange Adventures* #201 (June 1967):

First, the Mod Gorilla Boss is a thief with no respect for public or private property. He used his gorilla strength to smash open a postal inspector's door and rip through a jewelry store's barred window, with his human henchmen following closely behind. Were that not bad enough, the big brute even snatched a beauty queen's tiara off her head—during a parade! The fiend!

Second, you don't have to be a deputy of the Fashion Police to criticize him for his garish wardrobe: a white suit with black stripes, yellow striped shirt, and black tie with pink polka dots. In the spring of '67 when the Mod Gorilla Boss appeared, the British-spawned "mod" fashion trend was already passé (but then again, DC Comics in the 1960s was usually one step behind current trends, although its stodgy middle-aged editorial staff sometimes struggled to be hip).

Third, on the Carmine Infantino/George Roussos-drawn cover of *Strange Adventures*

© 2007 DC Comics.

#201, the Mod Gorilla Boss is groping Animal-Man inappropriately. Nuff said!

And fourth—and this might come as a surprise to even the most dedicated gorilla-comics devotee—the Mod Gorilla Boss is a notorious liar. A furry fibber. A primate prevaricator. On the cover he boasted, "You may be the man with animal powers, A-Man, but *I'm* the *real McCoy*!" Not so. As Animal Man discovered in this story (SPOILER ALERT!), the Mod Gorilla Boss was a *man*, baby! A man who used chemical injections to temporarily become an ape! But then again, "I'm a dumpy human being artificially transformed into a gorilla!" doesn't make the most exciting cover copy, so maybe we shouldn't list lying among his crimes.

Despite a rushed art job by Jack Sparling, one-hit wonder Mod Gorilla Boss is quite renowned among fans of gorilla comics. Then again, with a suit that exemplifies tackiness, this super-gorilla is hard to forget.

Monster Ape and Mole Man, kindred spirits. Original art to page 10 of *Captain America* #136 (Apr. 1971). Art by Gene Colan and Bill Everett.

Animal Man vs. the Mod Gorilla Boss. From *Strange Adventures* #201 (June 1967). Art by Jack Sparling.

MONSTER APE

While democracy-hating Nazis, autocrats, and super-spies have been the bread and butter of Captain America's rogues' gallery, surprisingly the Star-Spangled Avenger has battled his share of gorillas during his illustrious career. Chief among them was the white-furred fury called Monster Ape, seen in *Captain America* vol. 1 #135–136 (Mar.–Apr. 1971).

Writer Stan Lee and penciler Gene Colan's "More Monster Than Man" introduced Dr. Erik Gorbo, a biochemist in the employ of S.H. I.E.L.D. (Supreme Headquarters International Espionage Law-Enforcement Division), whose gawky appearance ostracized him from his peers. Rather than order the Charles Atlas muscle-building course (which he could have done right off the back of almost *any* comic book back in that day), Gorbo concocted a serum from gorilla blood with the intention of boosting his strength and stamina—once he became a Hercules, he

thought, he'd impress that cutie Julia, who held a desk job at S.H.I.E.L.D. But Stan the Man didn't give Gorbo's story a happily-ever-after ending: The serum instead turned the scientist into an intelligent gorilla with an empathic connection to and control over other animals. With metered injections, Gorbo was able to undergo Jekyll/Hyde-like transformations to Monster Ape and back to his own form, and started committing crimes in his gorilla identity.

In the second chapter of the two-issue story, Gorbo and Captain America fell into the subterranean world of the Mole Man, and fellow outcasts Monster Ape and Mole Man became fast friends. Gorbo turned on the Mole Man, however, to stop the super-villain's intended attack upon S.H.I.E.L.D. headquarters, and gave his life to spare the life of his would-be girlfriend Julia.

SURRENDER MONKEY

"Surrender monkey" is a derogatory term used by war supporters to describe those who would avoid battle or would "cut and run" from an existing conflict. Add the adjective "cheese-eating" and you've got a slam against the French.

From this writer Peter Milligan and penciler Mike Allred drew inspiration for Surrender Monkey, the beret-sporting French mutant hero who was, at face value, a chimpanzee-man. First seen in issue #13 (Oct. 2003) of Marvel's atypical X-Men title, *X-Statix*, Surrender Monkey was a Frenchman named Edouard Pompidou whose mutant power was the knowledge of when to turn tail and run. He was recruited to join up with the super-villain team Euro-Trash, and ultimately his secrets were revealed: Surrender Monkey wasn't really a monkey. Nor was he a mutant. Or French. He was an AWOL C.I.A. operative named Brad Bentley who broke rank to enjoy the European highlife. Poor Surrender Monkey—he was killed in action in Sept. 2004's *X-Statix* #24 (although comics history suggests that whenever Milligan or another writer needs a beret-sporting French mutant, Surrender Monkey might just retreat from the great beyond back into print).

Simon transferred his intellect into the hulking body of a white gorilla, and in this feral form became an executioner, tracking down and killing those former soldiers whom he blamed for his incarceration. With Thomas Wayne long dead (if you're not aware of his murder, then you've never read a Batman comic or seen a Batman movie…), Xavier Simon targeted Bruce Wayne as a surrogate for his rancorous mission. Not only was Simon smart enough to take over an ape's body, he also deduced Batman's Wayne identity, and came close to relocating his mind into Batman's buff bod.

ULTRA-HUMANITE

As you've read in this chapter, human-to-ape mind transferences are relatively common in comics. Yet no character has swapped bodies with the panache of the Ultra-Humanite. Most readers know the Ultra-Humanite from his robust form of an albino gorilla. That persona, first seen in a Justice League/Justice Society crossover in *Justice League of America* #195–197 (Oct.–Dec. 1981), was "Ultra's" latest in a long line of looks. Historically, the Ultra-Humanite was one of Superman's original foes, dating waaaaay back to *Action Comics* #13 (June 1939, Superman's 13th appearance in *Action*), where he was a bald super-scientist (before the introduction of Lex Luthor) who learned to cheat death by shifting his intellect into other bodies. His first mind-merger was into the curvy figure of Hollywood actress Dolores Winter, making Ultra-Humanite comics' original transgender character.

Over the years Ultra has hopped into a variety of forms, including a giant ant and a dinosaur, but none has quite resonated with audiences more than the big, white gorilla. The simian Ultra-Humanite got a lot of play in the 1980s in writer Roy

Batman battles the man-turned-gorilla Xavier Simon on page 15 of *Detective Comics* #482 (Feb.–Mar. 1979). Art by Jim Starlin and P. Craig Russell. © 2007 DC Comics. Courtesy of Steve Lipsky.

XAVIER SIMON

The frightening, no-nonsense Bat-villain Xavier Simon bore little resemblance to the Dark Knight's previous primate enemies, Gorilla Boss and the Living Beast-Bomb. According to writer/penciler Jim Starlin in a two-part Batman story in *Detective Comics* #481 and 482 (Dec. 1978–Jan. 1979 and Feb.–Mar. 1979), Simon served in the military alongside Bruce (Batman) Wayne's father, Thomas, during World War II, but was jailed for rape after Thomas and other soldiers testified against him. Years later,

Thomas' *All-Star Squadron* and *Infinity, Inc.* titles, but continuity rewritings in the mid-'80s temporarily displaced the villain. Although he was offed in a 2002 *JSA* story arc, Ultra-Humanite was seen on TV in a trio of episodes of the Cartoon Network's *Justice League Unlimited*. At this writing, in DC's post-*Infinite Crisis* universe, the Ultra-Humanite was mentioned in *Justice League of America* vol. 2 #1 (Oct. 2006), suggesting to hopeful gorilla-comics fans that he might be headed for a reappearance.

An Ultra-Humanite flashback on Jerry Ordway's pencil art to page 16 of *All-Star Squadron* #26 (July 1983).

© 2007 DC Comics. Courtesy of Tom Ziuko.

COVER GALLERY

COMICS STARS GO APE!

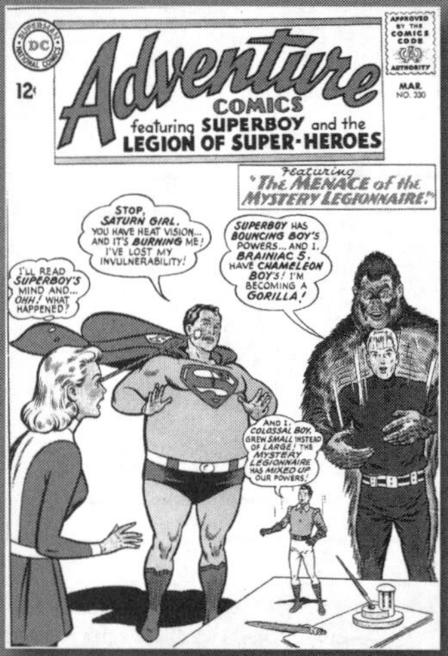
Adventure Comics
12¢
MAR. NO. 330
featuring SUPERBOY and the LEGION OF SUPER-HEROES
Featuring "The MENACE of the MYSTERY LEGIONNAIRE!"
STOP, SATURN GIRL. YOU HAVE HEAT VISION... AND IT'S BURNING ME! I'VE LOST MY INVULNERABILITY!
SUPERBOY HAS BOUNCING BOY'S POWERS... AND I, BRAINIAC 5, HAVE CHAMELEON BOY'S! I'M BECOMING A GORILLA!
I'LL READ SUPERBOY'S MIND AND... OHH! WHAT HAPPENED?
AND I, COLOSSAL BOY, GREW SMALL INSTEAD OF LARGE! THE MYSTERY LEGIONNAIRE HAS MIXED UP OUR POWERS!

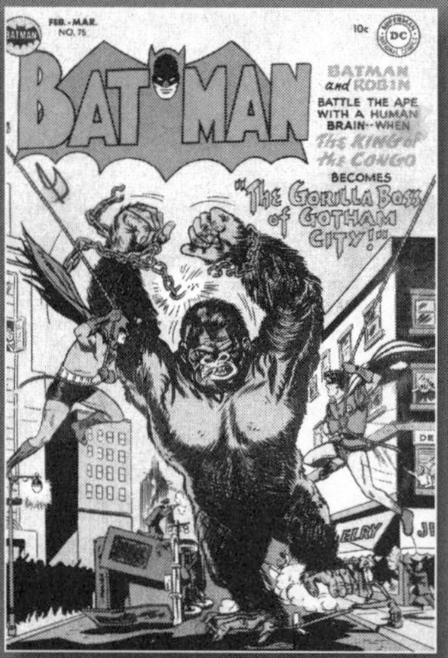
FEB.-MAR. NO. 75
10¢
BATMAN
BATMAN and ROBIN BATTLE THE APE WITH A HUMAN BRAIN--WHEN THE KING of the CONGO BECOMES
"The GORILLA BOSS of GOTHAM CITY!"

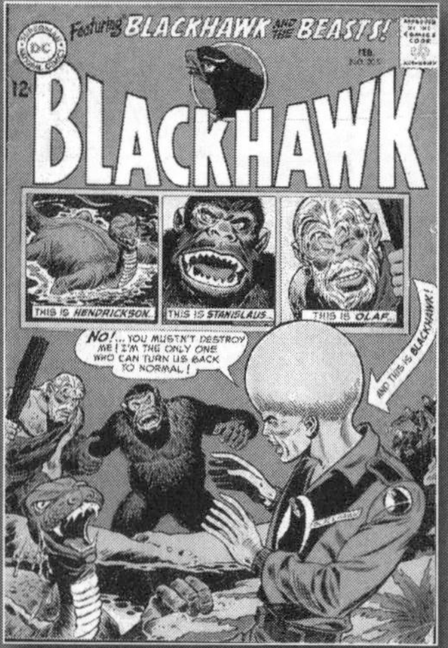
Featuring BLACKHAWK AND THE BEASTS!
12¢
BLACKHAWK
THIS IS HENDRICKSON.
THIS IS STANISLAUS...
THIS IS OLAF...
AND THIS IS BLACKHAWK!
NO!... YOU MUSTN'T DESTROY ME! I'M THE ONLY ONE WHO CAN TURN US BACK TO NORMAL!

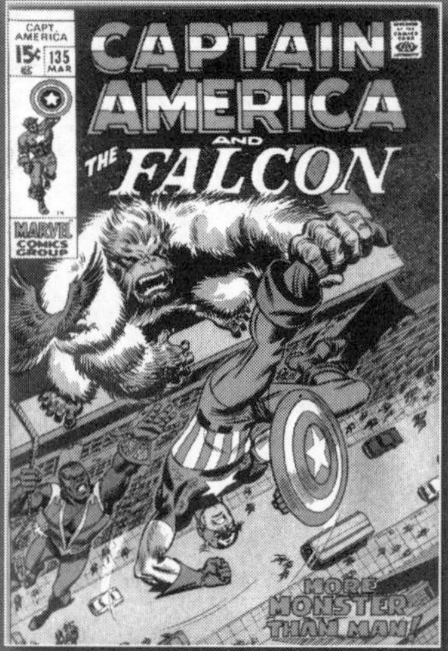
CAPT AMERICA
15¢ 135 MAR
CAPTAIN AMERICA AND THE FALCON
MARVEL COMICS GROUP
MORE MONSTER THAN MAN!

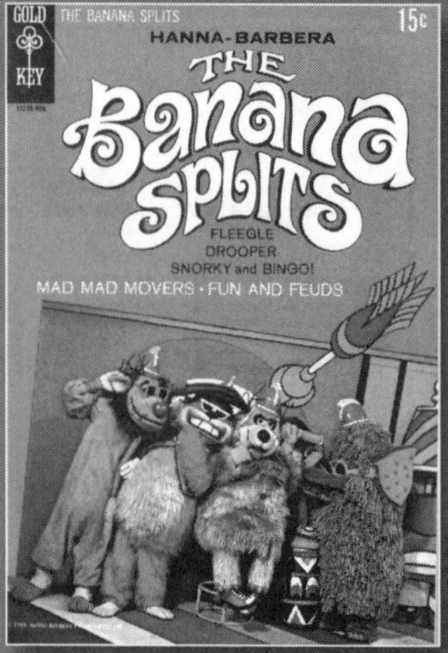
GOLD KEY
THE BANANA SPLITS
15¢
HANNA-BARBERA
THE Banana SPLITS
FLEEGLE
DROOPER
SNORKY and BINGO!
MAD MAD MOVERS · FUN AND FEUDS

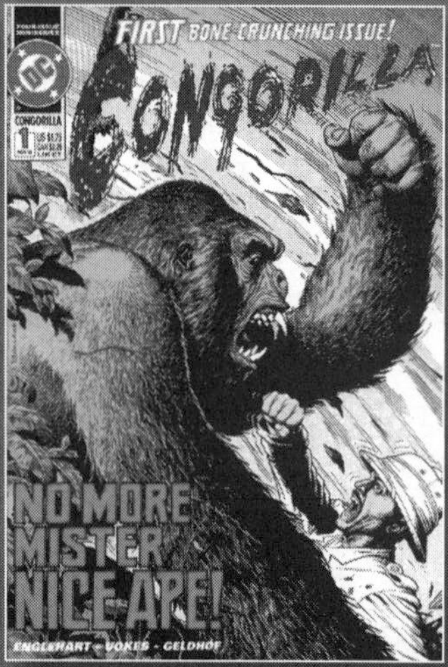
FIRST BONE-CRUNCHING ISSUE!
CONGORILLA
CONGORILLA 1
NO MORE MISTER NICE APE!
ENGLEHART · VOKES · GELDHOF

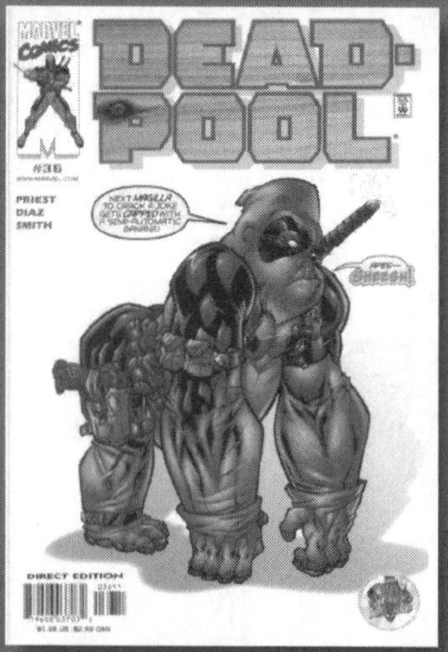
MARVEL COMICS
DEAD-POOL
PRIEST
DIAZ
SMITH
DIRECT EDITION

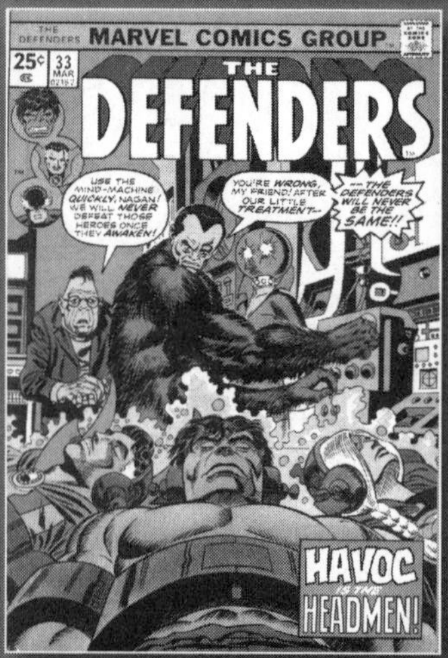
THE DEFENDERS
MARVEL COMICS GROUP
25¢ 33 MAR
THE DEFENDERS
USE THE WIND-MACHINE QUICKLY, NAGAN! WE WILL NEVER DEFEAT THOSE HEROES ONCE THEY AWAKEN!
YOU'RE WRONG, MY FRIEND! AFTER OUR LITTLE TREATMENT--
--THE DEFENDERS WILL NEVER BE THE SAME!!
HAVOC IS THE HEADMEN!

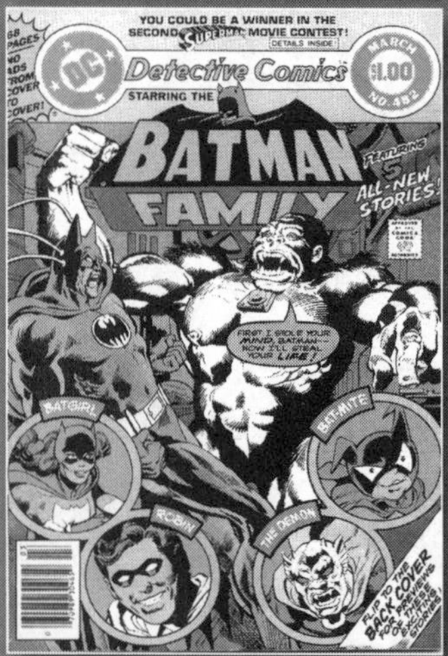
YOU COULD BE A WINNER IN THE SECOND SUPERMAN MOVIE CONTEST!
DETAILS INSIDE
DC
Detective Comics
MARCH
$1.00
STARRING THE BATMAN FAMILY
ALL-NEW STORIES!
FIRST I STOLE YOUR MIND, BATMAN--NOW I'LL STEAL YOUR LIFE!
BATGIRL
BAT-MITE
ROBIN
THE DEMON

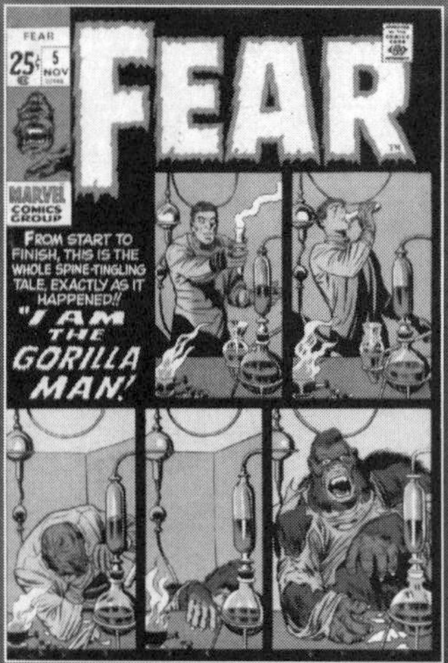
FEAR
25¢ 5 NOV
FEAR
MARVEL COMICS GROUP
FROM START TO FINISH, THIS IS THE WHOLE SPINE-TINGLING TALE EXACTLY AS IT HAPPENED!
"I AM THE GORILLA MAN!"

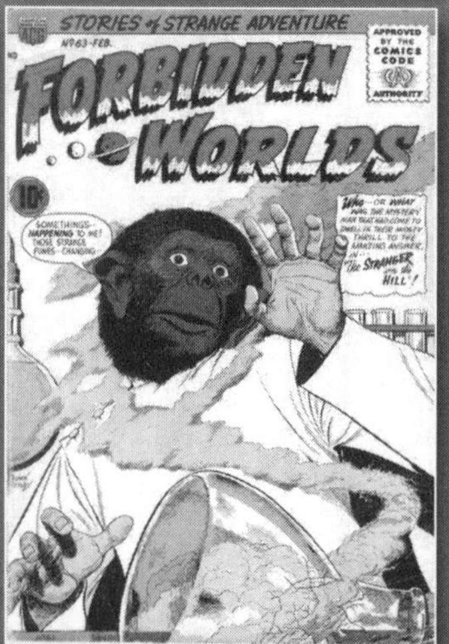
STORIES of STRANGE ADVENTURE
APPROVED BY THE COMICS CODE AUTHORITY
No 63-FEB.
FORBIDDEN WORLDS
10¢
SOMETHING'S HAPPENING TO ME!
THE STRANGER ON THE HILL!

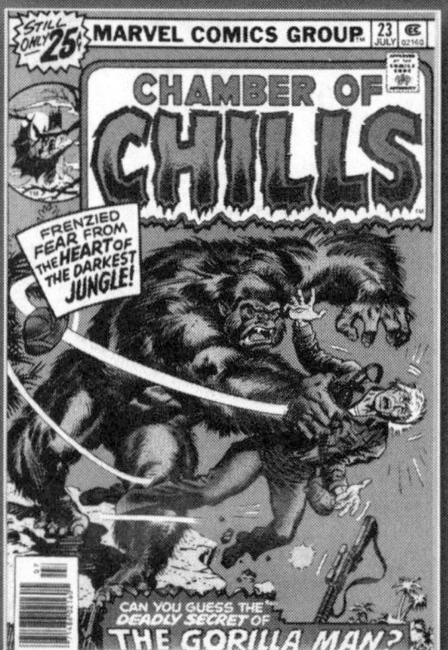
STILL ONLY 25¢
MARVEL COMICS GROUP
23 JULY
CHAMBER OF CHILLS
FRENZIED FEAR FROM THE HEART OF THE DARKEST JUNGLE!
CAN YOU GUESS THE DEADLY SECRET OF THE GORILLA MAN?

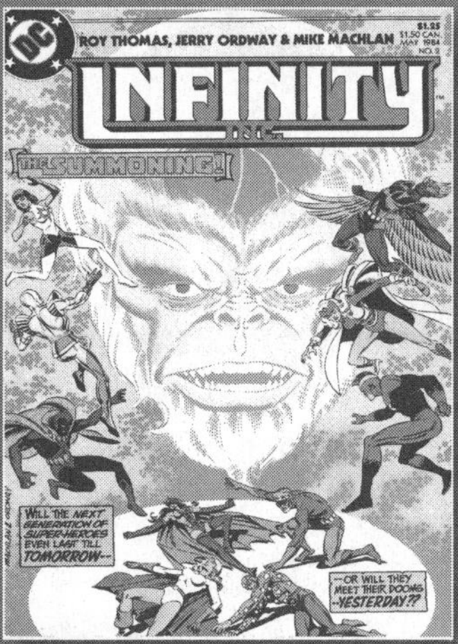
ROY THOMAS, JERRY ORDWAY & MIKE MACHLAN
INFINITY INC.
THE SUMMONING!
WILL THE NEXT GENERATION OF SUPER-HEROES EVEN LAST TILL TOMORROW--
--OR WILL THEY MEET THEIR DOOMS... YESTERDAY?!

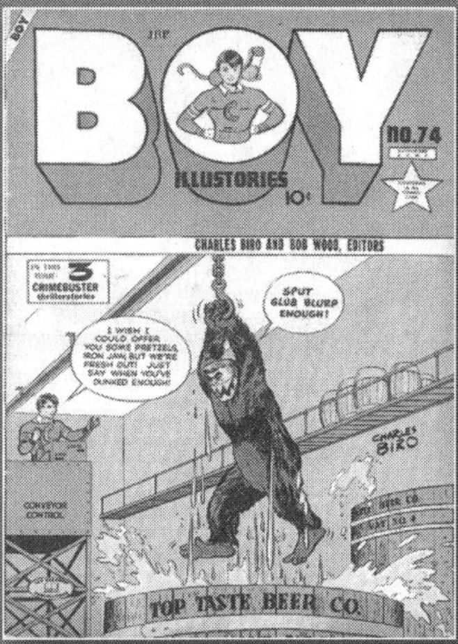
BOY ILLUSTORIES
NO.74
10¢
CHARLES BIRO AND BOB WOOD, EDITORS
CRIMEBUSTER
I WISH I COULD OFFER YOU SOME PRETZELS IRON JAW, BUT THEY'RE FRESH OUT! JUST SAY WHEN YOU'VE DUNKED ENOUGH!
GLUB GLUB BLURP ENOUGH!
TOP TASTE BEER CO.

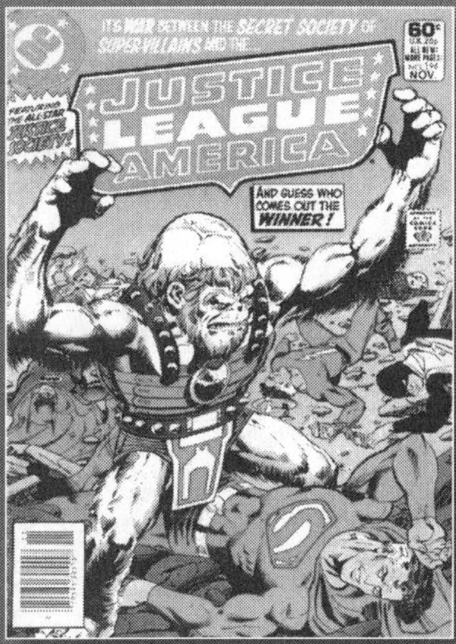
IT'S WAR BETWEEN THE SECRET SOCIETY OF SUPER-VILLAINS AND THE...
60¢
JUSTICE LEAGUE OF AMERICA
AND GUESS WHO COMES OUT THE WINNER!

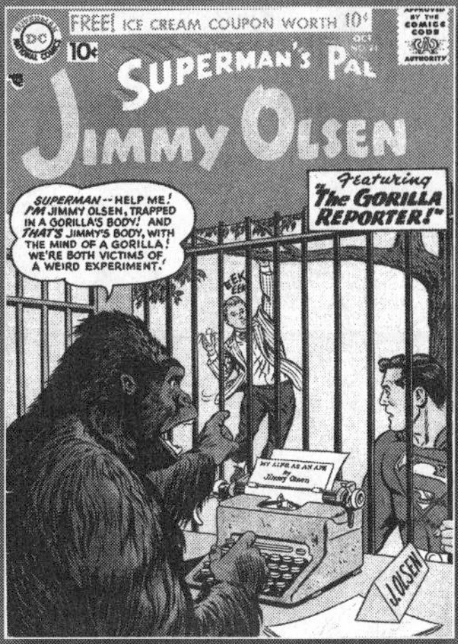
FREE! ICE CREAM COUPON WORTH 10¢
10¢
SUPERMAN'S PAL JIMMY OLSEN
Featuring "The GORILLA REPORTER!"
SUPERMAN--HELP ME! I'M JIMMY OLSEN, TRAPPED IN A GORILLA'S BODY! AND THAT'S JIMMY'S BODY, WITH THE MIND OF A GORILLA! WE'RE BOTH VICTIMS OF A WEIRD EXPERIMENT.
J. OLSEN

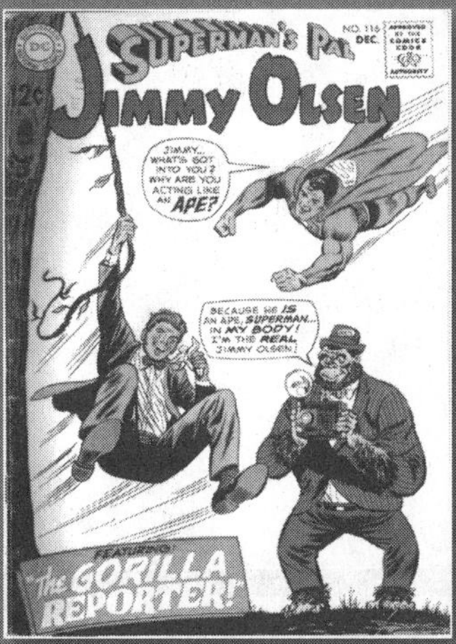
SUPERMAN'S PAL JIMMY OLSEN
12¢
JIMMY... WHAT'S GOT INTO YOU? WHY ARE YOU ACTING LIKE AN APE?
BECAUSE HE IS AN APE, SUPERMAN... IN MY BODY! I'M THE REAL JIMMY OLSEN!
"The GORILLA REPORTER!"

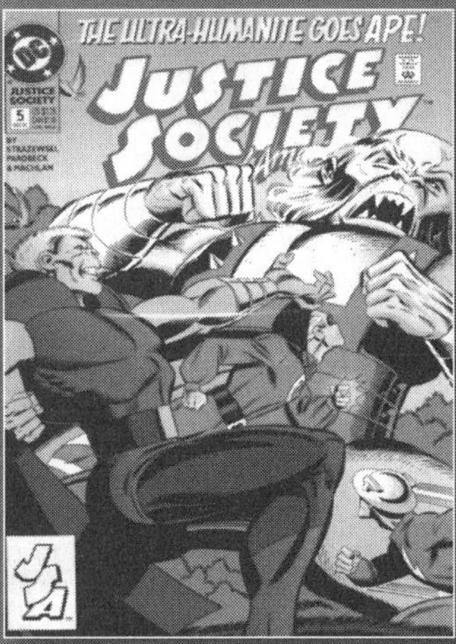
THE ULTRA-HUMANITE GOES APE!
JUSTICE SOCIETY
JSA

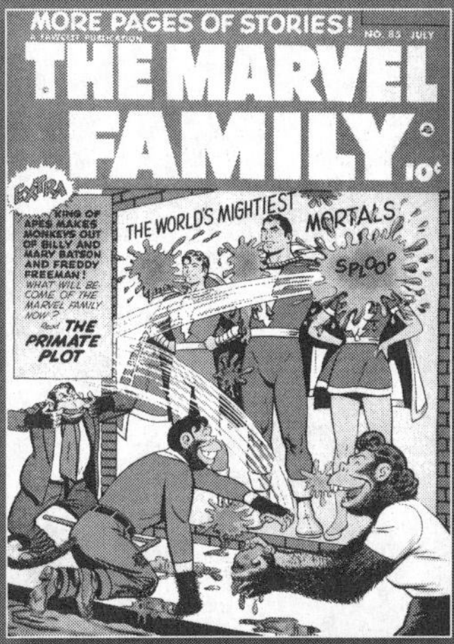
MORE PAGES OF STORIES!
THE MARVEL FAMILY
10¢
EXTRA
KING OF APES MAKES MONKEYS OUT OF BILLY AND MARY BATSON AND FREDDY FREEMAN! WHAT WILL BECOME OF THE MARVEL FAMILY NOW?
THE PRIMATE PLOT
THE WORLD'S MIGHTIEST MORTALS
SPLOOP

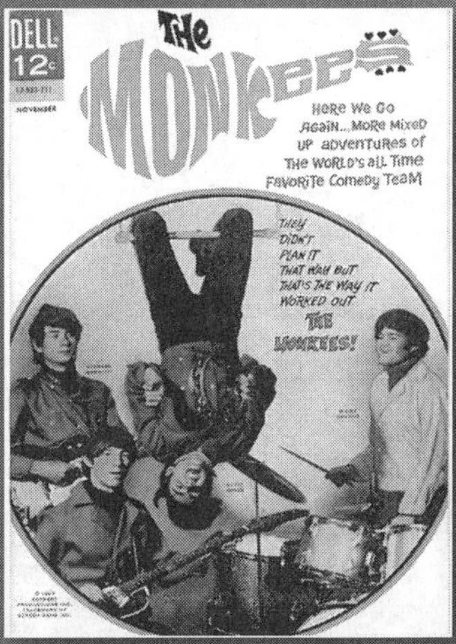
DELL
12¢
The MONKEES
Here We Go Again... More Mixed up adventures of The World's All Time Favorite Comedy Team
THEY DIDN'T PLAN IT THAT WAY BUT THAT'S THE WAY IT WORKED OUT
THE MONKEES!

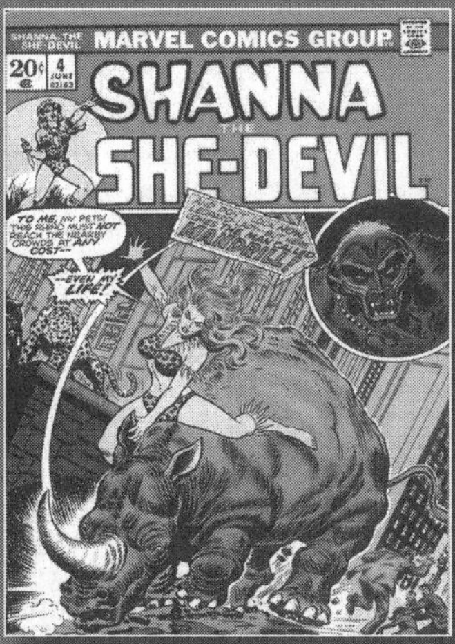
MARVEL COMICS GROUP
20¢
SHANNA THE SHE-DEVIL
TO ME, MY PETS! THIS BEAUTY MUST NOT REACH THE SHADOWY GROUND AT ANY COST--

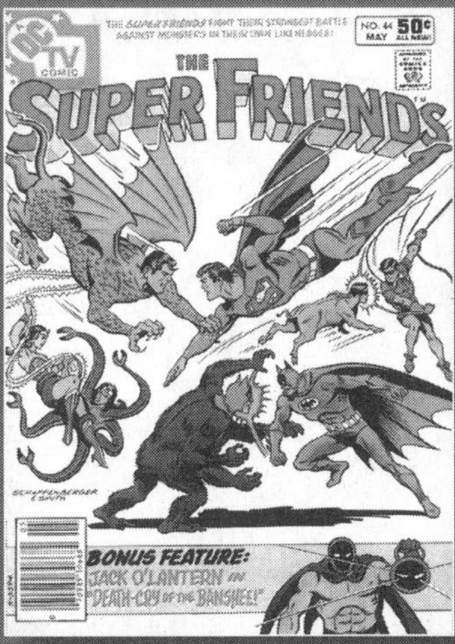
THE SUPER FRIENDS FIGHT THEIR STRONGEST BATTLE AGAINST MONSTERS IN THEIR OWN LIKENESSES!
50¢
THE SUPER FRIENDS
BONUS FEATURE: JACK O'LANTERN in "DEATH-CRY OF THE BANSHEE!"

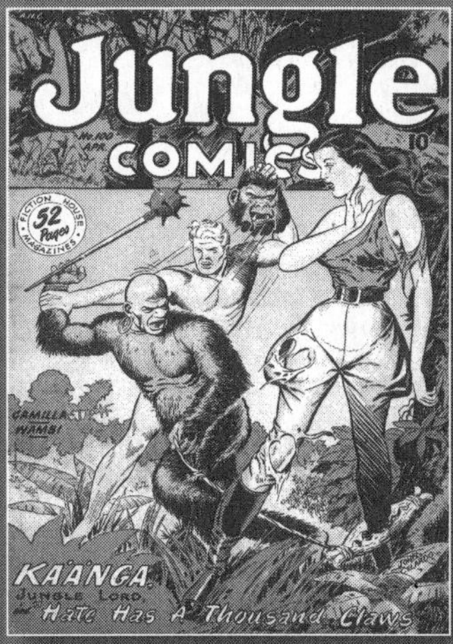
Jungle COMICS
10¢
52 Pages
KAÄNGA JUNGLE LORD, in Hate Has A Thousand Claws

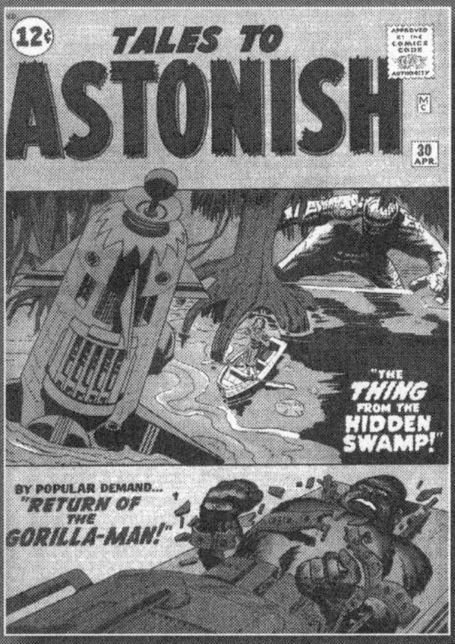
12¢
TALES TO ASTONISH
30 APR.
"THE THING FROM THE HIDDEN SWAMP!"
BY POPULAR DEMAND... "RETURN OF THE GORILLA-MAN!"

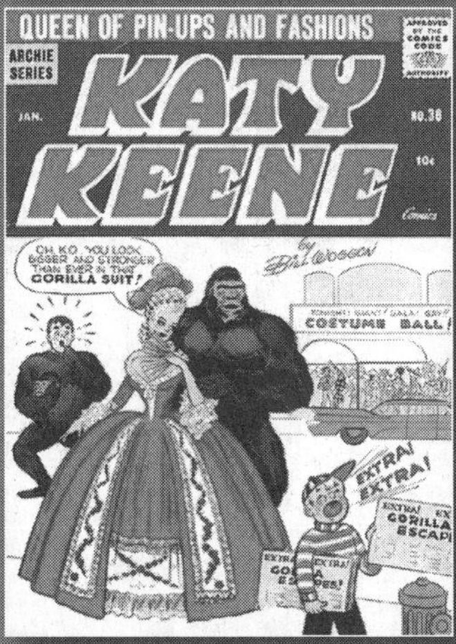
QUEEN OF PIN-UPS AND FASHIONS
ARCHIE SERIES
KATY KEENE
NO. 30
10¢
OH, KO, YOU LOOK BIGGER AND STRONGER THAN EVER IN THAT GORILLA SUIT!
COSTUME BALL!
EXTRA! EXTRA!

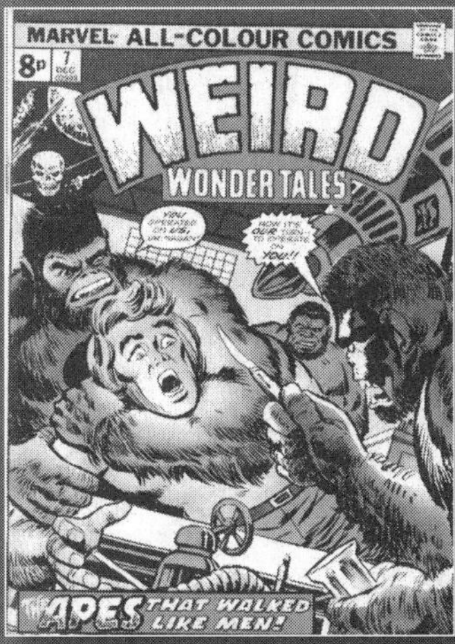
MARVEL ALL-COLOUR COMICS
8p
WEIRD WONDER TALES
THE APES THAT WALKED LIKE MEN!

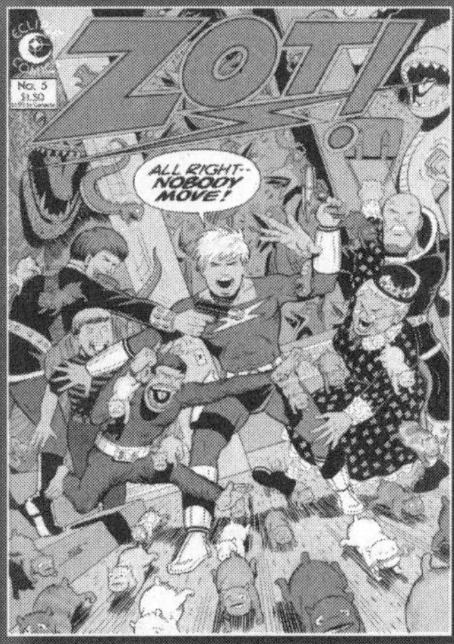
ZOT!
ALL RIGHT-- NOBODY MOVE!

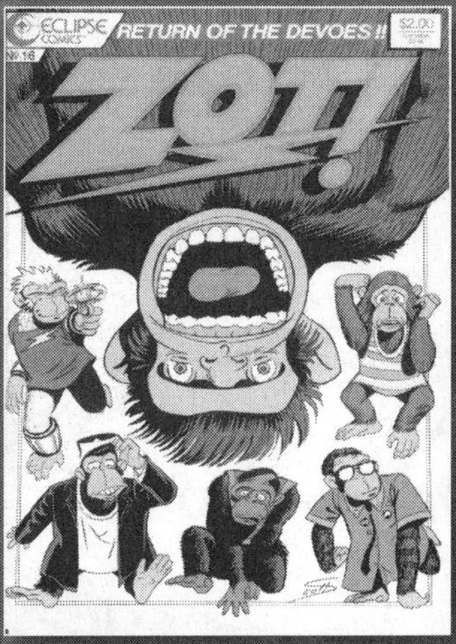
ECLIPSE COMICS
RETURN OF THE DEVOES!!
$2.00
ZOT!

APE
Q with NICK CARDY

Conducted by telephone on August 22, 2006

SPOTTED AMONG THE APES IN:

Jungle Comics (Sheena), *Tarzan* daily strip, *Congo Bill*,
"Experiment 1000" in *House of Secrets #6*,
miscellaneous gorilla covers

OTHER CAREER HIGHLIGHTS:

Lady Luck (for Will Eisner's *The Spirit*),
*The Legends of Daniel Boone,
Aquaman, Teen Titans, Bat Lash,
The Brave and the Bold*,
hundreds of 1970s DC Comics covers,
the illustrated biography *The Art of Nick Cardy*
by John Coates with Nick Cardy
(Vanguard Productions, 1999)

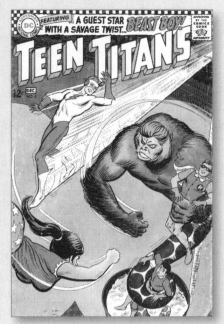

Most fans think of you as an artist of pretty girls, or of *Aquaman* or *Teen Titans*, but you drew a lot of apes during your career. Do you remember the first time you drew an ape in a comic?

I'm trying to think back to where I did an ape in the early years. At Fiction House, I did a *Jumbo* thing, but I don't have any copies of any of those.

The earliest example I found was your cover to Fiction House's *Jumbo Comics* #53, from 1943, with Sheena fighting a trio of mandrills.

The thing is, I know I've drawn gorillas. When I started *Tarzan*, I said, "Oh, boy, now I'm gonna do animals."

When you took on the *Tarzan* strip in 1950, your first five dailies featured a scruffy trapper who was snaring monkeys by placing food inside hollowed-out coconuts.

It was the first week... There was the scene where Tarzan was gently removing a monkey's hands out of the coconut, and I made that an emblem for Tarzan.

It was a nice drawing, you know? There was the rope part, where Tarzan was swinging through the trees over a hippopotamus, and this little monkey comes screaming at him—but Tarzan's with the monkey *just that week*. After that, Tarzan goes into the *desert…*

So you only got to draw Tarzan of the Apes *with* apes for five days…!

Yeah. And when Tarzan was in the desert, I put animals in the story—like whenever you see a African movie where a truck is going along on a safari, and you see elephants and things in the foreground. But in the desert, there aren't so many animals, so I brushed up on a lot of horses.

Nick Cardy's first week of 1950s *Tarzan* continuities, the artist's only opportunity to draw apes during his stint on the strip. © 2007 ERB.

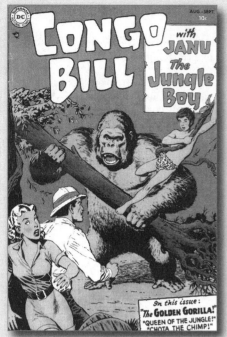

© 2007 DC Comics.

But your next jungle series, *Congo Bill*, gave you plenty of opportunities to draw apes.

I remember there was a cover of *Congo Bill* with an ape holding a tree, using it to go after the hero and the girl (*Congo Bill* #1, Aug.–Sept. 1954). Another one was a girl sitting by a tree with baboons or mandrills or something behind her.

They were mother-and-baby baboons, with "The Girl Who Loved Danger" (*Congo Bill* #3, Dec. 1954–Jan. 1955).

Then there was a whole story with apes. Did you see that?

That's my favorite *Congo Bill* story! "Gorilla City" (issue #6, June–July 1955), with Bill and Janu the Jungle Boy held captive by talking gorillas.

[The gorillas] didn't want to hurt anybody, they just wanted to take off. They were repairing a rocket or something.

(SPOILER ALERT!) That was the big surprise at the end of the story: They weren't intelligent Earth apes, they were aliens.

It was almost like Planet of the Apes got lost in space. [*laughter*]

What reference did you use when drawing apes?

When I did gorillas or apes, I went to the Museum of Natural History in New York City, and they referred me to the room with all the records of people who worked for the museum who had been on safaris. They had records… you could see their photos. When I did *Tarzan*, I wanted to make sure that the monkeys I drew were from Africa, and not monkeys from South America… or, you don't put tigers in Africa, you see. But the *writer* put them in!

Who was the *Congo Bill* writer? Those stories were done before DC listed story credits.

I don't know who wrote them… I don't remember. He was a good storyteller, but he knew absolutely nothing at all about animals, nothing at all! There's one scene where Congo Bill and his sidekick, little Janu, are looking for something and he's telling Janu to "Get on the hyena! We need help, and the hyena is the fastest animal in the jungle. Go get help." Before I drew Janu on the hyena, I said, "The hyena isn't the fastest; everybody knows that the cheetah is the fastest!" The writer said, "Oh, for—you're bothering me with little details," so I went ahead and drew what he asked for.

There's another scene; I think it's in the same story. Congo Bill and Janu were supposed to cross a plain, but they couldn't cross it because there was a rhinoceros. The writer wanted me to draw the rhinoceros attacking a zebra, their favorite meat. I tried to tell him that rhinoceroses are herbivorous—they don't eat meat!

But *I* got the fan mail that said, "Don't you know that cheetahs are the fastest animals?"… and all that. [*laughter*]

Let's not forget that you drew Chota

the Chimp, the pet of Bill's sidekick Janu the Jungle Boy. Chota was *Congo Bill*'s answer to Cheeta, the comic-relief chimp of the *Tarzan* movies.

Oh, yeah. I didn't remember Chota until you just mentioned him. I did well over 500 covers for DC, you see! [*laughs*]

Four out of the seven issues of *Congo Bill* had some kind of ape on the cover. Was there *really* an editorial directive in the 1950s from DC to spotlight gorillas on covers, or is that just an urban legend?

When Julie Schwartz was an editor at DC, he said, "I found that if you put a gorilla on a cover, it will sell." And I don't know if it was his idea or not, because everybody takes credit, you know?

You did a few gorilla covers for Julie Schwartz.

I remember some covers I did with gorillas. One is where a gorilla is running toward the reader and he's running past the jury and he's whacking the banister—he's breaking it and he's saying, "I'm not guilty!" (*Strange Adventures* #239, Nov.–Dec. 1972). And there's another one where a gorilla is borrowing books from a librarian (*From Beyond the Unknown* #23, July–Aug. 1973).

You actually drew a *story*, as well as its cover, featuring an intelligent gorilla: "Experiment 1000," in *House of Secrets* #6 (Sept.–Oct. 1957; reprinted in *The Unexpected* #160, Nov. –Dec. 1974).

© 2007 DC Comics.

House of Secrets #6 (Sept.–Oct. 1957).
The talking gorilla in the Cardy-illustrated "Experiment 1000" is Bill, a lab ape that gained brains from exposure to experimental compounds. © 2007 DC Comics.

Is that the cover where there are two human beings coming into a room, with guns, and a gorilla is going out the window?

That's it. You seem to enjoy drawing apes.

© 2007 DC Comics.

I love drawing apes because first of all, I like to draw them the way they are, the way they live, the way they act, and their expressions. You have these apes with very big eyebrows; while they're sitting there and someone's talking, you can see their eyes shift and see expressions in their eyes. Their heads don't shift, just their eyes, following you.

Second, they're gentle; when a little baby comes along to this big mammoth ape, with his wrist, he just pushes him away. And he comes back and tries to climb on his back, he doesn't push the kid off, he just gradually gets up and strolls through the trees and he sits there. It's such a nonviolent feeling, except when another male comes along and starts fooling around—then it's *war*.

Did you ever see that movie… this is a true thing… where they had gorillas in big pits [at the zoo], and they had big water moats to keep the people separated from the gorillas, but you could see them in their native habitat? And a little boy fell in, and the gorillas came down and looked at the boy like he was one of their own. They were really concerned about the little boy. I think that one gorilla picked the child up and held it in his arms. It showed that they weren't beasts and always killing. The human beings are the only ones who do that.

I do recall that being on the news a few years back.

Another thing, when you're drawing an animal, you have to know what its gait is. You can't make a horse run like a camel. Because a camel runs with two sides of his legs at one time, whereas most other animals alternate the left foot and hind foot. They start with their left front leg and the right back leg coming up to meet under the body. So every animal has his own thing. Gorillas have their own thing—when they make a dash, they're fast. And another thing, gorillas always go on all fours.

With animals, I always try to do accurate things. The gorillas that I did were a far cry from what you saw in *Abbott and Costello*, you know.

No fat guys in baggy gorilla suits. [laughter]
    Unless I've overlooked something, throughout the '60s and '70s the rest of your apes comics art was on covers only.

I remember an *Aquaman* cover with ape arms coming in at Aquaman (issue #28, July–Aug. 1966) and a *Superboy* cover (#183, Mar. 1972) with Superboy as a baby in the jungle, lording over gorillas. And I did an *Action* cover (*Action Comics*

© 2007 DC Comics.

#424, June 1973) with a gorilla (Grodd) spinning Superman around by his cape.

Nick, about the only DC books that *didn't* have apes on their covers were the *romance* comics. You never did a romance comic with a girl kissing a gorilla, did you?

Well, no. She would've been really hard up!

© 2007 DC Comics.

Q with JEFF PARKER

Conducted via email on August 29, 2006

SPOTTED AMONG THE APES IN:

writer/artist of "Ape Company" in *Heroic Tales #10* (Lone Star Press, 2001), writer of *Agents of Atlas* miniseries starring Gorilla Man (Marvel, 2006–2007), miscellaneous monkey drawings (including commissions and an Altoid/Curious George ad)

OTHER CAREER HIGHLIGHTS:

The Interman, X-Men: First Class (writer)

What got you interested in drawing monkeys?

I don't know—I can't understand why everybody wouldn't want to draw them! But maybe it was a steady diet of Silver Age DC comics as a child, which presented a world where monkeys figure in disproportionately higher than otherwise. Repeat viewings of *Planet of the Apes* are a likely suspect, too. I bet I'm saying exactly the same things everyone else is, huh.

Well, those *are* some popular influences. So, when did you do your first ape drawing?

As a four-year-old, I think I tried to imitate H. A. Rey's Curious George when I wasn't copying *Dennis the Menace*.

How did you come up with the Ape Company concept?

That's one of those stories that just starts playing itself completely in your head, and if you don't make it come to life, your Muse may abandon you forever. I was laying in bed laughing as the whole thing came to me, and I got up in the middle of the night and laid it all out in thumbnail form.

Are each of the "Congo-Happy Joes" of Ape Company ape-analogs of Easy Company soldiers?

No, it's just a general gestalt of all the Joe Kubert stories I ever read.

Where on a map of Europe would I find Ape Company's St. Simian?

France—it's a real place! It's actually Simeon, but once I bumbled across that I had to bend reality to my needs—how could I not?

What type of research did you conduct before drawing the primates of Ape Company?

Even on something that's a lark like that, I pore through books and try to get up to snuff on nomenclature and equipment and all. I think the more fantastic your premise, the more you need to shore it up with real-life detail.

No monkey medic could patch up poor Red. From Parker's "Ape Company."

© 2007 Jeff Parker.

Have you ever, uh, petted a monkey?

Just an organ-grinder's monkey, which pulled down my sock at the mall after I gave it money. Now it seems weird to me that I ever saw an actual organ grinder with a monkey—where did I grow up…?

Did you pitch Ape Company to any publishers other than Lone Star Press?

No. There were no suitable anthologies happening that year, but I knew fellow chimpfan Bill Williams of Lone Star (*www.lonestarpress.com*) would enjoy it.

Any chance that Ape Company will return?

I think the world can only take about ten pages of an ape troop. Incidentally, that is the actual group term for a bunch of apes, a troop. Coincidence?

That's also the group term for a bunch of scouts!
Are you familiar with Joe Kubert and Robert Kanigher's Sgt. Gorilla from "You Can't Pin a Medal on a Gorilla," from *Star Spangled War Stories* #126 (Apr.–May 1966)?

I wasn't until later. Some band should use the name Sgt. Gorilla!

You obviously like gorillas with guns, since Gorilla Man packs lots of heat in *Agents of Atlas*. Since the character's original appearances predate you, when did you discover Gorilla Man?

Probably in the *What If?* that featured the

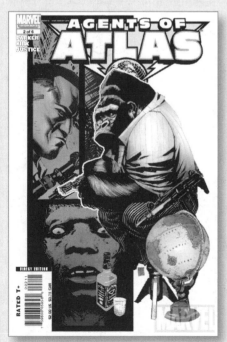

© 2007 Marvel Characters, Inc.

Secret Avengers (issue #9, June 1978), though there's decent odds that I read the reprint of his origin in *Chamber of Chills* (#23, Aug. 1976). I can't remember, though. It's as if he's always been there.

ALL YOU REALLY NEEDED WAS ME ANYWAY. AND A @#%*ING PARKING PLACE!

HER ENEMIES KEPT HER BODY IN ICE, THREATENING TO DESECRATE IT IF HER DAUGHTER TRIED TO CLAIM THE LEMURIAN THRONE.

© 2007 Marvel Characters, Inc.

What, out of your varied resumé, do you credit with leading Marvel editor Mark Paniccia to offer scripting *Agents of Atlas* to you?

It really comes down to another proposal I did that didn't go anywhere, for a *Doc Samson* miniseries. My pitch was laden with pulp sensibilities brought to the modern day, which Mark thought would wear well with the '50s Avengers.

Did *Agents of Atlas* penciler Leonard Kirk share your passion for drawing apes?

Leonard Kirk essentially *is* Gorilla Man, for all intents and purposes. I'm sure he does sweat over the drawing, but he brings the character to life in a way that looks effortless and completely natural. There were some prime Gorilla Man characterizations by Kirk in issue #3.

Past storylines (by other writers) have included Gorilla Man's hope to be restored to his original human form of Kenneth Hale. Do you think that Hale's now comfortable with permanently being a gorilla?

He wouldn't turn down the chance to be human, but at this point he's been a gorilla longer than he was a man. So you're not going to hear him grouse about it too much these days. Thanks to Marvel Boy's headband, we see [Hale] occasionally as the Fred Ward-esque Joe he used to be.

Do you have any plans—or hopes—for Gorilla Man as a solo character, post-*Agents of Atlas*?

I really like him best in context of the team, but I have a feeling now that he's being established, he'll be popping into other Marvel books.

Aside from Gorilla Man, who's your favorite comic-book ape?

Grodd. I love that he wants to conquer the world and that somehow his natural enemy is a man with super-speed. And I love that his home is called Gorilla City.

If you had to choose comics' all-time best ape artist, who would it be?

There's so many good ones: Kubert, obviously; Hal Foster; and, of course, Frank Cho draws a mean monkey. But I would love to see a short project that called for Mark Schultz to draw a ton of apes, he's so good with them. All animals, really.

Tell me about your near-miss "curiously strong" Altoids ad with Curious George.

Actually, that got used! Much later, so I never saw it, but they ended up doing the double-brand ad where George is holding a giant tin of the breathmints. I was visiting the Harris Publications offices and Maureen McTeague had the full-page ad from a magazine up on her wall and I blurted, "I did that!" When you're working in advertising, so many of the things you storyboard or plan out take forever before they get to the final stage, and then there's no one around to tell the people at the starting point how it all turned out. It was

BBRRAAKKAKAKAKAKAKAKAKAKAK! THREE!

THE HELL IS UP WITH THAT JEEP, MAGE? WE LOST ANY MEN?

Ken Hale, the gorilla with guns, from *Agents of Atlas*; written by Jeff Parker, penciled by Leonard Kirk, inked by Kris Justice.

© 2007 Marvel Characters, Inc.

a day of me drawing little images of George and Altoids cans that I assumed was dropped. [*Editor's note:* To see Jeff Parker's Curious George/Altoids art, visit *www.parkerspace.com* and click the monkey-head icon.]

Were you wearing a yellow hat when you drew George?

In spirit. Though I would never wear a hat specifically to trap a monkey like his friend "the Man" did. Why does he wear a sombrero anyway? He's French!

Kamandi, the Last Boy on Earth encounters a gorilla soldier in this Jack Kirby pencil illustration, probably an unused cover to

We expected a future of flying cars, push-button dinners, and silver lamé jumpsuits!
Instead we became the naked prey! All on a topsy-turvy world of talking apes...

WHERE MAN ONCE STOOD SUPREME!

Planet of the Apes exploits our deepest fears—that our evolutionary cousins, the ones we've kept in cages and in cute theatrical costumes, will one day revolt and make monkeys out of us all. Can you *blame* them, after *B. J. and the Bear*?

Planet of the Apes (or POTA, an acronym first coined on a Marvel Comics letters page, as Marvel UK scholar Robin Kirby reminds us) may be packaged as a sci-fi property, and its rich continuity of musty scrolls and pedantic lawgivers may attract the fantasy buff, but make no mistake about it, it's the ultimate *horror story*. Sort of like Al Gore's *An Inconvenient Truth*. We should have seen this coming. It's a madhouse! A *madhouse!*

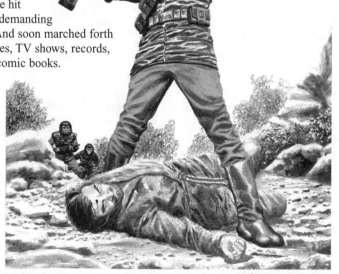

Planet of the Apes is also the poster child for franchise expansion. It started with a somewhat maligned novel that limped toward becoming a surprise hit movie, which led to men in suits demanding more movies with apes in suits. And soon marched forth an invasion of POTA action figures, TV shows, records, lunchboxes, jigsaw puzzles, and comic books.

Let's test your POTA IQ: Can you name the first artist to draw Planet of the Apes in comic-book form?

You might guess Mike Ploog, or George Tuska. Maybe cover painter Bob Larkin.

Wrong, wrong, and wrong again.

Before this question is answered, let's backtrack for a quick recap of the genesis of the world where apes rule and humans are hunting targets.

POTA © 2007 20th Century Fox.

YOU LED ME AROUND ON A LEASH!

French author Pierre Boulle (1912–1994) was best known for his 1952 novel *The Bridge on the River Kwai* (which spawned an Oscar-winning film adaptation in 1957) when, in 1963, he published *La planète des singes*—or, as translated into English, *Monkey Planet*. The author's tenth novel, the story that would soon become known as *Planet of the Apes* featured journalist Ulysse Mérou, who accompanied scientist Professor Antelle and physician Arthur Levain on a space/time sojourn to the solar system of the sun Betelgeuse. They ultimately found the planet Earth-esque planet Soror, home to primitive humans and intelligent apes. Boulle's simian society was more civilized than the movie version etched into the pop-culture psyche: Its apes dressed in clothing contemporary to that of the author's late-20th-century day, resided in homes and toiled in highrises, and drove automobiles. Yet the basic building blocks of the world we know today as the Planet of the Apes were there: a societal divide among chimpanzees, orangutans, and gorillas; the research-scientist chimps Zira and Cornelius; the scholarly orangutan Dr. Zaius; and the wild-girl love interest Nova.

Planet of the Apes began spinning its way to the big screen a few years later, when

Hollywood producer Arthur P. Jacobs scored the film rights for Boulle's book. Without a script or even a treatment, the infectiously enthusiastic Jacobs wooed Charlton Heston to the project through a verbal pitch accompanied only by several production drawings. Heston lured director Franklin J. Schaffner to the in-development film, but despite the superstar actor's involvement, trepidation existed within Tinseltown: Science fiction was not commercially successful at the time (remember, this was pre-Lucas Hollywood), concern was voiced over the prohibitive cost of the movie, and there was an outright fear that audiences would not take talking apes seriously.

To counter the latter concern, a short test film co-starring Heston as a trapped-in-a-world-he-never-made human, astronaut Colonel Thomas (yes, *Thomas*), and legendary screen gangster Edward G. Robinson as Dr. Zaius was prepped, currying the support of 20th Century Fox head Richard Zanuck. Zanuck procured the necessary funding ($5.8 million, considerably less than what Jacobs might've hoped for), and the producer grabbed *The Twilight Zone*'s twist-ending master Rod Serling to pen the screenplay (Boulle himself also lobbied for that assignment). Ultimately Heston's Colonel Thomas became Colonel Taylor, Maurice Evans was recast as Zaius due to Robinson's adverse reaction to ape makeup, and Roddy McDowall and Kim Hunter were signed to portray popular primates Cornelius and Zira. Screenwriter Michael Wilson reworked the story into its final shooting script, although Serling is responsible for its signature moment, Taylor's discovery that this planet of apes is in fact Earth of the future. Shot between May and August of 1967, *Planet of the Apes*—producer Jacobson's follow-up release to his 1967 kiddie movie *Dr. Dolittle*, which, coincidentally, starred a man who talked to the animals—opened on February 8, 1968. It eventually earned a jaw-dropping (for the day) box office of $32.6 million.

HUMAN SEE, HUMAN DO

As Jacobs had to toil to convince Zanuck to make his movie version of *Apes*, comic-book houses similarly required persuasion to adapt the movie to funnybooks. Gold Key Comics, responsible for the lion's share of movie and TV adaptations of the late 1960s, skipped the first movie. Once the buoyant box office of *POTA* inspired 20th Century Fox to hurry a sequel into production, Gold Key jumped on board.

Beneath the Planet of the Apes, starring James Franciscus as human flyboy Brent (accompanied by a reluctant Heston reprising, in a limited capacity, his Taylor role), hit theaters in June 1970, with a Gold Key adaptation produced by (in answer to the POTA IQ question) the Alberto Giolitti studio. As noted in Chapter 2,

The first POTA comic book, Gold Key's *Beneath the Planet of the Apes* adaptation from 1970.

POTA © 2007 20th Century Fox.

Giolitti and his studio of artists were also responsible for Gold Key's 1968 adaptation of *King Kong*. For some, the Gold Key comic's photo cover is more exciting than the pedestrian interiors (presumably, Giolitti's studio also provided the script, adapting from the screenplay), but this one-shot does indeed hold the distinction of being POTA's first foray into the comics world.

A PLANET WHERE APES EVOLVED FROM MEN?

The second artist to draw the series was… no, not Larkin, Ploog, or Tuska… but *Jack Kirby*. Okay, that that's not entirely accurate, but Kirby's title *Kamandi, the Last Boy on Earth* was launched with a Nov. 1972 cover date, and *Apes*' imprint upon "the King's" DC Comics creation is indisputable.

As related by Kirby's one-time protégé Mark Evanier in *The Jack Kirby Collector* #40 (Summer 2004), in late 1971 (or thereabouts) Kirby and then-publisher of DC, Carmine Infantino, were chatting by phone about the growing film and merchandising success of Planet of the Apes; since Gold Key's adaptation of the second film, the franchise had expanded with *Escape from the Planet of the Apes* (1971), and 1972's *Conquest of the Planet of the Apes* was on its way. Infantino had inquired about DC obtaining the rights to a *POTA* comic but was unsuccessful in his pursuit (probably due to the expense of the license), so the

© 2007 DC Comics.

pair agreed that a new concept that borrowed (but not *too* closely) from the Apes mythology might be a worthwhile project for Kirby. Before long, Kirby dusted off his unrealized *Kamandi of* the Caves 1950s' comic *strip* and recreated it into a comic *book* starring a long-haired, teenage protagonist fighting to stay alive on a future Earth populated by "Beasts That Act Like Men!" and "Men Who Act Like Beasts!" One need to look no further than Kirby's iconic cover to *Kamandi* #1 for proof of POTA's mark upon Kirby's dystopian world—its depiction of a junked Statue of Liberty might have earned Rod Serling a "special thanks" credit. And while apes were far from the only intelligent animals in Kamandi's world—other creatures in the mix included tigers, dogs, rats, and bats—gorillas occasionally tangled with the Last Boy on Earth, even in non-Kirby Kamandi adventures including the Batman/

The Norman Mingo cover to *MAD* #173 (Mar. 1973). *MAD* © 2007 EC Publications. POTA © 2007 20th Century Fox.

Kamandi team-up in *The Brave and the Bold* #120 (July 1975) and the time-displacement tale in *Superman/ Batman* #16 (late Feb. 2005).

And so the actual second comics artist to draw POTA was… Norman Mingo, on the cover of *MAD* magazine #173 (Mar. 1973). That issue featured a lampoon of the Apes craze, "The Milking of the Planet That Went Ape," by drawn by POTA's third comics artist, Mort Drucker.

YOU MANIACS! YOU BLEW IT UP!

During the winter of 1973, the first three *POTA* movies were broadcast on network television, netting colossal ratings— especially the first film. This was noticed by the editor-in-chief of Marvel Comics, Roy Thomas, who was fundamental in Marvel's then-recent transformation of licensed properties, most notably Conan the Barbarian, into successful comic books. "I recall going to lunch with a representative of the movie company one day in Manhattan," Thomas says. "The movie *Planet of the Apes* had had spectacular ratings when it had been shown for the first time recently on TV, and a deal was struck for what soon became both color and black-and-white comics versions, as a TV series was to follow." This was during the era of Marvel's line of black-and-white magazines, containing slightly edgier material and distributed beyond the spinner racks housing the kid-friendly four-color titles.

Marvel's plan was to produce both adaptations of the *Apes* movies and new material which expanded the film mythos, augmented by text and photo features that explored the cinematic versions of POTA. Thomas picked Marvel's go-to writer *du jour*, Gerry Conway, for the project. After crafting a brief outline for non-movie continuity, Conway bowed out of the project due to overcommitment. That problem was easily solved: Relative

newcomer Doug Moench was assigned the *Apes* startup, because Thomas had observed "that Doug could use a series, could turn out lots of work, and was a good writer whom I saw as best better suited to non-super-hero work."

That reassignment was a mere bump in what would quickly become a rocky road to the first issue's release, as what Thomas calls "a couple of mini-disasters for the company" occurred. The ink was barely dry on Marvel's contract with 20th Century Fox when the licensor forbade the use of Charlton Heston's likeness, to avoid profit sharing with or a lawsuit from the actor. Penciler George Tuska drew a generic heroic figure as Colonel Taylor in Moench's first installment of the original movie's adaptation. Moench also introduced his long-running "Terror on the Planet of the Apes" storyline, drawn by Mike Ploog. Nervous over Fox's sluggish delay in approving issue #1, Marvel rushed the magazine to the printer—and was soon informed of Fox's objections to Tuska's Taylor being too Heston-like, despite the artist's

This Bob Larkin cover painting graced the first issue of Marvel's B&W *Planet of the Apes* #1 (Aug. 1974). POTA © 2007 20th Century Fox.

precautions. Marvel was forced to shred the first print run, frantically redraw the Taylor faces in the adaptation, and return to press. Yet at last, in the summer of 1974, the black-and-white comics magazine *Planet of the Apes* #1 (Aug. 1974) finally hit the stands.

HONORBOUND TO EXPAND THE FRONTIERS OF KNOWLEDGE

Curiously, despite 20th Century Fox's gorilla-fisted policing of the rendering of Taylor, their scrutiny of Doug Moench's original stories was a game of "see no evil, hear no evil, speak no evil." As Marvel's *POTA* series progressed through its 29-issue run, the Counterculture writer ran amuck with offbeat storylines in the backup strip (which supported the film adaptations in most issues), covering a range of controversial topics and tiptoeing from what the licensor probably might have wanted (see the accompanying Q & Ape with Moench). By creative whim or deadline necessity, the writer occasionally sidestepped his initial serial, "Terror on the Planet of the Apes" (issues #1–4, 6, 8, 11, 13–14, 19–20, 23, 26–28), for the single tales or series "Evolution's Nightmare" (#5), "Kingdom on an Island of the Apes" (#9–10, 21), "Future History Chronicles" (#12, 15, 17, 24, 29), and "Quest for the Planet of the Apes" (a two-parter in #22). The majority of these stories were illustrated either by Ploog or by Tom Sutton. Will Eisner-trained Ploog's lush backgrounds and supple linework made Moench's *Apes* tales intoxicatingly seductive yet at the same time stark and haunting, while Sutton approached the material and the B&W format's larger pages with gusto, saturating each page, and each panel, with extraordinarily detailed artwork.

Moench also adapted each of the movies for Marvel's *POTA* magazine: *Planet of the Apes* was serialized in issues #1–6, *Beneath the Planet of the Apes* in #7–11, *Escape from the Planet of the Apes* in #12–16, *Conquest of the Planet of the Apes* in #17–21, and *Battle for the Planet of the Apes* in #22–28. The first two movie adaptations were reprinted—edited, with panel alterations, from copies of the original art made before the addition of the characteristic washtones used in the black-and-white magazines—in the newsstand-distributed color comic *Adventures on the Planet of the Apes*, which ran 11 issues beginning with an Oct. 1975 cover-dated first issue. Two additional comics publishers cribbed elements from POTA for new titles: Atlas/Seaboard's *Planet of Vampires* #1 (Feb. 1975) lasted three issues, while Charlton's *Doomsday + 1* #1 (July 1975), with art by newcomer John Byrne, lasted six (with reprint revivals following in later years as Byrne's star rose). And Gerry Conway finally got to write talking apes (as well as other beasts) by introducing them into his futuristic DC title *Hercules Unbound* in its fourth issue (Apr.–May 1976).

Recalling the TV airing which prompted Marvel's licensing of POTA, Roy Thomas reveals, "I understood later that apparently bad weather over much of the country had contributed a lot to the high ratings by keeping an inordinate number of people indoors that night… and there never was the kind of boom for *Apes* that we all thought. Still, the books did okay for a while." In addition to performing below expectations, the problems that plagued the book from the get-go continued, including "when two issues (after I was no longer editor-in-chief, thank goodness) evidently had the same cover date, so that one of them had an on-sale date of about 20 minutes."

And *then* there was the ravenous demand for material…

ALL MY LIFE I'VE AWAITED YOUR COMING

The Brits' Beatles invaded the US in 1964, and ten years later the Yanks returned the favor by shipping them their Apes.

Marvel's *POTA* #1 was quickly followed by the September 13, 1974 premiere of the CBS-TV *Planet of the Apes* series, a short-lived program that might have lasted longer than its 14 episodes were its production costs not so high. When the series "was first shown across the ITV network in Britain" (except, strangely, Scotland), "viewers couldn't get enough of the show," writes Rob Kirby in his forthcoming [to be published by Quality Communications, with online teasers at *www.qualitycommunications.co.uk*] history/index book on Marvel's UK comics line, originally magazine-sized black-and-white color comics reprinting material produced in the States and distributed across the British Isles. On October 26, 1974, the first UK edition of *Planet of the Apes* was released—and published *weekly*! "It seems that nobody had given any consideration to the fact that they didn't yet have a sufficiently large enough inventory of material for the UK comic to stay comfortably behind the States," Kirby writes. "Inevitably, the reprints in our weekly version began catching up with the most recent stories appearing in the US monthly magazine, and after only 22 weeks both comics had achieved synchronicity."

APING APES

While Marvel UK churned out new covers to meet the demands of a weekly schedule, after electing to use almost none of the US painted covers, even the lightning-fast typing hands of Doug Moench couldn't maintain this breakneck pace. More story content was needed, and needed *yesterday*.

Enter: Apeslayer!

Lifting material from its own *Amazing Adventures* series, featuring the sci-fi/sword-of-sorcery hybrid "Killraven" concept in stories loosely based upon H. G. Wells' *War of the Worlds*, "Killraven" became "Apeslayer" beginning in issue #23 (March 29, 1975). "In double-quick time they had to re-dialogue and overdraw photo-stats of the original artwork," writes Rob Kirby, "converting the cast into new characters and their protagonists into apes of various guises." As weird as this sounds, Apeslayer wasn't the first time a comic-book publisher performed such an act of grave-robbing—just a few years earlier, to satisfy a demand for *Archie*-like teen titles, DC raided its vaults and transformed its cobwebbed early '60s TV tie-in *The Many Loves of Dobie Gillis* into *Windy and Willy*, which spun off into its own series after a preview in *Showcase* #81 (Mar. 1969). DC's series at least benefited from its original artist, *Angel and the Ape* co-creator Bob Oksner, performing the necessary cosmetic surgery to make over Dobie and his beatnik sidekick Maynard G. Krebs into the hip Willy and the hippie Windy, but Apeslayer's alteration of the Killraven art of Neal Adams, Howard Chaykin, and Herb Trimpe was jarring for those familiar with the originals. Thankfully, the insertion of the Apeslayer stories corrected the disparity between the US' and UK's inventory, sparing readers further comics cannibalizations such as "The Tomb of Ape-ula" or "Peter Primate, the Spectacular Spider-Monkey." To feed the UK's demand Moench was then asked to instigate his run of "Terror" stories and other original serials.

The British Bullpen reprinted every American *POTA* story at least once, printing the film adaptations from copies of the original artwork, made by the UK department the minute new artwork arrived in the office before it was washtoned for US use (which is probably where *Adventures* got its artwork from, Rob Kirby suggests). This led to some small differences of dialogue, as well as several additional pages of strip material later deleted from the US editions due to page restrictions—"making the US edition effectively the reprint one!" Kirby points out.

Also, beginning in 1974, four of the movie adaptations were adapted anew in a series of Power Records narrated-comics releases (which omitted the fourth, *Conquest*; some surmise that its exclusion was due to its violent content being deemed unsuitable for children). Alan Maxwell, co-editor of the UK Apezine *Simian Scrolls*, states that some of the adaptations are credited to "Arvid Knudsen and associates," but that "at least part of the first Power adaptation was drawn by Ernie Chan (Chua)." Power repackaged the POTA records in several forms, which included new sleeve artwork by Chan and Neal Adams.

While Marvel didn't adapt material from the *Apes* CBS-TV into comics form, Brown Watson did, releasing three hardcover *POTA Annuals* in the mid-1970s. Additionally, the TV series was adapted into Spanish-language comics by a publisher in Argentina.

In 1976 the Apes fad began to peter out. The UK's title merged with another sagging series, becoming *Planet of the Apes and Dracula Lives!* with issue #88 (June 23, 1976). This staved off cancellation of *POTA/DL!* until #123 (Feb. 3, 1977), when the Apes strip was then shunted into Marvel's premiere anthology

The Neal Adams/Frank Chiaramonte splash to the Killraven story in *Amazing Adventures* #18 (May 1973) was reworked into Apeslayer for the UK's *POTA* #23 (Mar. 29, 1976).
Apeslayer © 2007 Marvel Characters, Inc. . Courtesy of Rob Kirby.

The Mighty World of Marvel, before being dropped from the comic 16 weeks later following #246 (June 15, 1977)—outdistancing Stateside Marvel's *POTA*, which ended with issue #29 (Feb. 1977). And with the summer 1977 release of Brown Watson's *POTA Annual* #3, Apes comics were now banished to back-issue bins, flea markets, and memories.

SOME APES, IT SEEMS, ARE MORE EQUAL THAN OTHERS

Charles Marshall's memories of POTA's 1970s boom—the stuff of his childhood—led to the realization of his dream project.

In 1990, Marshall was the chief writer of an *Apes* revival for Adventure Comics, an imprint of Malibu Graphics (a.k.a. Malibu Comics). Hoping to capitalize on nostalgia, Adventure's POTA rebirth was from its inception conceived as a franchise: a black-and-white monthly *Planet of the Apes* title aggressively supported by a variety of miniseries. Whereas Moench embellished POTA movie continuity with his fanciful diversions, Marshall took on the responsibility of being *Apes*' next "storygiver." He set the monthly a century after the events of the last movie, *Battle for the Planet of the Apes*, and peppered the film continuity with story material that fed into the first two movies. "I know what's out there and I know what's behind me," Marshall revealed in an interview in *Comics Scene* #13 (June 1990). "I'm just trying to fill up the middle."

In this vein, in *POTA* #1 (Apr. 1990) Marshall and penciler

Kent Burles introduced descendants of the *Battle* characters, such as the chimp Alexander (the grandson of Cornelius and Zira's son Caesar) and a bloodthirsty gorilla named General Ollo (a disciple of the war doctrines of General Aldo). In the four-issue miniseries *Ape City* (Aug.–Nov. 1990), Marshall and penciler M. C. Wyman—in Moench-like "Terror" fashion—unveiled original ideas that included baboon ninjas, a giant ape named Cong, and Terminator-like Vindicators sent from the past on a mission to avert Earth's monkey-planet future. Marshall and Wyman also teamed up for Adventure's first color comic, 1991's four-issue *Ape Nation*, perhaps the oddest comic-book crossover ever (not counting *Archie Meets the Punisher*), between the Planet of the Apes and Alien Nation continuities.

The jewel in the Adventure crown came in the form of a 1991 POTA miniseries titled *Urchak's Folly*, written and penciled by Australian cartoonist Gary Chaloner, an Apes fan since his youth, attracted to the Marvel's series, in part, by his fascination with the art of Mike Ploog. "I'm a long-time admirer of Will Eisner's work and currently working on *Will Eisner's John Law* [an online comic available at *johnlaw.us.com*]," says Chaloner in a November 2006 email. "[Since] Ploog was an Eisner assistant, the stylistic connection must have attracted me."

Chaloner's *Urchak's Folly* was an homage to Apes novelist Pierre Boulle's other classic. "It's *Bridge on the River Kwai* with a time-travel twist," Chaloner explains. "A man from the Victorian era,

Thorne, is transported to the future ruled by apes. In a large, mysterious valley, he's captured by a group of militant gorillas, led by the insane Urchak, whose expedition west from Ape City has been blocked by a river. The gorillas have enslaved a group of trogs—half-human, half-ape—and are forcing them to build a huge bridge across the river. The trogs are led by a woman who is making her way east, to Ape City, to await the arrival of a messiah… a man called Taylor."

Chaloner endeavored to make *Urchak's Folly* compatible with the Adventure Comics continuity, but "tried hard for it to be a stand-alone story. I also relied heavily on continuity from the feature films, mentioning Taylor [and featuring] a journal that recounts events concerning Zira and Cornelius." *Urchak's Folly* earned Chaloner the 1992 OzCon Award for Favorite Writer.

Adventure's *POTA* monthly was initially well received, its first issue selling out and going into multiple printings. But its readership quickly dwindled, the entire franchise jeopardized by fluctuating market conditions and mired in Marshall's earnest but overly ambitious plan to expand the Apes mythos—or in this case, monkey around with fans' memories. "The art and stories varied wildly and in trying to expand the POTA universe they took some pretty wild diversions," observes Alan Maxwell. "The series is not remembered fondly by too many fans." Adds Chaloner, "Perhaps those stories weren't close enough to the films, both visually and thematically. It's always a tough call working on a project that has such a loyal fanbase. If you are even a little off-target with your vision, then it won't go over with the fans." After an Annual, a *Blood of the Apes* miniseries, and reprints of some of Moench's Marvel material (the first three movie adaptations and a *Terror* collection), Adventure/Malibu's *POTA* was cancelled in 1992 with issue #24. The publisher's Apes line ended in 1993 with the miniseries *The Forbidden Zone*.

BEWARE THE BEAST MAN, FOR HE IS THE DEVIL'S PAWN

For the rest of the 1990s, fans were teased and tormented as a new *Apes* movie was in development. Filmmakers as diverse as Oliver Stone and James Cameron were attached at various times, and *Planet of the Apes* was considered as a starring vehicle for both Arnold Schwarzenegger and George Clooney.

Eventually it was announced that master visionary Tim Burton would direct a "reimagining" of *Planet of the Apes*. Burton was known for his freakish cinematic eye candy—but *not* for cohesive storytelling. Would the director of *Beetlejuice* transport moviegoers to the star system of Boulle's Betelgeuse? Or did he have something else in mind?

Burton's heavily hyped *Apes* bowed on July 27, 2001, with Mark Wahlberg as reluctant (and unlikeable) human hero Captain Leo Davidson and Tim Roth as the savage ape General Thade. As you'd expect from a Burton film, the makeup, costumes, and sets were astonishing. But the director had blundered into a real-life Forbidden Zone, attempting to "fix" what was never broken. His brutal reimagining strayed too far from viewers' expectations,

A rare Ape study by artist Tom Sutton, in preparation for his *POTA* illustration stint.
Courtesy of Heritage Auctions.

as a result being butchered by critics and soon fading from screens.

Visually, though, this reimagining was a sight to behold. Its multilayered treehouse of an Ape City, complex military costumes, buxom wild women, and mean-ass monkeys were the kind of stuff comics artists go Pavlov over. It made perfect sense for Dark Horse Comics, the publisher that had created comic-book hits out of 20th Century Fox's *Aliens* and *Predator* franchises, to see another winner in *Planet of the Apes*. Scott Allie ably penned the compulsory movie adaptation, drawn by Davidé Fabbry, and writer Ian Edginton and artist Paco Medina, like Moench and Ploog before them, ventured beyond the movie in the three-issue miniseries *POTA: The Human War*. Apes anticipation was sufficient enough to warrant a monthly series written by Edginton that launched with a Sept. 2001 cover date; Dan Abnett succeeded Edginton with issue #4. "Ian and I wanted the characters to have real warmth and depth and not be cut-out, two-dimensional figures," Abnett remarked in a *Simian Scrolls* interview.

Dark Horse, like movie-goers, soon realized that Burton's baby just wasn't the Planet of the Apes everyone would have liked to have seen, and concocted an escape clause: "Ian Edginton did reveal that they had been toying with combining the worlds of the remake with that of the original, classic POTA," says Alan Maxwell, "but alas, the comic didn't last long enough to ever see that come to fruition." Dark Horse's *POTA* series was canned with issue #6 (Feb. 2002).

A sketch by the artist who drew Marvel's adaptation of the first POTA movie, George Tuska.

Art © 2007 George Tuska. Courtesy of John Roche.

CHALK UP ANOTHER VICTORY TO THE HUMAN SPIRIT

Shrugging off the Burton version as if it were only a bad dream, *Revolution on the Planet of the Apes* (RPOTA) #1 (Dec. 2005), from Canadian publisher Mr. Comics, began a six-issue exploration of Caesar's rise to power in the advent of the Ape rebellion depicted in the final two movies. Each issue featured a 16-page lead "Revolution" story and a supplemental five-page backup story set in different periods of the Apes timeline, provided by a collective of writers and artists including Joe O'Brien, Salgood Sam, Tom Fowler, Attila, Sam Agro, Art Lyon, cover painter Denis Rodier, and Ty Templeton, the series' co-writer and point person. Fortunately for Apes fans, Templeton and company's *Revolution* augmented, not violated, the Apes mythos, and was well received by devotees.

Mr. Comics' acquisition of POTA was, however, a second-banana choice. "Originally, I suggested that Mr. Comics approach Fox for the rights to *Family Guy* (back when it was still in cancellation)," reveals Templeton, no stranger to licensed titles from his previous *Batman Adventures* and *Simpsons* contributions.

Publisher Steve Ballentyne obtained the *Family Guy* rights, but was stalemated when Fox did not respond to Mr. Comics' proposal materials. "I've been told it was because [*Family Guy* creator] Seth MacFarlane was hard to get on board the project, or because he wasn't interested in seeing *Family Guy* in comic form while his show was off the air," Templeton explains.

After waiting for months without a *Family Guy* green light, Ballentyne, hot for a licensed property for his line, wanted to capitalize upon his relationship with Fox's licensing department and asked Templeton asked if there was a different Fox property Mr. Comics might acquire. *Nightmare on Elm Street* was considered, but Templeton was not interested because of his unfamiliarity with that Freddy Krueger series. "When our publisher suggested POTA, I told him that *Planet* was one of my favorite films and I could have a ball writing that title," says Templeton. "I suspect my enthusiasm for the characters (as well as our publisher's familiarity with the movies) was the deciding factor."

Revolution on the Planet of the Apes #6 (Aug. 2006) concluded, for the time being, Mr. Comics' new POTA material, although a collected edition reprinting the series, with bonus extras included, followed.

Will there be a continuation?

"I have a very rough outline for a sequel to *Revolution*," Templeton says, "which follows the social and political creation of the Ape City we see in *Battle for the Planet of the Apes*. It focuses on the fight for control of the society between the gorillas and the chimps (which the orangutans sit out, smart little buggers that they are)." The sequel was foreshadowed in the backup story in *Revolution #5*, "where we see that gorillas and chimps eventually have a civil war for control of the Planet of the Apes," Templeton reveals. The RPOTA sequel, with a working title of *Empire of the Planet of the Apes*, "will expand on that, featuring Caesar and Aldo in the lead features, and in the backup stories follow the story of how Cornelius, Zira, Zaius, and Milo all met up."

Empire's publication is in question at this writing. "We broke a little below even on our original run of the title," Templeton reveals, "and hope to actually turn a profit with the collected book. Without the sales, we have to pull up stakes."

Even if that happens, the resiliency of the Planet of the Apes concept suggests that another Apes revolt into comic books is one day bound to follow. So be on your best behavior and treat *all* animals humanely, won't you?

(Special thanks to John Roche, Rob Kirby, and Alan Maxwell for information, art, and fact checking; and to Dave Ballard, Gary Chaloner, Ty Templeton, Philip Simon, and Amy Huey.)

COVER GALLERY

PLANET OF THE APES

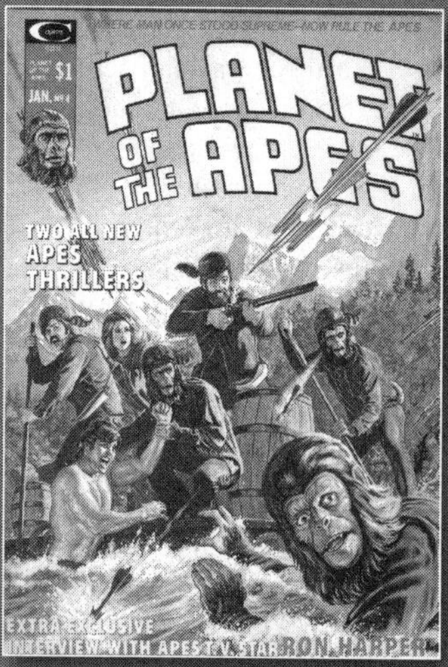
WHERE MAN ONCE STOOD SUPREME--NOW RULE THE APES
$1
PLANET OF THE APES
TWO ALL NEW APES THRILLERS
EXTRA EXCLUSIVE INTERVIEW WITH APES T.V. STAR RON HARPER
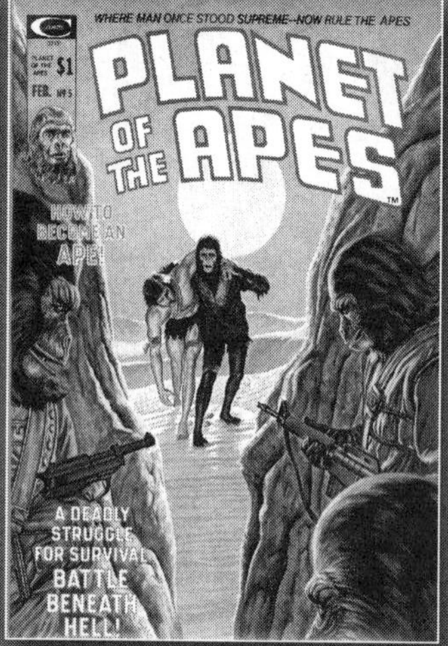
WHERE MAN ONCE STOOD SUPREME--NOW RULE THE APES
$1
PLANET OF THE APES
A DEADLY STRUGGLE FOR SURVIVAL
BATTLE BENEATH HELL!
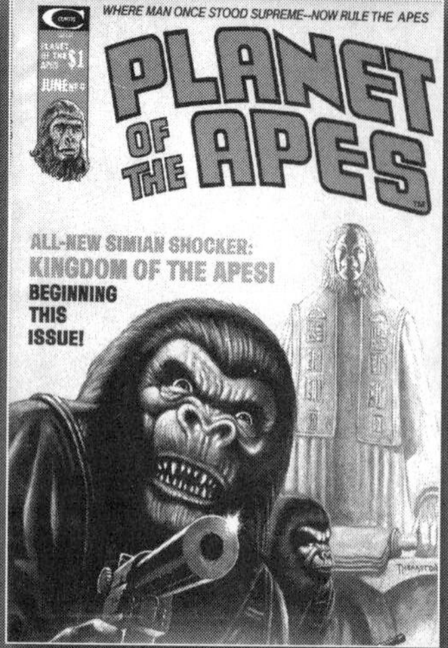
WHERE MAN ONCE STOOD SUPREME--NOW RULE THE APES
$1
PLANET OF THE APES
ALL-NEW SIMIAN SHOCKER: KINGDOM OF THE APES!
BEGINNING THIS ISSUE!
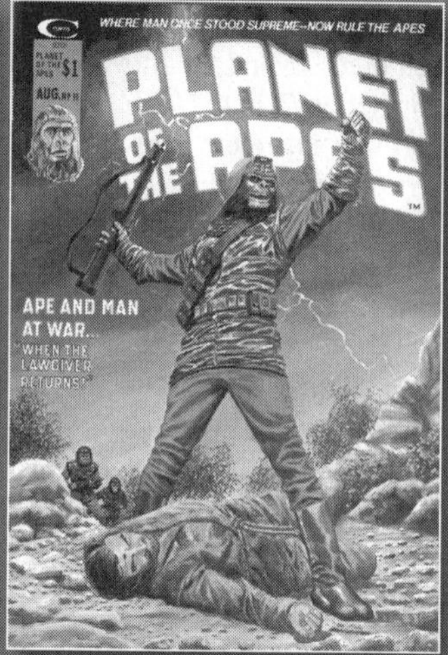
WHERE MAN ONCE STOOD SUPREME--NOW RULE THE APES
$1
PLANET OF THE APES
APE AND MAN AT WAR..
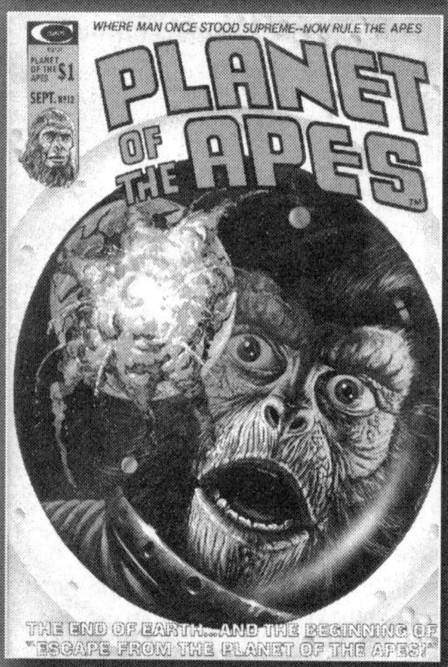
WHERE MAN ONCE STOOD SUPREME--NOW RULE THE APES
$1
PLANET OF THE APES
THE END OF EARTH... AND THE BEGINNING OF "ESCAPE FROM THE PLANET OF THE APES!"
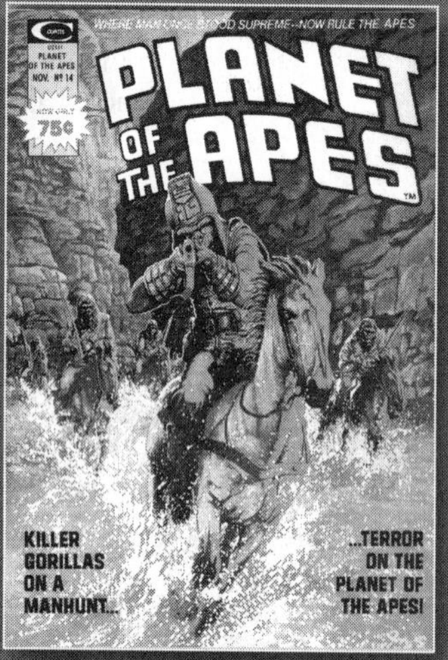
WHERE MAN ONCE STOOD SUPREME--NOW RULE THE APES
75¢
PLANET OF THE APES
KILLER GORILLAS ON A MANHUNT...
...TERROR ON THE PLANET OF THE APES!
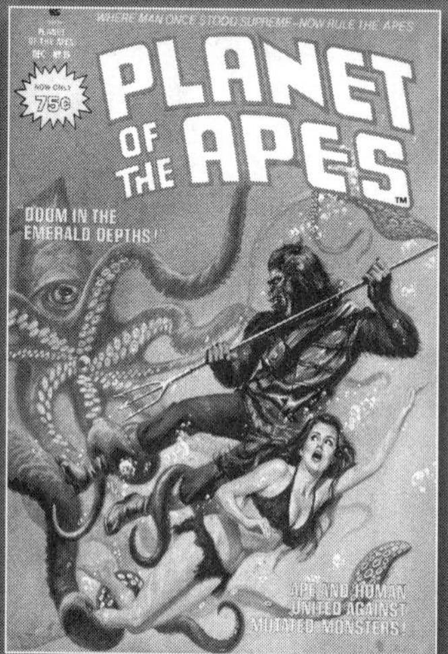
WHERE MAN ONCE STOOD SUPREME--NOW RULE THE APES
75¢
PLANET OF THE APES
DOOM IN THE EMERALD DEPTHS!
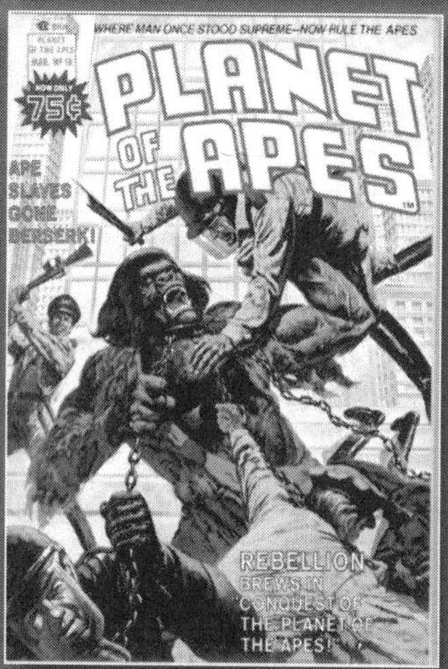
WHERE MAN ONCE STOOD SUPREME--NOW RULE THE APES
75¢
PLANET OF THE APES
APE SLAVES GONE BERSERK!
REBELLION BREWS IN CONQUEST OF THE PLANET OF THE APES!
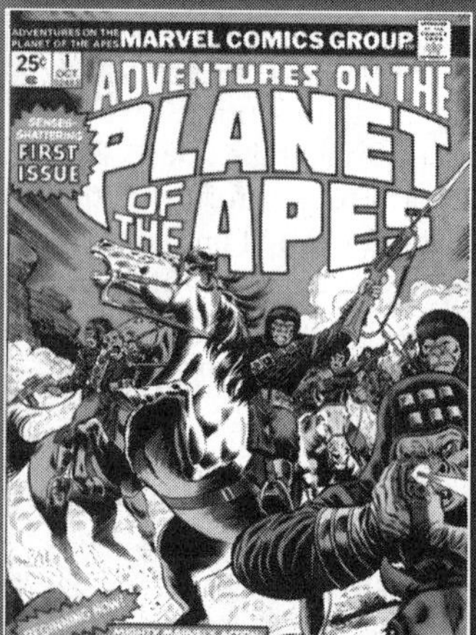
MARVEL COMICS GROUP
25¢
ADVENTURES ON THE PLANET OF THE APES
FIRST ISSUE
"PLANET OF THE APES!"
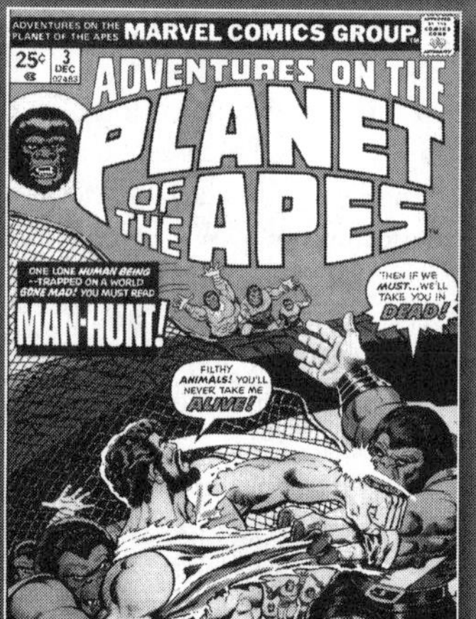
MARVEL COMICS GROUP
25¢
ADVENTURES ON THE PLANET OF THE APES
MAN-HUNT!
THEN IF WE MUST...WE'LL TAKE YOU IN DEAD!
FILTHY ANIMALS! YOU'LL NEVER TAKE ME ALIVE!
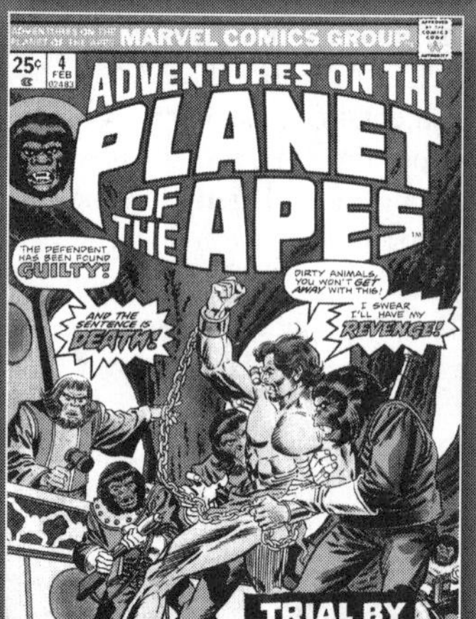
MARVEL COMICS GROUP
25¢
ADVENTURES ON THE PLANET OF THE APES
THE DEFENDANT HAS BEEN FOUND GUILTY!
AND THE SENTENCE IS DEATH!
DIRTY ANIMALS. YOU WON'T GET AWAY WITH THIS!
I SWEAR I'LL HAVE MY REVENGE!
TRIAL BY FEAR!
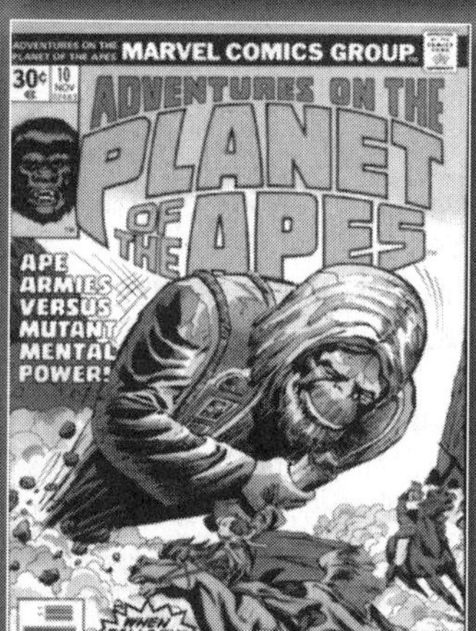
MARVEL COMICS GROUP
30¢
ADVENTURES ON THE PLANET OF THE APES
APE ARMIES VERSUS MUTANT MENTAL POWER!
WHEN FALLS THE LAW GIVER!

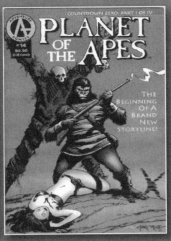

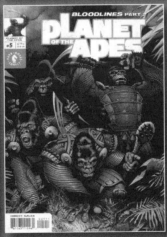

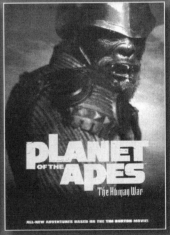

Where Man Once Stood Supreme!

Ape
Q with DOUG MOENCH

Conducted via email on October 16, 2006

SPOTTED AMONG THE APES IN:

Planet of the Apes (Marvel, 1970s),
Detective Comics #562, Batman #535

OTHER CAREER HIGHLIGHTS:

"Weirdworld" (Marvel), *Master of Kung Fu, Godzilla: King
of the Monsters, Werewolf by Night, Moon Knight, Batman*
(monthly, *Detective,* and various miniseries), *Aztec Ace,
Six from Sirius, The Spectre, James Bond: Serpent's Tooth*

**Gerry Conway was originally intended to be Marvel's *Planet of
the Apes* writer. How did you end up with the assignment?**

Roy Thomas called me into his office and offered it. Why me, I
don't really know, since I was still new. You'd have to ask Roy.
Marv Wolfman knew me from Warren [Publishing] and was
instrumental in my hire, so maybe Roy was operating on
Marv's further recommendation. Or maybe Roy just liked
the other stuff I'd begun writing for Marvel.

    Anyway, Gerry had written a paragraph or two broadly
outlining his *Apes* intentions before realizing his schedule
was already on overload. Something had to give, so he
gave up the assignment not yet really begun. At the time,
he lived on West End Avenue just two corners around
from my Riverside Drive apartment on the same block, so
it was easy to stop off that evening on the way home from
Marvel. But rather than offering further input, liberated
Gerry generously said: "It's yours, have fun, go for it." So
we began our friendship discussing other things, after which
I went ape going for it.

**Is it true you wrote some of the *Apes* film adaptations
without having seen the movies?**

True, although the choice was before-the-fact and could
not, in those days, be undone. I'd seen the first two movies
upon release in Chicago theaters long before moving to
New York, meaning long before I knew I'd ever write for
Marvel, let alone adapt all five movies into comics
form. Although I'd loved the first movie and enjoyed the
second, lukewarm-to-bad reviews led me to skip the
final three.

Detail from Doug Moench's "Ogre and the Ape" tale in
Batman #535 (Oct. 1996). Art by Kelley Jones. © 2007 DC Comics.

Along comes 1973 and I'm invited to work for Marvel in New York, then asked to adapt all five *Apes* movies. Now, of course, I really should catch the last three, but I'm stuck in that remote epoch before home video. My only hope is that the last three films will be shown on TV or in some Manhattan revival theater before I finish adapting the first two. But if such happened, I simply missed it, forcing me to work solely from the screenplays, adjusting the first two to the best of my memory and working the last three blind.

Have you seen the movies since?

After finishing all five adaptations for better or worse, accurately or not, I simply had no need or inclination. The subliminal effect of lukewarm-to-bad reviews can be stubborn, plus I'd had more than my fill of the screenplays.

Since you worked from screenplays instead of the edited films, your *Conquest* and *Battle* adaptations contain scenes not present in the movies. Do you recall any of those deleted or unfilmed scenes that made it into your stories?

Nope, since I've never seen the movies. Even as I started the adaptations, of course, I assumed "my" versions would include unavoidable differences, screenplay scenes either cut from the finished movies or never filmed in the first place. It's rare for any screenplay, after all, to reach the screen exactly as written. There was less chance I'd *omit* scenes contained in the finished films—since I was working from "final draft" screenplays for movies of a type unlikely to contain significant on-set improvisation—but I still cringed, knowing the possibility existed. All I could do was hope that any differences would be minor while telling the editors to flag any striking discrepancies. They never said a peep, although their memories of the last three films were obviously fuzzy, since other people have mentioned fairly major differences since

publication. My bad, but committed a good five years before home video was invented and maybe ten years before all five *Apes* titles reached tape and/or laser disc.

Of the artists who drew your *Apes* movie adaptations—George Tuska/Mike Esposito on *POTA*, Alfredo Alcala on *Beneath* and *Conquest*, Rico Rival on *Escape*, and a host of Filipino artists on *Battle*—who do you think best handled the material?

A fair assessment would require full review the work, but digging out all the back issues is too daunting a prospect right now. Limited to flawed memory, I'd say the Tuska storytelling was best, although I preferred the actual art done by Alcala and Rival.

What did you think of Tim Burton's 2001 reimagining of *Planet of the Apes*?

Yikes. Didn't see that one either, maybe the only Tim Burton film I've missed.

You're best known among *Apes* fans for your original serials that explored themes and characters beyond the movies. Was going beyond the films part of the Marvel plan for *Apes*, or did you propose this to then-editor-in-chief Roy Thomas?

Original material was planned by Roy and Gerry from the start, with the broad intentions for one such series covered in Gerry's paragraph or two. I've always assumed that the chosen format—large black-and-white magazine rather than regular color comic—*dictated* original material as much as permitted it. With so many pages to fill each issue (something like 66, I believe), the title would have been consigned to a brief run with nothing but adaptations, even with five films to draw on. Given the page count, each issue boasted photo-illustrated movie articles as well as a 20-page adaptation installment and another 20-or-so pages of original material—at a time when the regular color comics offered a paltry 17 pages of story sandwiched between way too many ads.

Yo, Roy (and no doubt Stan): Righteous choice on the format!

Your first non-movie storyline was "Terror on the Planet of the Apes," with artist Michael Ploog. You and Mike meshed beautifully as a team… what's the secret behind your creative harmony?

Well, I prefer that others assess the quality, but I'll take a stab at our collaboration. Like everyone, I love beautiful art, but what I truly prize is solid visual storytelling. Any artist combining the two qualities—style and storytelling—is aces with me. Indeed, they rank as giants in the field.

Just off the top of my head, and unfairly omitting slews of European and Japanese artists, I'd include: Eisner, Barks, Caniff, Kurtzman-teamed-with-Elder-and-others, Steranko, Corben, Wrightson, Gulacy. And Ploog. Quite a range, but they all share two attributes: Attractive art and killer storytelling. Eyeball kicks laid down in coherent sequence. Can't beat it.

Like most of those on the list, Mike Ploog's style is "cartoony-but-realistic." And, especially like Eisner, Corben, and Wrightson, Mike can even be "cartoony-but-scary." Exaggeration packs a wallop and, when done well, it paradoxically makes the unreal more "real" than reality. As for Mike's storytelling, well, he learned and earned his chops as an assistant to Will Eisner himself. 'Nuff, as they say, said.

Now then. Bad storytelling tends to make the reader squint and frown while trying to puzzle or decipher or deduce just who the devil might be whom and what's what, not to mention where and when, proving there are artists abroad in this land who, I swear, have never seen a single Hitchcock film.

But we always know bad storytelling when we see it, because it always hurts the eye. No sequential flow, no rhyme or reason, no way to tell where the characters are, who's who in relation to whom, what's happening and why anyone should care, the reader definitely included. Maybe the POV angles, cropping, and composition are all wrong to the point of omitting or obscuring crucial visual information. Maybe establishing shots are nonexistent, with nothing to introduce or anchor what follows. Maybe all the wrong "key moments" have been selected for illustration, all the right moments occurring unseen "between panels." Maybe the characters display facial expressions and body language inappropriate to the scene's actions or emotional thrust. At its worst, this devolves to a scattering of unrelated pin-up shots with characters striking poses utterly irrelevant to whatever they're supposed to be saying and/or doing.

The very antithesis of the comic strip's hieroglyphic *modus operandi*, bad storytelling is infinite in variety, but always confusing. You need a roadmap to figure it out.

But good storytelling, by contrast, *is* a roadmap. The page explains itself. It conveys what's happening, at least roughly, in visual terms absorbed at a glance. Reading the words should add a whole new dimension (even to the point of "reversing" what *seemed* to be happening at a glance) rather than laboriously explaining what should be immediately and visually apparent.

I hate bad storytelling. It forces me to waste time pursuing nothing but flawed compromise. Often the best I can achieve is a finished product which at least makes sense —but only if you *read* it, not at a glance. Working with a good story-teller, on the other hand, always and automatically makes my writing better. It frees me, in fact, to pursue my full potential while making the finished product the best it can be, adding only those words which are vital to advancing the story or which enhance the effect or impact of the art. Inadequate visuals force me to compen-sate with words, conveying too much of a story's necessary information in clunky narration and/or contrived dialogue. I always try to disguise the contrivance and limit the clunk-iness, but neither should be necessary. In a "perfect" comic, one blending words and pictures in smooth synergy, such artifices give way to an elegant whole greater than the sum of its individual parts. And at its best, such alchemy renders magic.

Which is exactly what I felt when working with Mike Ploog. "Creative harmony," indeed.

And let us not forget an ancillary benefit of working with Mike: The eureka realization that PLOOG makes a perfect sound effect for a stone tossed into water.

Didn't you base a character in "Terror" upon Ploog?

Indeed. Michael J. Ploog the man may not be especially tall, but he's a larger-than-life character with twinkling eyes, big beard, and bigger boisterous laugh. He hails from Wyoming. He was a Marine. He rode bucking broncos. Just looking at him, you'd figure fifty other things, all the way from safecracker to chef, before artist.

Recalling the character Mike Keel from my beloved childhood *Davy Crockett* series, I decided to create two lovably obnoxious and incessantly cantankerous

pals who run a riverboat, one ape and one human, both larger than life and equally prone to endlessly over-the-top braggart raps and rants. The kind of guys who don't just laugh; they *roar*, putting their whole bodies into it. When they slap your back, you're face-down in the mud with a dislocated shoulder blade. Calling them Gunpowder Julius and Steely Dan, I told Mike in my art instructions: "They're both you in buckskin and coon-caps, but I'm not sure it'll

A Mike Ploog-drawn Ape commissioned illo.
POTA © 2007 20th Century Fox. Art © 2007 Michael Ploog.
Courtesy of John Roche.

show more in the gorilla or the human."

After moving to New York— first time I walked home from Marvel, in—I came upon a Broadway refreshment stand of a type then unknown in Chicago. It offered a drink, and a most delicious one at that, called *Orange Julius*. The odd name struck me at the time and later bubbled to the fore when naming my riverboat gorilla, probably because "Julius" (as in Caesar, and like "Brutus") fit the *Apes* Roman Empire theme. Had I

made the ape an orangutan, I could have stolen the "Orange Julius" name whole-sale, but I wanted a big bad gorilla rather than a patrician wuss orangutan. And since the two rogues were using their boat to pole barrels of gun-powder downriver, Gunpowder Julius the gorilla became.

Leaving Ploogie to become Steely Dan by default, named when few had heard of the jazz-rock group. Had I known how famous they'd become, I never would've cribbed the name. At the time it fit to a T, although I never asked Mike if he dug the music.

You re-teamed with Mike Ploog on "Weirdworld" in 1976, 1977, and 1986, but 20 years later, readers are waiting for another Moench/Ploog reunion. Will it happen?

It's almost happened several times, and I'm still game with a vengeance. Any time, anywhere. All Mike has to do is call when he's ready.

You spun *Planet of the Apes'* inherent racism allegory into a '70s-charged youth-culture direction with your intro-duction of the human/chimp heroic duo of Jason and Alexander. What was the genesis of those characters?

The basic genesis was covered in Gerry Conway's one or two paragraphs before he opted out. The theme was already implicit—actually, explicit—in the movies. And since all stories thrive on conflict, it was a natural. Take one representative from each of two groups in conflict and force them together by circumstance. Make them teenagers, old enough to be aware that they should hate each other but young enough to overcome the hate, ultimately forging a friendship which transcends racism—or, in this case, "specieism." Finally, since the true bad guys are gorillas, make the young ape a more sympathetic chimp. I was given simplicity itself, and I simply ran with it.

Any "'70s youth-culture" trappings probably derived from the fact that I'd just emerged from the '60s youth culture myself. Indeed, for me, "the sixties" was more like 1964–1974—say, from the end of JFK and the beginning of the Beatles to the end of Nixon and the beginning of bad music. So, by that marker, I was *still* part of the '60s youth culture when starting the *Apes* book in 1973.

And by the way, while I can't swear

to it at this point, I believe Gerry included the names Jason and Alexander in his one or two—although I came up with the series title "Terror on the Planet of the Apes."

What inspired your major *Apes* villain, the gorilla general Brutus?

The obvious need for a major recurring villain and the fact that the name so perfectly comported with the preexisting Roman Empire gorilla-naming scheme. Needing a real brute, what else would I call him? In fact, I found it hard to believe the name had not occurred to any of the writers working on *five* different movies. I quickly skimmed the screenplays. Nope, no "Brutus" anywhere. How the hell could they miss something so sublimely obvious? Didn't matter. Brutus was mine, baby, all mine.

You penned a scene with a lip-locked human and ape in issue #19 that was, for its time, as groundbreaking in comics as the Kirk/Uhura smooch was on TV's *Star Trek* a few years earlier. What type of fan reaction was sparked by that scene?

We may have received some hate mail, but nothing that I recall. The *Apes* letter pages were probably handled by one of the assistant editors so I'm not sure I even saw the mail. I have the vague sense of a general that-was-cool consensus amongst the bullpen. But if I'm right, even that reaction was mild and passing.

The core *Apes* premise was obviously ripe for—and rife with—racial allegory, so I knew exactly what I was doing with that "miscegenation" scene. On the other hand, given black girlfriends in my past, I really didn't think it was that big a deal, let alone "groundbreaking." In the fifties, sure, but the times, they'd already been a-changin' for more than a decade and I assumed nothing could stop the inevitable, not after the stunning assassinations of JFK, MLK, and RFK. If the zeitgeist had not yet reached full enlightenment and tolerance, it was at least trending toward the only state of mind that made sense, one increasingly freed of superficial hate. My optimism, as it turned out, was clearly infused with a more-than-liberal dose of blissful ignorance. I knew dark forces were still in play, but I'd badly underestimated them. Looking back, I'm dismayed at how naïve I was. And looking around at the here and now, I'm staggered and appalled. Indeed, the last six years of grim reality have blown my mind on a daily basis. It's as if the sixties never happened, with every positive gain rolled back almost totally.

9/11 didn't change everything, but it could have, and could have changed everything for the better. The whole world stood with America on 9/12, and that universal good will (including, remember, candlelight vigils in *Tehran*) could have been marshaled to discredit, overwhelm, and defeat hate and horror to the point of virtual extinction. It was not only possible but easily *within reach*, simply by doing the right things in the right ways. By living up to our Constitution and laws, by going after the guilty, *all* the guilty and no one *but* the guilty. By rejecting fear and hate, rising from the ashes to stand in strength and courage while refusing to scapegoat anyone. Instead, fear and hate were exploited, actively promoted. *Pimped.*

9/11 never should have happened in the first place. It could and should have been prevented. Worse, once it was allowed to occur, everything done in alleged response was both wrong and wrongly done. As a result, the profoundly un-American *reaction* to 9/11 changed everything—and changed it all for the worse. No longer naïve by 2001, I fully expected—fully dreaded and predicted on the day of 9/11 itself—everything that has since come to pass. And more yet to come. The whole thing feels like a flashback to those childhood bad vibes, with nary a sane grownup in sight.

In this case, however, no ESP required. Just experience, a current contempt born of past familiarity. Today's administration is crammed with my generation's benighted jerks, the losers of the sixties now ruling supreme. They're people I knew all too well, the ones who always hated my kind, always wanting to make war, not love, while somehow avoiding the draft. Back then, I simply avoided them. Now, they've manipulated fear and xenophobia to regress us all the way back to their Reactionary Stone Age wet dream. Dark days indeed, with all too many of us blind to the light lost. While hoping my sense of foreboding is exaggerated, I fear it may only scratch the surface of some alternate-universe Germany in the 1930s, with Jews and Gypsies traded for Muslims and Mexicans. This is epic stupidity and ignorance, against which all resistance is pathetically weak.

Whoa. Big downer sparked by one simple long-ago kiss between a human and an ape. Sorry. But if reality sucks right now, it was once wonderful and maybe we can get it back.

And by the way, he said climbing off his soapbox, I was unaware of any Kirk/ Uhura kiss until reading your question. While I've caught most of the *Star Trek* movies, I'm one of those rare sentient beings on the planet who has never seen more than accidental snippets of the various TV series. Back when the original show was first broadcast, I'd already left home and moved in with three girls, none of whom owned a TV, nor did I. So after a childhood drenched in absurd gobs of television, I spent my late teens (up to 21 or 22) watching literally nothing, exclusively obsessed with reading and music. Beatles, Stones, Yardbirds, Who, Pretty Things, Animals, Small Faces, Kinks, Hendrix, Cream, Traffic, Dylan, Donovan, Zeppelin, Sly Stone. And can someone please tell me, what happened to music after the mid-'70s? ("Disco," I believe they called it.) Anyway, when one of the girls scored a TV in 1967, the one and only impetus was John Lennon's pending debut of "All You Need Is Love" on the world's first global live feed. After that, the little black-and-white set went dark and pretty much stayed that way until man set foot on the moon in 1969. Worth it for those two events alone, but no *Star Trek*.

Now, alas, I find myself in second childhood with a 58" screen, albeit reserved for football, movies, and what passes these days for "news."

Although "Terror" was the dominant non-movie serial, running through the majority of *POTA*'s 29 issues, you wrote several other stories or storylines, starting with "Evolution's Nightmare" in issue #5. Was this deviation from "Terror" predicated upon deadline problems with Ploog or your desire to go into different directions?

More like anticipation of potential deadline problems down the road, rather than Mike actually being late.

Even so, the true reason for "Evolution's Nightmare" was more complicated. Granted his shot at penciling, Bullpen assistant Ed Hannigan asked if I'd write a single self-contained *Apes*

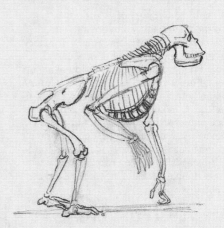

story
with no
deadline
(because no one,
including Ed himself, knew how long
he'd need to draw it in his spare time),
slated for the drawer as backup against
future deadline problems. I said sure and
turned out the story overnight. If it ran in
#5, then Ed was apparently quicker than
anyone expected and the future came
sooner than later. Sorry to lack precision,
but I was so busy in those days that I
simply rolled with whatever, barely noticing which story reached print when.

I do remember Ed's original art,
mounted on stiff boards so gigantic they
couldn't fit on my desk. Or any other
desk, for that matter. I had to
prop them on a makeshift
easel while scripting the
dialogue. Normally, original
art is 1½ times larger than the
printed page. Ed's pages may
well have been *triple* size.

My memory of the
finished job is that it turned
out pretty well, certainly not
bad for a guy's first job.

**Tom Sutton first worked
with you on issue #12's
"Future History
Chronicles," then eventually
took over "Terror" from
Ploog. Was that an editorial
pairing or did you two want
to work together?**

I could be wrong, but seems
to me I'd already worked with Tom on
something or other, maybe a horror story
for Warren or Skywald. In any case, I
can't remember the details of hooking up
on "Future History Chronicles." If Tom
called me, I probably recommended him
to the *Apes* editor. If not, then the editor
recommended Tom to me. Either way, I
know we discussed the first episode on the
phone because I clearly remember Tom
going apesh*t at the prospect of that city-
ship double-spread. On which he did an
incredible job.

Not just incredible, but *also* humon-
gous. Just like Ed Hannigan's originals,

the Sutton "Future History" pages were
way oversized, if not mounted on stiff
boards. And since these were the only two
times I've ever grappled with such
unwieldy originals, what was the deal
with *Apes?*

**You wrote some wild stuff in "Terror,"
including talking brains, water-breath-
ing apes, drug hallucinations, and ape/
human hybrids. Were there any stories
you proposed that were rejected by either
20th Century Fox or Marvel's editors?**

Nothing was ever rejected by anyone,
although Archie Goodwin did ask me to
change one title. It was the Mount
Rushmore story, with some ape hermit
living inside the huge hollowed-out head
of a dead human president—knowing me,
probably Abe Lincoln—wherein he
hoarded a cache of precious artifacts from
his past/our present. Things like soup cans
and traffic signs and flashlights, mundane
crap treated like treasure. The entrance
into this den of treasure-trash—into
Lincoln's brain—was a chiseled nostril.
So when a character sneezed inside the
head, I naturally cut to an exterior shot
with the ATCHOO coming from *Lincoln's*

POTA © 2007 20th Century Fox.

nose. Anyway, while I can't recall the
revised—and published—version, I sure
do remember my original title…

"Up the Nose-Tube to Monkey-Junk."

Gotta be one of my all-time favorite
titles, spunky and funky while perfectly
describing the story. Too canny for me,
Archie knew that "junk" was drug slang
while cocaine snorting was catching on at
the time. Obviously, I was also aware of
the *double entendre*—but only, I swear, a
split-second after coming up with the title
purely for its sound and sheer literalness.

Sorry, Arch, but I can't help feeling a
kick at finally getting my title into print.

**Marvel's *Planet of the Apes* was more
popular in the UK than in the US. Why
do you think the UK went ape?**

No bloody clue, mate, but the damn Brits
drove me bonkers by publishing their
version *weekly*. Try mightily though I
might, it was virtually impossible to feed
them sufficient gobs of material, forcing
me to blast through all five screenplay
adaptations before chancing upon showings
of the last three movies. I had to devote
every Friday, in fact, to churning out yet
another installment of 20 full-script pages,
more than most other Marvel writers
produced in a week. Hell, Don McGregor
considered 20 pages a good *month*.

And yet, for all the pressure and
intensity, I *loved* it. My brain exploded on
a permanent high, buzzing and crackling
nonstop. Doing a "mere" *Master of Kung
Fu* plot plus five or ten pages of "mere"
Werewolf By Night dialogue—or 17 pages
of nothing but *Inhumans* dialogue, or a
ten-page original-story full-script for
Vampire Tales or *Monsters Unleashed*, or
even 25 pages of dialogue for *Doc Savage*
or whatever—made every other day of the
week a 12-hour breeze by comparison.
The more I worked, the easier and faster the
stuff flowed.

Thank you, damn
Brits. (P.S.: I'm half-
Scottish, so my love is pure
with the passion of a brave
heart.)

**Your stories were
published in multiple
formats, including the UK
editions and the newsstand
comic *Adventures on the
Planet of the Apes*. Were
you paid a reprint or
special rate for their
multiple use?**

Hell, no. This was still a
year or three before Neal
Adams and I, along with
others in ACBA [Academy of
Comic Book Arts], started
pushing the publishers to adopt the novel
practice of paying any kind of "royal-
ties"—which didn't happen until more
years after that. Most of my Marvel work,
in fact, was done under pre-royalty, pre-
reprint, and pre-foreign-compensation
conditions. Recently, however, I've begun
receiving pleasant-surprise reprint/royalty
checks for the various *Essentials*
volumes, and how sweet it is. So only if
Marvel negotiates the rights for *Essential
Apes* reprints will I finally receive more
than my then-measly page rate for all that
long-ago material. But hey, it sure was
fun at the time—and maybe, in the

cosmic scheme of things, reward enough.

If you were ever to write another *Planet of the Apes* storyline, which artist would you like to work with?

Oh, I'd probably just hop in my time machine to team up with 35-year-old Frank Frazetta.

Ten years after you finished *Planet of the Apes*, you wrote a Batman story that featured a gorilla cover—penciled by your "Evolution's Nightmare" artist Ed Hannigan—for *Detective* #562 (May 1986), part of the "Film Freak" storyline. And ten years later, you co-created (with Kelley Jones) the Ape and the Ogre in *Batman* #535 (Oct. 1996), a story of evolution and de-evolution. Was *Planet of the Apes* in the back of your mind when you wrote those issues?

Nope. My brain separates and compartmentalizes things to an extraordinary degree. And it's not bad memory. In fact, my memory seems quite vivid, but only if and when it kicks in. Often, it just doesn't. Two examples from not long ago:

Halfway through an Angelina Jolie film, it abruptly occurred to me: *Hey, I had champagne with this woman at the Paramount Hotel, so how could anyone forget being in the presence of lips like that?*

And only when turning off a David Letterman show after the news did I recall: *Wait a minute, did I not have dinner with Paul Shaffer (and Richard Belzer and Robert Klein) at the Friar's Club? Indeed I did. We even discussed Bob Dylan and Batman as Shaffer nibbled from my plate while his returned order was being corrected in the kitchen.*

This sort of thing can feel weird. Other than the Beatles, Dylan, and the Stones, I've probably listened to more of the Who than anything else, yet hanging out with them for a long and highly memorable 1967 night seldom occurs to me. And James Bond movies, Sherlock Holmes movies, the Shadow movie, the Conan movie—all have been oddly jolted at some point by the realization that I've *written these characters*.

From Moench's "Ogre and the Ape" tale in *Batman* #535 (Oct. 1996). Art by Kelley Jones. © 2007 DC Comics.

I can even see a Batman commercial without immediately making any personal connection.

Why, I don't know, but the here-and-now me tends to divorce himself from my own past.

Another ten years have passed— you're due another ape comic, you know…

If so, I probably won't remember *Planet of the Apes* until reaching the last page.

But in closing, maybe I should note my one and only regret while apologizing for the blown opportunity, a story delayed and delayed until we simply ran out of issues. It would've been an homage riff on my favorite movie, the High Adventure discovery by Jason and Alexander of a shockingly mutated ape in the wilds of the New Jersey Pine Barrens. The mutated ape—and the story—would have then moved to the radioactive ruins of New York. The nature of the mutation? Nothing but size. Indeed, while possessing human-level thought and speech, the gorilla would have fully matched the stature of King Kong.

**(throughout)
Tom Sutton ape studies, in preparation for his *POTA* gig.**
Courtesy of Heritage Auctions.

THE TWOMORROWS LIBRARY

THE KRYPTON COMPANION

Unlocks the secrets of Superman's Silver and Bronze Ages, when kryptonite came in multiple colors and super-pets flew the skies! Features all-new interviews with NEAL ADAMS, MURPHY ANDERSON, NICK CARDY, JOSÉ LUIS GARCÍA-LÓPEZ, KEITH GIFFEN, JIM MOONEY, DENNIS O'NEIL, BOB OKSNER, MARTY PASKO, BOB ROZAKIS, JIM SHOOTER, LEN WEIN, MARV WOLFMAN, and others, plus tons of rare and unseen art! By BACK ISSUE MAGAZINE'S Michael Eury!

(224-Page Trade Paperback) $29 US

JUSTICE LEAGUE COMPANION VOL. 1

A comprehensive examination of the Silver Age JLA by MICHAEL EURY, tracing its development, history, and more through interviews with the series' creators, an issue-by-issue index of the JLA's 1960-1972 adventures, classic and never-before-published artwork, and other fascinating features. Contributors include DENNY O'NEIL, MURPHY ANDERSON, JOE GIELLA, MIKE FRIEDRICH, NEAL ADAMS, ALEX ROSS, CARMINE INFANTINO, NICK CARDY, and many, many others. Plus: An exclusive interview with STAN LEE, who answers the question, "Did the JLA really inspire the creation of Marvel's Fantastic Four?" With an all-new cover by BRUCE TIMM (TV's Justice League Unlimited)!

(224-page trade paperback) $29 US

STREETWISE
TOP ARTISTS DRAWING STORIES OF THEIR LIVES

An unprecedented assembly of talent drawing NEW autobiographical stories:
• Barry WINDSOR-SMITH • C.C. BECK
• Sergio ARAGONÉS • Walter SIMONSON
• Brent ANDERSON • Nick CARDY
• Roy THOMAS & John SEVERIN
• Paul CHADWICK • Rick VEITCH
• Murphy ANDERSON • Joe KUBERT
• Evan DORKIN • Sam GLANZMAN
• Plus Art SPIEGELMAN, Jack KIRBY, more!
Cover by RUDE • Foreword by EISNER

(160-Page Trade Paperback) $24 US

BEST OF DRAW! VOL. 1

Compiles material from the first two sold-out issues of DRAW!, the "How-To" magazine on comics and cartooning! Tutorials by, and interviews with: DAVE GIBBONS (layout and drawing on the computer), BRET BLEVINS (drawing lovely women, painting from life, and creating figures that "feel"), JERRY ORDWAY (detailing his working methods), KLAUS JANSON and RICARDO VILLAGRAN (inking techniques), GENNDY TARTA-KOVSKY (on animation and Samurai Jack), STEVE CONLEY (creating web comics and cartoons), PHIL HESTER and ANDE PARKS (penciling and inking), and more!

(200-page trade paperback) $26 US

BEST OF DRAW! VOL. 2

Compiles material from issues #3 and #4 of DRAW!, including tutorials by, and interviews with, ERIK LARSEN (savage penciling), DICK GIORDANO (inking techniques), BRET BLEVINS (drawing the figure in action, and figure composition), KEVIN NOWLAN (penciling and inking), MIKE MANLEY (how-to demo on Web Comics), DAVE COOPER (digital coloring tutorial), and more! Cover by KEVIN NOWLAN!

(156-page trade paperback) $22 US

ALL-STAR COMPANION VOL. 1

ROY THOMAS has assembled the most thorough look ever taken at All-Star Comics:
• Covers by MURPHY ANDERSON!
• Issue-by-issue coverage of ALL—STAR COMICS #1—57, the original JLA–JSA teamups, & the '70s ALL—STAR REVIVAL!
• Art from an unpublished 1945 JSA story!
• Looks at FOUR "LOST" ALL—STAR issues!
• Rare art by BURNLEY, DILLIN, KIRBY, INFANTINO, KANE, KUBERT, ORDWAY, ROSS, WOOD and more!!

(208-page Trade Paperback) $26 US

THE LEGION COMPANION

• A history of the Legion of Super-Heroes, with DAVE COCKRUM, MIKE GRELL, JIM STARLIN, JAMES SHERMAN, PAUL LEVITZ, KEITH GIFFEN, STEVE LIGHTLE, MARK WAID, JIM SHOOTER, JIM MOONEY, AL PLASTINO, and more!
• Rare and never-seen Legion art by the above, plus GEORGE PÉREZ, NEAL ADAMS, CURT SWAN, and others!
• Unused Cockrum character designs and pages from an UNUSED STORY!
• New cover by DAVE COCKRUM and JOE RUBINSTEIN, introduction by JIM SHOOTER, and more!

(224-page Trade Paperback) $29 US

BEST OF THE LEGION OUTPOST

Collects the best material from the hard-to-find LEGION OUTPOST fanzine, including rare interviews and articles from creators such as DAVE COCKRUM, CARY BATES, and JIM SHOOTER, plus never-before-seen artwork by COCKRUM, MIKE GRELL, JIMMY JANES and others! It also features a previously unpublished interview with KEITH GIFFEN originally intended for the never-published LEGION OUTPOST #11, plus other new material! And it sports a rarely-seen classic 1970s cover by Legion fan favorite artist DAVE COCKRUM!

(160-page trade paperback) $22 US

TITANS COMPANION

A comprehensive history of the NEW TEEN TITANS, with interviews and rare art by MARV WOLFMAN, GEORGE PÉREZ, JOSÉ LUIS GARCÍA-LÓPEZ, LEN WEIN, & others, plus a Silver Age section with NEAL ADAMS, NICK CARDY, DICK GIORDANO, & more, plus CHRIS CLAREMONT and WALTER SIMONSON on the X-MEN/TEEN TITANS crossover, TOM GRUMMETT, PHIL JIMENEZ & TERRY DODSON on their '90s Titans work, a new cover by JIMENEZ, & intro by GEOFF JOHNS! Written by GLEN CADIGAN.

(224-page trade paperback) $29 US

BLUE BEETLE COMPANION

The history of a character as old as Superman, from 1939 to his tragic fate in DC Comics' hit INFINITE CRISIS series, and beyond! Reprints the first appearance of The Blue Beetle from 1939's MYSTERY MEN COMICS #1, plus interviews with WILL EISNER, JOE SIMON, JOE GILL, ROY THOMAS, GEOFF JOHNS, CULLY HAMNER, KEITH GIFFEN, LEN WEIN, and others, never-before-seen Blue Beetle designs by ALEX ROSS and ALAN WEISS, as well as artwork by EISNER, CHARLES NICHOLAS, JACK KIRBY, STEVE DITKO, KEVIN MAGUIRE, and more!

(128-page Trade Paperback) $21 US

ALL-STAR COMPANION VOL. 2

ROY THOMAS' new sequel, with more secrets of the JSA and ALL-STAR COMICS, from 1940 through the 1980s:
• Wraparound CARLOS PACHECO cover!
• More amazing information, speculation, and unseen ALL-STAR COMICS art!
• Unpublished 1940s JSA STORY ART not printed in Volume One!
• Full coverage of the 1980s ALL-STAR SQUADRON, with scarce & never-published art!

(240-Page Trade Paperback) $29 US

WALLY WOOD & JACK KIRBY CHECKLISTS

Each lists PUBLISHED COMICS work in detail, plus ILLOS, UNPUBLISHED WORK, and more. Filled with rare and unseen art!

(68/100 Pages) $8 US EACH

T.H.U.N.D.E.R. AGENTS COMPANION

The definitive book on WALLACE WOOD's super-team of the 1960s, featuring interviews with Woody and other creators involved in the T-Agents over the years, plus rare and unseen art, including a rare 28-page story drawn by PAUL GULACY, UNPUBLISHED STORIES by GULACY, PARIS CULLINS, and others, and a JERRY ORDWAY cover. Edited by CBA's JON B. COOKE.

(192-page trade paperback) $29 US

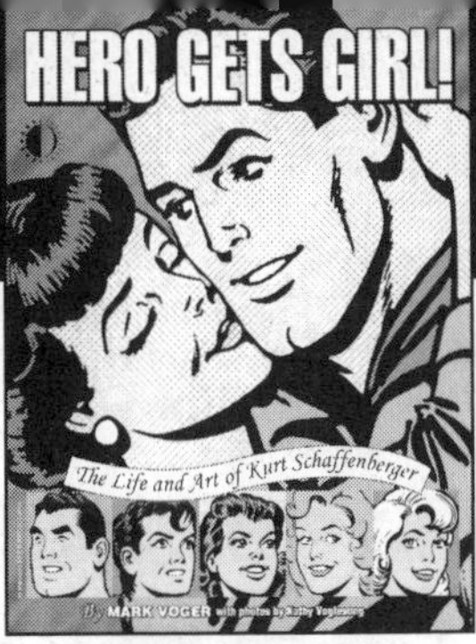
HERO GETS GIRL!
The Life and Art of Kurt Schaffenberger
MARK VOGER

HERO GETS GIRL! THE LIFE & ART OF KURT SCHAFFENBERGER

MARK VOGER's biography of the artist of **LOIS LANE** & **CAPTAIN MARVEL!**

- Covers **KURT'S LIFE AND CAREER** from the 1940s to his passing in 2002!
- Features **NEVER-SEEN PHOTOS & ILLUSTRATIONS** from his files!
- Includes recollections by **ANDERSON, EISNER, INFANTINO, KUBERT, ALEX ROSS, MORT WALKER** and others!

(128-page Trade Paperback) **$19 US**

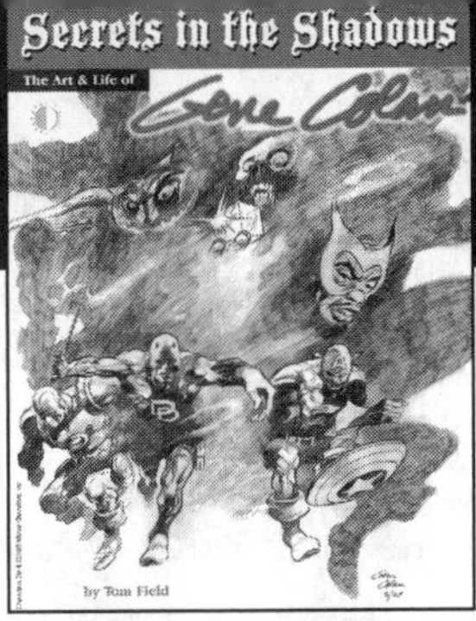
Secrets in the Shadows
The Art & Life of
Gene Colan
by Tom Field

SECRETS IN THE SHADOWS: GENE COLAN

The ultimate retrospective on **COLAN**, with rare drawings, photos, and art from his nearly 60-year career, plus a comprehensive overview of Gene's glory days at Marvel Comics! **MARV WOLFMAN, DON MCGREGOR** and other writers share script samples and anecdotes of their Colan collaborations, while **TOM PALMER, STEVE LEIALOHA** and others show how they approached the daunting task of inking Colan's famously nuanced penciled pages! Plus there's a **NEW PORTFOLIO** of never-before-seen collaborations between Gene and such masters as **JOHN BYRNE, MICHAEL KALUTA** and **GEORGE PÉREZ**, and all-new artwork created specifically for this book by Gene! Available in Softcover and Deluxe Hardcover (limited to 1000 copies, with 16 extra black-and-white pages and 8 extra color pages)!

(168-page softcover) **$26 US**
(192-page trade hardcover) **$49 US**

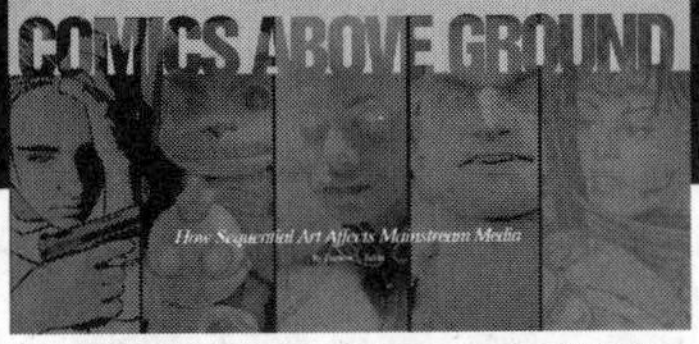
COMICS ABOVE GROUND
How Sequential Art Affects Mainstream Media

COMICS ABOVE GROUND
SEE HOW YOUR FAVORITE ARTISTS MAKE A LIVING OUTSIDE COMICS

COMICS ABOVE GROUND features top comics pros discussing their inspirations and training, and how they apply it in "Mainstream Media," including Conceptual Illustration, Video Game Development, Children's Books, Novels, Design, Illustration, Fine Art, Storyboards, Animation, Movies & more! Written by **DURWIN TALON** (author of the top-selling **PANEL DISCUSSIONS**), this book features creators sharing their perspectives and their work in comics and their "other professions," with career overviews, never-before-seen art, and interviews! Featuring:

- **BRUCE TIMM**
- **BERNIE WRIGHTSON**
- **ADAM HUGHES**
- **LOUISE SIMONSON**
- **DAVE DORMAN**
- **GREG RUCKA & MORE!**

(168-page Trade Paperback) **$24 US**

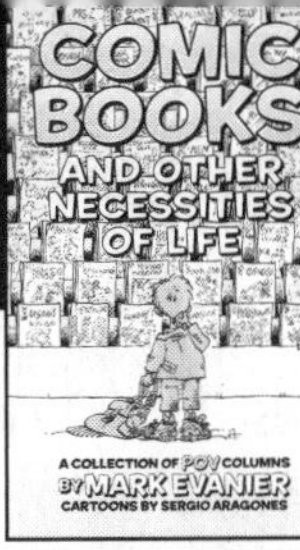
COMIC BOOKS
AND OTHER NECESSITIES OF LIFE
A COLLECTION OF POV COLUMNS BY MARK EVANIER
CARTOONS BY SERGIO ARAGONÉS

COMIC BOOKS & OTHER NECESSITIES OF LIFE

WERTHAM WAS RIGHT!

SUPERHEROES IN MY PANTS!

Each collects **MARK EVANIER'S** best essays and commentaries, plus new essays and illustrations by **SERGIO ARAGONÉS!**

(200-page Trade Paperbacks)
$17 US EACH
ALL THREE BOOKS: $34 US

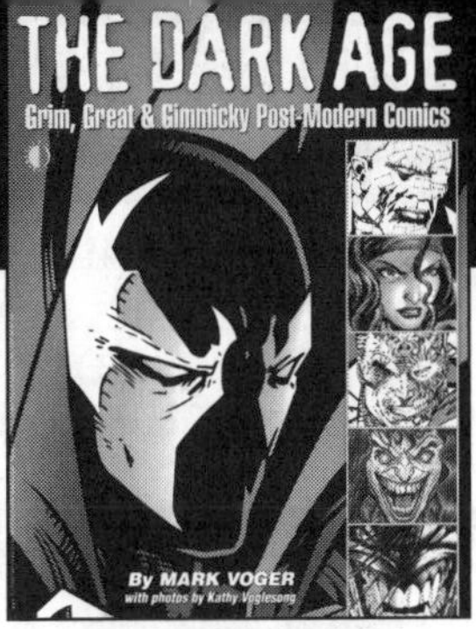
THE DARK AGE
Grim, Great & Gimmicky Post-Modern Comics
By MARK VOGER
with photos by Kathy Voglesong

THE DARK AGE

Documents the '80s and '90s era of comics, from **THE DARK KNIGHT RETURNS** and **WATCHMEN** to the "polybagged premium" craze, the **DEATH OF SUPERMAN**, renegade superheroes **SPAWN, PITT, BLOODSHOT, CYBERFORCE**, & more! Interviews with **TODD McFARLANE, DAVE GIBBONS, JIM LEE, KEVIN SMITH, ALEX ROSS, MIKE MIGNOLA, ERIK LARSEN, J. O'BARR, DAVID LAPHAM, JOE QUESADA, MIKE ALLRED** and others, plus a color section! Written by **MARK VOGER**, with photos by **KATHY VOGLESONG.**

(168-page trade paperback) **$24 US**

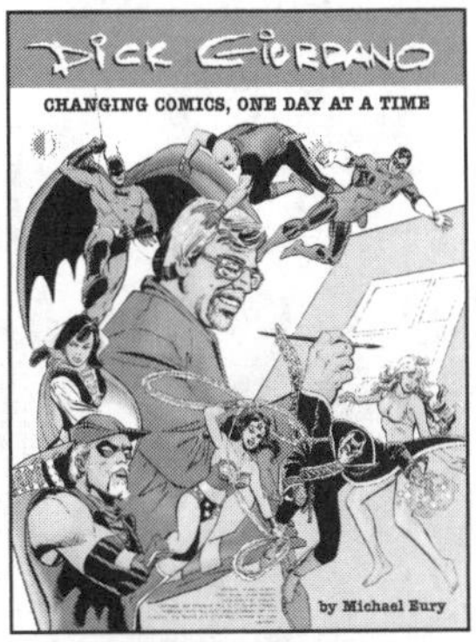
DICK GIORDANO
CHANGING COMICS, ONE DAY AT A TIME
by Michael Eury

DICK GIORDANO CHANGING COMICS, ONE DAY AT A TIME

MICHAEL EURY's biography of comics' most prominent and affable personality!

- Covers his career as illustrator, inker, and editor, peppered with **DICK'S PERSONAL REFLECTIONS** on his career milestones!
- Lavishly illustrated with **RARE AND NEVER SEEN** comics, merchandising, and advertising art (includes a color section)!
- Extensive index of his published work!
- Comments & tributes by **NEAL ADAMS, DENNIS O'NEIL, TERRY AUSTIN, PAUL LEVITZ, MARV WOLFMAN, JULIUS SCHWARTZ, JIM APARO** & others!
- With a Foreword by **NEAL ADAMS** and Afterword by **PAUL LEVITZ!**

(176-pg. Paperback) **$24 US**

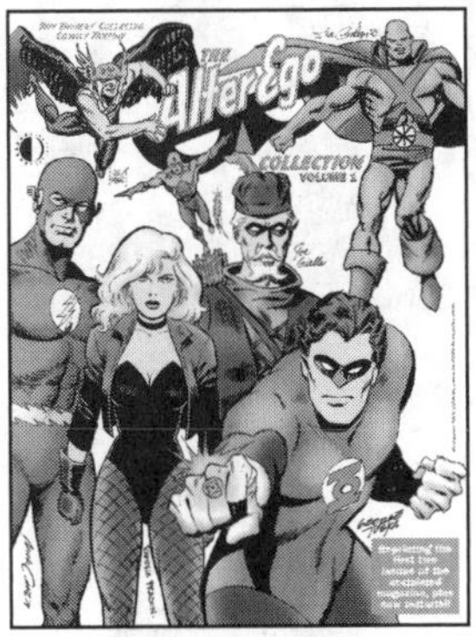
Alter Ego
COLLECTION VOLUME 1

ALTER EGO COLLECTION, VOL. 1

Collects the first two issues of **ALTER EGO**, plus 30 pages of **NEW MATERIAL!** JLA Jam Cover by **KUBERT, PÉREZ, GIORDANO, TUSKA, CARDY, FRADON, & GIELLA**, new sections featuring scarce art by **GIL KANE, WILL EISNER, CARMINE INFANTINO, MIKE SEKOWSKY, MURPHY ANDERSON, DICK DILLIN**, & more!

(192-page trade paperback) **$26 US**

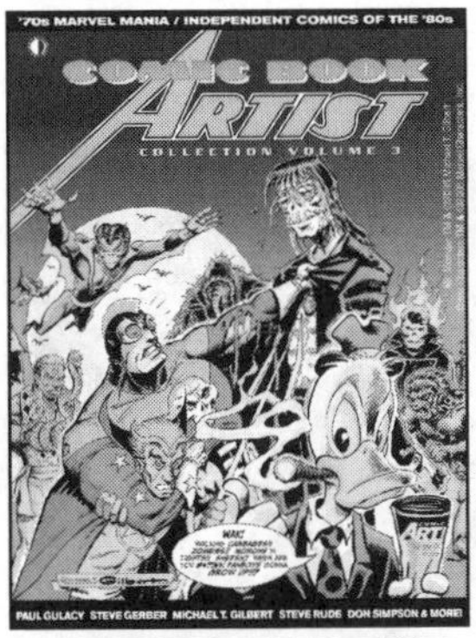
'70s MARVEL MANIA / INDEPENDENT COMICS OF THE '80s
COMIC BOOK ARTIST
COLLECTION VOLUME 3
PAUL GULACY STEVE GERBER MICHAEL T. GILBERT STEVE RUDE DON SIMPSON & MORE!

COMIC BOOK ARTIST COLLECTION, VOL. 3

Reprinting the Eisner Award-winning **COMIC BOOK ARTIST** #7 and #8 ('70s Marvel and '80s independents), featuring a new **MICHAEL T. GILBERT** cover, plus interviews with **GILBERT, RUDE, GULACY, GERBER, DON SIMPSON, CHAYKIN, SCOTT McCLOUD, BUCKLER, BYRNE, DENIS KITCHEN**, plus a **NEW SECTION** featuring over 30 pages of previously-unseen stuff! Edited by **JON B. COOKE.**

(224-page trade paperback) **$29 US**

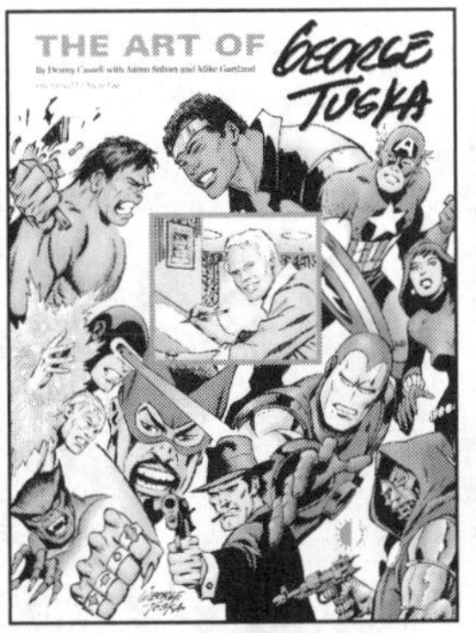
THE ART OF GEORGE TUSKA

ART OF GEORGE TUSKA

A comprehensive look at Tuska's personal and professional life, including early work with Eisner-Iger, crime comics of the 1950s, and his tenure with Marvel and DC Comics, as well as independent publishers. The book includes extensive coverage of his work on **IRON MAN, X-MEN, HULK, JUSTICE LEAGUE, TEEN TITANS, BATMAN, T.H.U.N.D.E.R. AGENTS**, and many more! A gallery of commission artwork and a thorough index of his work are included, plus original artwork, photos, sketches, previously unpublished art, interviews and anecdotes from his peers and fans, plus George's own words!

(128-page trade paperback) **$19 US**

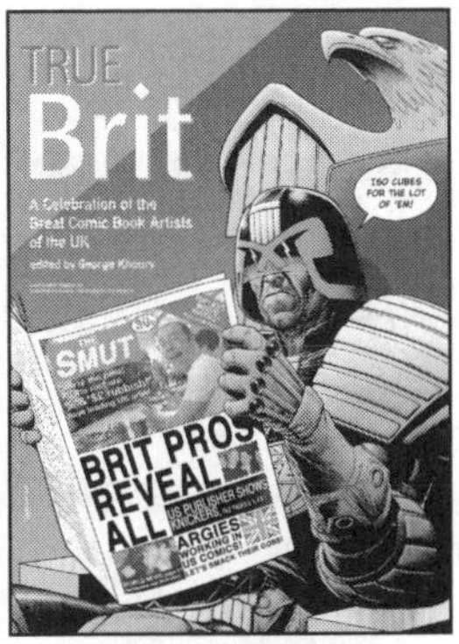
TRUE Brit
A Celebration of the Great Comic Book Artists of the UK
SMUT
BRIT PROS REVEAL ALL

TRUE BRIT
CELEBRATING GREAT COMIC BOOK ARTISTS OF THE UK

A celebration of the rich history of British Comics Artists and their influence on the US with in-depth interviews and art by:

- **BRIAN BOLLAND**
- **ALAN DAVIS**
- **DAVE GIBBONS**
- **BRYAN HITCH**
- **DAVID LLOYD**
- **DAVE MCKEAN**
- **KEVIN O'NEILL**
- **BARRY WINDSOR-SMITH**

and other gents!

(204-page Trade Paperback with COLOR SECTION) **$26 US**

COLLECTED JACK KIRBY COLLECTOR, VOL. 1-5

See what thousands of comics fans, professionals, and historians have discovered: The King lives on in the pages of **THE JACK KIRBY COLLECTOR!** These colossal **TRADE PAPERBACKS** reprint the first 22 sold-out issues of the magazine for Kirby fans!

- **VOLUME 1:** Reprints **TJKC #1-9** (including the Fourth World and Fantastic Four theme issues), plus over 30 pieces of Kirby art never before published in TJKC! • (240 pages) **$29 US**

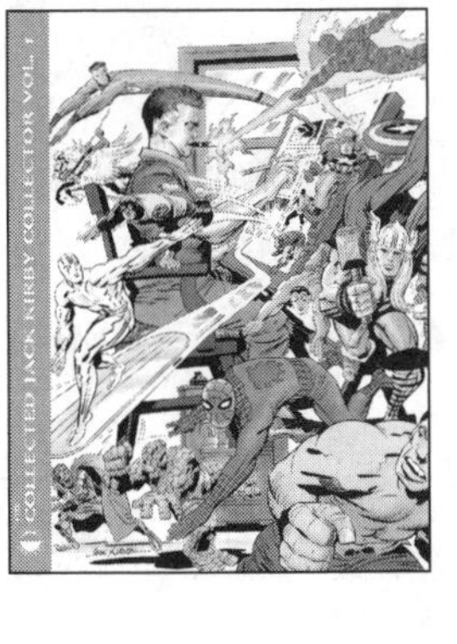
COLLECTED JACK KIRBY COLLECTOR VOL. 1

- **VOLUME 2:** Reprints **TJKC #10-12** (the Humor, Hollywood, and International theme issues), and includes a new special section detailing a fan's private tour of the Kirbys' remarkable home, showcasing more than 30 pieces of Kirby art never before published in TJKC! • (160 pages) **$22 US**
- **VOLUME 3:** Reprints **TJKC #13-15** (the Horror, Thor, and Sci-Fi theme issues), plus 30 new pieces of Kirby art! • (176 pages) **$24 US**
- **VOLUME 4:** Reprints **TJKC #16-19** (the Tough Guys, DC, Marvel, and Art theme issues), plus more than 30 pieces of Kirby art never before published in TJKC! • (240 pages) **$29 US**
- **VOLUME 5:** Reprints **TJKC #20-22** (the Women, Wacky, and Villains theme issues), plus more than 30 pieces of Kirby art never before published in TJKC! • (224 pages) **$29 US**

HOW TO CREATE COMICS
FROM SCRIPT TO PRINT

REDESIGNED and **EXPANDED** version of the groundbreaking **WRITE NOW! #8 / DRAW! #9** crossover! **DANNY FINGEROTH** & **MIKE MANLEY** show step-by-step how to develop a new comic, from script and roughs to pencils, inks, colors, lettering—it even guides you through printing and distribution, & the finished 8-page color comic is included, so you can see their end result! **PLUS:** over 30 pages of **ALL-NEW** material, including "full" and "Marvel-style" scripts, a critique of their new character and comic from an editor's point of view, new tips on coloring, new expanded writing lessons, and more!

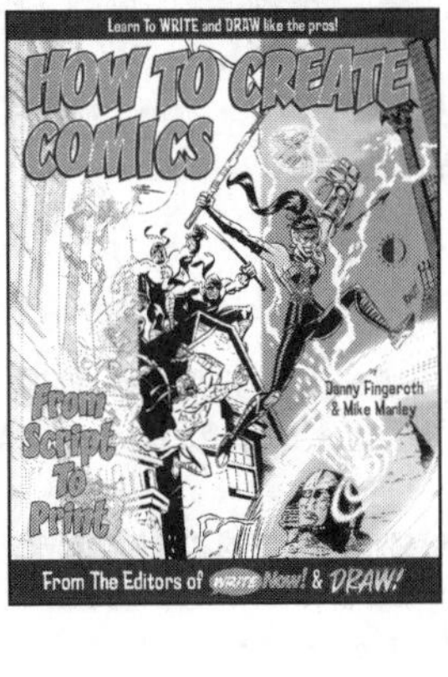
Learn To WRITE and DRAW like the pros!
HOW TO CREATE COMICS
From Script To Print
Danny Fingeroth & Mike Manley
From The Editors of WRITE Now! & DRAW!

(108-page trade paperback) **$18 US**

(120-minute companion DVD) **$35 US**

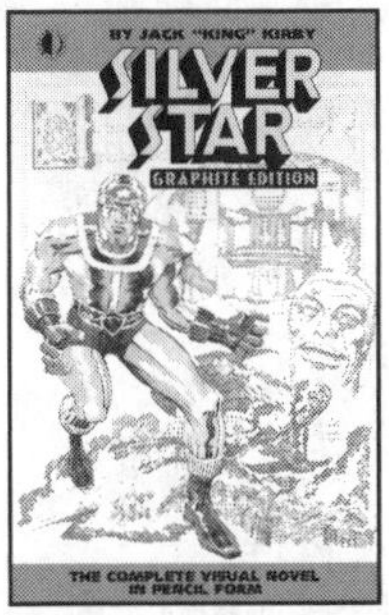
BY JACK "KING" KIRBY
SILVER STAR
GRAPHITE EDITION
THE COMPLETE VISUAL NOVEL IN PENCIL FORM

SILVER STAR: GRAPHITE

JACK KIRBY'S six-issue "Visual Novel" for Pacific Comics, reproduced from his powerful, uninked pencil art! Includes Kirby's illustrated movie screenplay, never-seen sketches, pin-ups, & more from his final series!

(160 pages) **$24 US**

CALL, WRITE, OR E-MAIL FOR A FREE COLOR CATALOG!

MODERN MASTERS SERIES

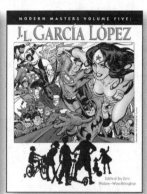
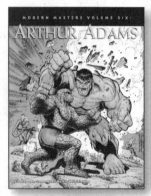

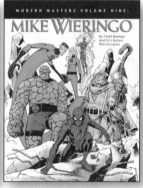

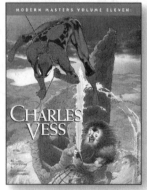

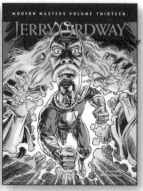